D0672865

Touchwood

A Collection of Ojibway Prose

Edited by Gerald Vizenor

Many Minnesota Project Number 3

NEW RIVERS PRESS 1987

Copyright © 1987 by New Rivers Press
Library of Congress Catalog Card Number: 86-63559
ISBN 0-89823-091-8
All rights reserved
Typesetting: Peregrine Graphics Services
Book Design: Gaylord Schanilec
Cover Painting: David Bradley

ACKNOWLEDGEMENTS:

The Ojibway Sacred Scrolls used throughout this volume are from the George A. Flaskerd collection now housed in the archival collections of the Minnesota Historical Society. They are reproduced here from the July 1963 issue of *The Minnesota Archaeologist.*

"Love Medicine" is from the book of that title by Louise Erdrich. Copyright © 1984 by Louise Erdrich. It is reprinted here by permission of Henry Holt and Company, Inc.

The selection from John Rogers' work is from *Red World and White* and is reprinted here with the permission of the University of Oklahoma Press.

Gerald Vizenor's "Shadows at La Pointe" has been reprinted from *The People Named the Chippewa: Narrative Histories.* "Laurel Hole in the Day" is from *Wordarrows.* Both volumes were published by the University of Minnesota Press and are reprinted here with their permission.

Touchwood has been printed with the aid of grants from the Metropolitan Regional Arts Council (with funds appropriated by the Minnesota State Legislature and with the assistance of funding from the McKnight Foundation), The First Bank System Foundation, and the National Endowment for the Arts (with funds appropriated by the Congress of the United States). The second printing was made possible by a grant from the Metropolitan Regional Arts Council (with funds appropriated by the Minnesota State Legislature), Robert Alexander and the Walt Whitman Reprint Fund, and by a gift from the Bois Forte Reservation Tribal Council.

New Rivers Press books are distributed by

The Talman Company
131 Spring Street, Suite 201E-N
New York, NY 10012
1-800-537-8894

Touchwood has been manufactured in the United States of America for New Rivers Press, 420 N. 5th Street/Suite 910, Minneapolis, MN 55401. Second printing, October 1994.

Touchwood

PETER JONES, of Kahkewaquonaby, the Ojibway missionary, said that his personal tribal name, which means "sacred feather" in translation, was given to him by his traditional grandfather. "The Indians have but one name, which is derived either from their gods or some circumstance connected with their birth or character," Jones wrote in the *History of Ojebway Indians: With Especial Reference to Their Conversion to Christianity*, published more than a century ago in England. "When an Indian is asked his name he will look at some bystander and request him to answer. This reluctance arises from an impression they receive when young, that if they repeat their own names it will prevent their growth, and they will be small in stature. On account of this unwillingness to tell their names, many strangers have fancied that they either have no names or have forgotten them. . . . "

Jones described traditional practices at a time when tribal cultures were burdened with disease and death, colonial revisions, primal survival; his comments were romantic, perhaps servile to his religious conversion, because this assumed reluctance to reveal personal names, whether such a practice was true or not, belies martial domination. Would we have revealed our names to the men who denied our cultures, or to those who were dedicated to either our destruction or conversion? Indeed, tribal names, dream names, and words that assured the sacred in communal and oral traditions were protected, but tribal cultures were seldom passive—never as submissive as the neocolonial transformers once imagined.

The tribal and mixedblood authors presented in this collection bear no apparent relucance to announce their names; rather, the historical essays and imaginative stories here seem to reveal a tacit promise to report the humor and solemn experience of the Ojibway, or the Anishinaabe, as the tribal culture is better known in the oral tradition. The Ojibwe claim more published writers than any other tribe on this continent.

The Anishinaabe [the plural is Anishinaabeg] are known to most of the world as the Ojibway and Chippewa; lexicon entries seldom explain the meaning of these different tribal names. *The American Heritage Dictionary of the English Language*, for example, defines Ojibwa as a "tribe of Algonquin speaking North American Indians inhabiting regions of the United States and Canada around Lake Superior. . . . Also called 'Chippewa,' and 'Chippeway.'"

John Nichols, an editor of *Ojibwewi-Ikidowinan: An Ojibwe Word Resource Book*, wrote that the "Ojibwe language is one language of a wide-spread family of North American Indian languages known as the Algonquian language family, one of many such families of languages. Ojibwe is spoken by perhaps forty-thousand to fifty-thousand people in the north-central part of the continent. Although the English name 'Chippewa' is commonly used both for the people and the ancestral language in Michigan, Minnesota, North Dakota, and Wisconsin, in the language itself the people are the *Anishinaabeg* and the language is called *Anishinaabemowin* or *Ojibwemowin*. . . . "

This collection is divided by two centuries; there is one transition selection between the historical writers of the nineteenth century and the three modern writers. William Whipple Warren, the mixedblood historian, interpreter, and legislator, leads the collection. William was born on May 27, 1825, son of Lyman Marcus Warren and Mary Cadotte, and attended mission schools at La Pointe on Madeline Island in Wisconsin. In January 1851, two years before his death, the young mixedblood took "his seat as a member of the House of Representatives" in Minnesota. The selection here, from *History of the Ojibway Nation*, was first published in 1885 by the Minnesota Historical Society.

The first selection by George Copway, from *The Life, History, and Travels of Kahgegabahbowh*, was published in 1847 by James Harmstead in Philadelphia. The second selection, from *The Traditional History and Characteristic Sketches of the Ojibway Nation*, was published in London, Edinburgh, and Dublin, by Charles Gilpin in 1850. Copway was born in 1818 near the Trent River in Canada where his parents were "attending the annual distribution of the presents from the government to the Indians." He wrote that his parents were of the Ojebwa nation, who lived on the lake back of Cobourg, on the shores of Lake Ontario, Canada West. . . . My father and mother were taught the religion of their nation. My father became a medicine man in the early part of his life, and always had by him the implements of war, which generally distinguished our head men. He was as good a hunter as any in his tribe. . . . "

John Rogers, or Way Quauh Gishig, was born in 1890 on the White Earth Reservation in Minnesota. He attended a federal boarding school at Flandreau, South Dakota. His memories as a child on the reservation appeared in *A Chippewa Speaks*, first published privately in 1957; his stories were republished under the title *Red World and White* by the University of Oklahoma Press in 1973. Joseph Whitecotten, in a forward to the last edition, wrote that the book "focuses on his boyhood, and depicts the thinking and learning processes of a youth caught between two cultural worlds." The romantic metaphor "caught between two worlds" pervades the interpretations of tribal experiences and reviews of books published by Native American Indian writers. Rogers, in spite of his adverse experiences in a racist world, wrote with a sense of adventure, and peace, about the changes he observed when he returned from boarding school. He was suspicious at times, dubious of the promises made by white people, but his published remembrance is not bitter or consumed with hatred for white people or their institutions. Rogers made the best of his experiences and was positive about his boarding school education; in this collection he is a transition between the first published tribal historians and modern prose writers.

"Shadows at La Pointe" was first published in *The People Named the Chippewa: Narrative Histories* (University of Minnesota Press, 1984). "Laurel Hole in the Day" first appeared in *Wordarrows: Indians and Whites in the New Fur Trade* (University of Minnesota Press, 1978), and later revised in *Roots: On the Reservation*, a publication of the Minnesota Historical Society. Gerald Vizenor teaches Native American literature at the University of California, Berkeley. He is enrolled at the White Earth Reservation.

Louise Erdrich is a member of the Turtle Mountain Band of Chippewa and grew up in Wahpeton, North Dakota. "Love Medicine" is a chapter from her novel *Love Medicine*, published by Holt, Rinehart and Winston in 1984. Her fiction has appeared in the *Atlantic Monthly, Redbook, North American Review,* and numerous other periodicals. *The Beet Queen*, her second novel, appeared in 1986. Peter Matthiessen wrote that *Love Medicine* was a "remarkable first novel, quick with agile prose, taut speech, poetry, and power, conveying unflinchingly the funkiness, humor, and great unspoken sadness of the Indian reservations, and a people exiled to a no-man's-land between two worlds."

Jim Northrup is the editor of the *Fond du Lac News*; he lives on the reservation with his family. He won the Lake Superior Contemporary Writers Series. Northrup is an imaginative listener; his direct and humorous stories are inspired by the rich language that people speak on the reservation. The wild and wondrous characters in his stories are survivors in the best trickster humor, no one is a passive victim.

B. Wallace was born and reared on Fond du Lac Reservation in northern Minnesota. She is the mother of two daughters and has worked in the education field for fifteen years. She is a graduate of the University of Minnesota, lives in south Minneapolis, and serves currently as Director of Augsburg College's American Indian Support Program. Like Jim Northrup, she believes that "Indian Humor" is critical to the survival of Indian people and encourages and welcomes the playful teasing of all tribal people and sees it as a very real extension of the trickster tradition, so prominent in many Indian cultures, past and present.

Gerald Vizenor
January 1987

Contents

History of the Ojibway Nation

Origin of the Ojibways

I AM FULLY AWARE that many learned and able writers have given to the world their opinions respecting the aboriginal inhabitants of the American Continent, and the manner in which they first obtained a footing and populated this important section of the earth, which, for so many thousand years, remained unknown to the major portion of mankind inhabiting the Old World.

It is, however, still a matter of doubt and perplexity; it is a book sealed to the eyes of man, for the time has not yet come when the Great Ruler of all things, in His widsom, shall make answer through his inscrutable ways to the question which has puzzled the minds of the learned civilized world. How came America to be first inhabited by man? What branch of the great human family are its aboriginal people descended from?

Ever having lived in the wilderness, even beyond what is known as the western frontiers of white immigration, where books are scarce and difficult to be procured, I have never had the coveted opportunity and advantage of reading the opinions of the various eminent authors who have written on this subject, to compare them to the crude impressions which have gradually, and I may say naturally, obtained possession in my own mind, during my whole life, which I have passed in a close connection of residence and blood with different sections of the Ojibway tribe.

The impressions and the principal causes which have led to their formation,

by William Warren

I now give to the public to be taken for what they are considered worth. Clashing with the received opinions of more learned writers, whose words are taken as standard authority, they may be totally rejected, in which case the satisfaction will still be left me, that before the great problem had been fully solved, I, a person in language, thought, beliefs, and blood, partly an Indian, had made known my crude and humble opinion.

Respecting their own origin the Ojibways are even more totally ignorant than their white brethen, for they have no Bible to tell them that God originally made Adam, from whom the whole human race is sprung. They have their beliefs and oral traditions, but so obscure and unnatural, that nothing approximating to certainty can be drawn from them. They fully believe, and it forms part of their religion, that the world has once been covered by a deluge, and that we are now living on what they term the "new earth." This idea is fully accounted for by their vague traditions; and in their Me-da-we-win or Religion, hieroglyphics are used to denote this second earth.

They fully believe that the Red man mortally angered the Great Spirit which caused the deluge, and at the commencement of the new earth it was only through the medium and intercession of a powerful being, whom they denominate Man-ab-o-sho, that they were allowed to exist, and means were given them whereby to subsist and support life; and a code of religion was more lately bestowed on them, whereby they could commune with the offended Great Spirit, and ward off the approach and ravages of death. This they term Me-da-we-win.

Respecting their belief of their own first existence, I can give nothing more appropriate than a minute analysis of the name which they have given to their race – An-ish-in-aub-ag. This expressive word is derived from An-ish-aw, meaning without cause, or "spontaneous," and in-aub-a-we-se, meaning the "human body." The word An-ish-in-aub-ag, therefore, literally translated, signifies "spontaneous man."

Henry R. Schoolcraft (who has apparently studied this language, and has written respecting this people more than any other writer, and whose works as a whole, deserve the standard authority which is given to them by the literary world), has made the unaccountable mistake of giving as the meaning of this important name, "Common people." We can account for this only in his having studied the language through the medium of imperfect interpreters. In no respect can An-ish-in-aub-ag be twisted so as to include any portion of a word meaning "common."

Had he given the meaning of "original people," which he says is in the interpretation of "Lenni Lenape," the name which the ancient Delawares and eastern sections of the Algic tribes call themselves, he would have hit nearer the mark. "Spontaneous man" is, however, the true literal translation, and I am of the impression that were the two apparently different names of Lenni Lenape and An-ish-aug-ag fully analyzed, and correctly pronounced by a person understanding fully the language of both sections of the same family, who call themselves respectively by these names, not only the meaning would be found exactly to coincide, but also the words, differing only slightly in pronunciation.

The belief of the Algics is, as their name denotes, that they are a spontaneous people. They do not pretend, as a people, to give any reliable account of their first creation. It is a subject which to them is buried in darkness and mystery, and of which they entertain but vague and uncertain notions; notions which are fully embodied in the word An-ish-in-aub-ag.

Since the white race have appeared amongst them, and since the persevering and hard-working Jesuit missionaries during the era of the French domination, carried the cross and their teachings into the heart of the remotest wilderness, and breathed a new belief and new tales into the ears of the wild sons of the forest, their ideas on this subject have become confused, and in many instances they have pretended to imbibe the beliefs thus early promulgated amongst them, connecting them with their own more crude and mytholgical ideas. It is difficult on this account, to procure from them what may have been their pure and original belief, apart from what is perpetrated by the name which we have analyzed. It requires a most intimate acquaintance with them as a people, and individually with their old storytellers, also with their language, beliefs, and customs, to procure their real beliefs and to analyze the tales they seldom refuse to tell, and separate the Indian or original from those portions which they have borrowed or imbibed from the whites. Their innate courtesy and politeness often carry them so far that they seldom, if ever, refuse to tell a story when asked by a white man, respecting their ideas of the creation and the origin of mankind.

These tales, though made up for the occasion by the Indian sage, are taken by his white hearers as their *bona fide* belief, and, as such, many have been made public, and accepted by the civilized world. Some of their sages have been heard to say, that the "Great Spirit" from the earth originally made three different races of men – the white, the black, and red race. To the first he gave a book, denoting wisdom; to the second a hoe, denoting servitude and labor; to the third, or red race, he gave the bow and arrow, denoting the hunter state. To his red children the "Great Spirit" gave the great island on which the white have found them; but because of having committed some great wickedness and angered their Maker, they are doomed to disappear before the rapid tread and advance of the wiser and more favored pale face. This, abbreviated and condensed into a few words, is the story, with variations, with which, as a general thing, the Indian has amused the curiosity of his inquisitive white brother.

It is, however, plainly to be seen that these are not their original ideas, for they know not, till they came amongst them, of the existence of a white and black race, nor of their characteristic symbols of the book and the hoe.

Were we to entertain the new belief which is being advocated by able and learned men, who have closely studied the Biblical with the physical history of man, that the theory taught us in the Sacred Book, making mankind the descendants of one man – Adam – is false, and that the human family are derived originally from a multiplicity of progenitors, definitely marked by physical differences, it would be no difficult matter to arrive at once to certain conclusions respecting the manner in which America became populated. But a believing mind is loth to accept the assertions, arguments, and opinions of a set of men who cast down at one fell swoop the widely-received beliefs inculcated in the minds of enlightened mankind by the sacred book of God. Men will not fall blindly into such a belief, not even with the most convincing arguments.

Throw down the testimony of the Bible, annul in your mind its sacred truths, and we are at once thrown into a perfect chaos of confusion and ignorance. Destroy the belief which has been entertained for ages by the enlightened portion of mankind, and we are thrown at once on a level with the ignorant son of the forest respecting our own origin. In his natural state he would even have the advantage of his more enlightened brother, for he deduces his beliefs from what he sees of nature and nature's work, and possessing no certain proof or knowledge of the manner of his creation, he simply but forcibly styles himself "spontaneous man." On the other hand, the white man, divest of Bible truths and history, yet possessing wisdom and learning, and a knowledge of the conflicting testimony of ages past, descended to him in manuscript and ancient monuments, possessing also a knowledge of the physical formation of all races of men and the geological formation of the earth, would still be at a loss to arrive at certain conclusions; and the deeper he bit into the apple of knowledge, the more confused would be his mind of attempting without the aid of God's word to solve the deep mysteries of Nature – to solve the mystery of the creation of a universe in which our earth is apparently but a grain of sand, and to solve the problem of his own mysterious existence.

We pause, therefore, before we take advantage of any apparent discrepancy or contradiction in the Bible which may be artfully shown to us by unbelieving writers, and to make use of it to more easily prove any favorite theory which we may imbibe respecting the manner in which America first became peopled.

Assume the ground that the human species does not come of one common head, and the existence of the red race is a problem no longer; but believe the word of the Holy Bible, and it will remain a mystery till God wills otherwise. In the meantime, we can but conjecture and surmise; each person has a right to form his own opinion. Some deduce from the writings of others, and others from personal observation, and by making known the causes which have led to the formation of his opinion, he will add to the general mass of information which has been and is gradually collecting, from which eventually more certain deductions will be arrived at.

Taking the ground that the theory respecting the origin of the human race taught us in the Holy Scriptures is true, I will proceed to express my humble opinion respecting the branch of the human race from which originates that particular type of the aboriginal race of America comprised by the term Algic or Algonquin, of which grand family the Ojibway tribe, of whom I shall more particularly treat, forms a numerous and important section.

During my long residence among the Ojibways, after numberless inquiries of their old men, I have never been able to learn, by tradition or otherwise, that they entertain the belief that all the tribes of the red race inhabiting America have ever been, at any time since the occupancy of this continent, one and the same people, speaking the same language, and practising the same beliefs and customs. The traditions of this tribe extend no further into the past than the once concentration or coalition under one head, of the different and now scattered tribes belonging to the Algic stock.

We have every reason to believe that America has not been peopled from one nation or tribe of the human family, for there are differences amongst its inhabitants and contrarieties as marked and fully developed as are to be found between European and Asiatic nations – wide differences in language, beliefs, and customs.

A close study of the dissimilarities existing between the Ojibways and Dakotas, who have more immediately come under my observation, has led me fully to believe that they are not descended from the same people of the Old World, nor have they ever in America formed one and the same nation of tribe. It is true that they assimilate in color and in their physical formation, which can be accounted for by their residence in the same climate, and sustaining life through the same means. Many of their customs are also alike, but these have been naturally similarized and entailed on them by living in the same wild hunter state, and many have derived from one another during their short fitful terms of peace and intercourse. Here all similitude between the two tribes ends. They cannot differ more widely than they do in language; and the totemic system, which is an important and leading characteristic among the Ojibways, is not known to the Dakotas. They differ also widely in their religious beliefs, and as far back as their oral traditions descend with any certainty, they tell of even having been mortal enemies, waging against each other a bloody and exterminating warfare.

Assuming the ground which has been proved both probable and practicable by different eminent authors, that the American continent has been populated from the eastern and northeastern shores of Asia, it is easy to believe that not only one, but portions of different Asiatic tribes found their way thither, which will account for the radical differences to be found in the languages of the several stocks of the American aborigines.

Taking these grounds, the writer is disposed to entertain the belief that, while the original ancestors of the Dakota race might have formed a tribe or portion of a tribe of the roving sons of Tartary, whom they resemble in many essential respects, the Anglics, on the other hand, may be descended from a portion of the ten lost tribes of Israel, whom they also resemble in many important particulars.

Of this latter stock only can I speak with any certainty. I am fully aware that the surmise which is here advanced is not new, but is one which has already elicited much discussion; and although later writers have presented it as an exploded idea, yet I cannot refrain from presenting the ideas on this subject which have gradually inducted themselves into my mind.

Boudinot and other learned writers, having at their command the books and observations on the Indian tribes which have been published from time to time since their first discovery, and possessing an intimate knowledge of Biblical history, have fallen into the same belief, and from a mass of book information they have been enabled to offer many able arguments to prove the Red Race of America descendants of the lost tribes of Israel. I have never had the advantage of seeing or reading these books, and only know of their existence from hearsay, and the casual remarks or references of the few authors I have been enabled to consult. The belief which I have now expressed has grown on me imperceptibly from my youth, ever since I could first read the Bible, and compare with it the lodge stories and legends of my Indian grandfathers, around whose lodge fires I have passed many a winter evening listening with parted lips and open ears to their interesting and most forcibly told tales.

After reaching the age of maturity, I pursued my inquiries with more system, and the more information I have obtained from them – the more I have become acquainted with their anomalous and difficult to be understood characters – the more insight I have gained into their religious and secret rites and faith, the more strongly has it been impressed on my mind that they bear a close affinity or analogy to the chosen people of God, and they are either descendants of the lost tribes of Israel, or they have had, in some former era, a close contact and intercourse with the Hebrews, imbibing from them their beliefs and customs and the traditions of their patriarchs.

To enter into a detailed account of all the numerous and trivial causes which have induced me to entertain this idea, would take up much space, and as the subject has been so much dwelt upon, by those who, from having made the subject the study of their lives, and who by their researches have gathered much of the requisite information to arrive at more just conclusions than the humble writer, I will confine myself to stating a few general facts, some of which may have missed the attention of my predecessors on this road of inquiry, and which none but those intimately acquainted with the Indians, and possessing their fullest confidence, are able to obtain.

It is a general fact that most people who have been discovered living in a savage and unenlightened state, and even whole nations living in partial civilization, have been found to be idolaters – having no just conception of a great first Cause or Creator, invisible to human eyes, and pervading all space. With the Ojibways it is not so; the fact of their firm belief and great veneration, in an overruling Creator and Master of Life, has been noticed by all who have had close intercourse with them since their earliest discovery. It is true that they believe in a multiplicity of spirits which pervade all nature, yet all these are subordinate to the one Great Spirit of good.

This belief is as natural (if not more so), than the belief of the Catholics in their interceding saints, which in some respects it resembles, for in the same light as intercessors between him and the great Spirit, does the more simple Red Man regard the spirits which in his imagination pervade all creation. The never-failing rigid fasts of the first manhood, when they seek in dreams for a guardian spirit, illustrates this belief most forcibly.

Ke-che-mun-e-do (Great Spirit) is the name used by the Ojibways for the being equivalent to our God. They have another term which can hardly be surpassed by any one word in the English language, for force, condensity, and expression, namely: Ke-zha-mun-e-do, which means pitying, charitable, overruling, guardian and merciful Spirit; in fact, it expresses all the great attributes of the God of Israel. It is derived from Ke-zha-wand-e-se-roin, meaning charity, kindness – Ke-zha-wus-so expressing the guardian feeling, and solitude of a parent toward its offspring, watching it with jealous vigilance from harm; and Shah-wau-je-gay, to take pity, merciful, with Mun-e-do (spirit). There is nothing to equal the veneration with which the Indian regards this unseen being. They seldom even ever mention his name unless in their Me-da-we and other religious rites, and in their sacrificial feasts; and then an address to him, however trivial, is always accompanied with a sacrifice of tobacco or some other article deemed precious by the Indian. They never use his name in vain, and there is no word in their language expressive of a profane oath, or equivalent to the many words used in profane swearing by their more enlightened white brethen.

Instances are told of persons while enduring almost superhuman fasts, obtaining a vision of him in their dreams; in such instances the Great Spirit invariably appears to the dreamer in the shape of a beautifully and strongly-formed man. And it is a confirmed belief amongst them, that he or she who has once been blessed with this vision, is fated to live to a good old age and in enjoyment of ease and plenty.

All other minor or guardian spirits whom they court in their first dream of fasting appear to them in the shape of quadrupeds, birds, or some inanimate object in nature, as the moon, the stars, or the imaginary thunderers; and even this dream-spirit is never mentioned without sacrifice. The dream itself which has appeared to the faster, guides in a great measure his future course in life, and he never relates it without offering a sacrificial feast to the spirit of the dream. The bones of the animal which he offers are carefully gathered, unbroken, tied together, and either hung on a tree, thrown into deep water, or carefully burnt. Their beliefs and rites, connected with their fasts and dreams, are of great importance to themselves, more so than has been generally understood by writers who have treated of the Algics.

These facts are mentioned here to show an analogy with the ancient and primitive customs of the Hebrews – their faith in dreams, their knowledge and veneration of the unseen God, and the customs of fasting and sacrifice. Minor customs, equally similar with the usages of the Hebrews as we read in the Bible, might be enumerated; for instance, the never-failing separation of the female during the first period of menstruation, their war customs, etc. But it is not the intention of the writer to enter with prolixity on this field of inquiry which has been so often trod by able writers.

The grand rite of Me-da-wa-win (or, as we have learned to term it, "Grand Medicine") and the beliefs incorporated therein, are not yet fully understood by the whites. This important custom is still shrouded in mystery, even to my own eyes, though I have taken much pains to inquire, and made use of every advantage, possessed by speaking their language perfectly, being related to them, possessing their friendship and intimate confidence, has given me, and yet I frankly acknowledge that I stand as yet, as it were, on the threshold of the Me-da-we-win lodge. I believe, however, that I have obtained full as much and more general and true information on this matter than any other person who has written on the subject, not excepting a great and standard author, who, to the surprise of many who know the Ojibways well, has boldly asserted in one of his works that he has been regularly initiated into the mysteries of this rite, and is a member of the Me-da-we Society. This is certainly an assertion hard to believe in the Indian country; and when the old initiators or Indian priests are told of it, they shake their heads in incredulity that a white man should ever have been allowed *in truth* to become a member of their Me-da-we lodge.

An entrance into the lodge itself, while the ceremonies are being enacted, has sometimes been granted through courtesy; but this does not initiate a person into the mysteries of the creed, nor does it make him a member of the society.

Amongst the Ojibways, the secrets of this grand rite are as sacredly kept as the secrets of the Masonic Lodge among the whites. Fear of threatened and certain death, either by poison or violence, seals the lips of the Me-da-we initiate, and this is the potent reason why it is still a secret to the white man, and why it is not generally understood.

Missionaries, travellers, and transient sojourners amongst the Ojibways, who have witnessed the performance of the grand Me-da-we ceremonies, have represented and published that it is composed of foolish and unmeaning ceremonies. The writer begs leave to say that these superficial observers labor under a great mistake. The Indian has equal right, and may with equal truth (but in his utter ignorance is more excusable), to say, on viewing the rites of the Catholic and other churches, that they consist of unmeaning and nonsensical ceremonies. There is much yet to be learned from the wild and apparently simple son of the forest, and the most which remains to be learned is to be derived from their religious beliefs.

In the Me-da-we rite is incorporated most that is ancient amongst them — songs and traditions that have descended, not orally, but in hieroglyphics, for at least a long line of generations. In this rite is also perpetuated the purest and most ancient idioms of their language, which differs somewhat from that of the common everyday use. And if comparisons are to be made between the language of the Ojibways and the other languages, it must be with their religious idiom. . . .

The tradition of the deluge, and traditions of wars between the different Totemic clans, all bear an analogy with tales of the Bible.

To satisfy my own curiosity I have sometimes interpreted to their old men, portions of Bible history, and their expression is invariably: "The book must be true, for our ancestors have told us similar stories, generation after generation, since the earth was new." It is a bold assertion, but it is nevertheless a true one, that were the traditions of the Ojibways written in order, and published in a book, it would as a whole bear a striking resemblance to the Old Testament, and would contain no greater improbabilities than may be accounted for by the loose manner in which these traditions have been perpetuated; naturally losing force and truth in descending orally through each succeeding generation. Discard, then, altogether the idea of any connection existing or having existed between the Ojibways and the Hebrews, and it will be found difficult to account for all the similarities existing between many of their rites, customs, and beliefs. Notwithstanding all that has been and may be advanced to prove the Ojibways descended from the lost tribes of Israel, or at least, their once having had close communion with them, yet I am aware that there are many stubborn facts and arguments against it, the principal of which is probably their total variance in language. Never having studied the Hebrew language, I have not had the advantage of comparing with it the Ojibway, and on this point I cannot express any opinion.

It is not supposable, however, that the ten lost tribes of Israel emigrated from the land of their captivity in one body, and proceeding direct to the eastern shores of Asia, crossed over to America (by some means which, through changes and convulsions in nature, have become extinct and unknown to the present age) there to resume the rites of their religion, practice the Mosiac laws, and isolated from the rest of mankind, perpetuated in their primitive purity their language and belief.

On the contrary, if the Algics are really descendants of these tribes, it must be only from a portion of them, as remnants of the lost tribes have been discovered in the Nestorians of Asia. To arrive in America, these portions must have passed through strange and hostile tribes of people, and in the course of their long wanderings and sojourns amongst them, they might have adopted portions of their languages and usages, losing thereby the purity of their own. It is natural to surmise that they were driven and followed into America by hostile tribes of Asia, and that they have been thus driven and followed till checked by the waves of the broad Altantic. This would account for the antagonistical position in which they and the Dakotas were first discovered, and which, as the Algics are now being pressed by the white race, on the track of their old emigration, has again been renewed more deadly than ever. Truly are they a wandering and accursed race! They now occupy a position wedged in as it were, between the onward resistless tide of European emigration, and the still powerful tribes of the Naud-o-wa-se-wug ("Like unto the Adders"), their inveterate and hereditary enemies. As a distinct people their final extinction appears inevitable, though their blood may still course on as long as mankind exists.

I cannot close these remarks on this subject (though they have already been lengthened further than was at first intended), without offering a few words respecting the belief of the Ojibways in a future state. Something can be deduced from this respecting their condition in former ages, and the direction from which they originally emigrated.

When an Ojibway dies, his body is placed in a grave, generally in a sitting posture, facing the west. With the body are buried all the articles needed in life for a journey. If a man, his gun, blanket, kettle, fire steel, flint and moccasins; if a woman, her moccasins, axe, portage collar, blanket and kettle. The soul is supposed to stand immediately after the death of the body, on a deep beaten path, which leads westward; the first object he comes to in following this path, is the great Oda-e-min (Heart berry), or strawberry, which stands on the roadside like a huge rock, and from which he takes a handful and eats on his way. He travels on till he reaches a deep, rapid stream of water, over which lies the much dreaded Ko-go-gaup-o-gun or rolling and sinking bridge; once safely over this as the traveller looks back it assumes the shape of a huge serpent swimming, twisting and untwisting its folds across the stream. After camping out four nights, and travelling each day through a prairie country, the soul arrives in the land of spirits, where he finds his relatives accumulated since mankind was first created; all is rejoicing, singing and dancing; they live in a beautiful country interspersed with clear lakes and streams, forests and prairies, and abounding in fruit and game to repletion – in a word, abounding in all that the red man most covets in this life, and which conduces most to his happiness. It is that kind of a paradise which he only by his manner of life on this earth, is fitted to enjoy. Without dwelling further on this belief, which if carried out in all its details would occupy under the head of this chapter much unnecessary space, I will now state the conclusions which may possibly be deduced from it.

The Ojibway believes his home after death to lie westward. In their religious phraseology, the road of souls is sometimes called Ke-wa-kun-ah, "Homeward road." It is, however, oftener named Che-ba-kun-ah, (road of souls). In the ceremony of addressing their dead before depositing them in the grave, I have often heard the old men use the word Ke-go-way-se-kah (you are going homeward). This road is represented as passing mostly through a prairie country.

Is it not probable from these beliefs that ages ago the Ojibways resided westward, and occupied a country "flowing in milk and honey" – a country abounding in all that tends to their enjoyment and happiness, and to which they look back as the tired traveller on a burning desert looks back to a beautiful oasis which he has once passed, or as the lonely wanderer looks back to the once happy home of his childhood? May they not forcibly have been driven from this former country by more powerful nations – have been pressed east and still further eastward from Asia in to America, and over its whole extent, arrested by the waves of the Atlantic Ocean? And, like a receding wave, they have turned their faces westward towards their former country, within the past four centuries forced back to European discovery and immigration.

With their mode of transmitting traditions from father to son orally, it is natural to suppose that their present belief in the westward destination of the soul has originated from the above-surmised era in their ancient history. And the tradition of a once happy home and country, being imperfectly transmitted to our times through long lines of generations, has at last merged into the simple and natural belief of a future state, which thoroughly pervades the Indian mind, and guides, in a measure, his actions in life, and enables him to smile at the approach of death. . . .

MIGRATION OF THE OJIBWAY

The history of the Ojibway tribe, till within the past five centuries, lies buried in darkness and almost utter oblivion. In the preceding chapter we have feebly attempted to lift the veil which covers their past, by offering well-founded facts which can be excusably used in the formation of conjectures and probabilities. All is, however, still nothing but surmise and uncertainty, and what of this nature has been presented, has not been given, nor can it be considered as authentic history. We will now descend to times and events which are reached by their oral traditions, and which may be offered as certain, though not minute history. Through close inquiry and study of their vague figurative traditions, we have discovered that the Ojibways have attained to their present geographical position, nearly in the centre of the North American continent, from the shores of the Atlantic Ocean, about the Gulf of the St. Lawrence River. The manner in which I first received a certain intimation of this fact, may illustrate it more forcibly to the reader, and is presented as follows: —

I was once standing near the entrance of an Ojibway Me-da-we-gaun, more commonly known as the "Grand Medicine Lodge," while the inmates were busy in the performance of the varied ceremonies of this, their chief medical and religious rite. The lodge measured in length about one hundred feet, and fifteen in width, was but partially covered along the sides with green boughs of the balsam tree, and the outside spectator could view without hindrance the different ceremonies enacting within. On a pole raised horizontally above its whole length were hung pieces of cloth, calico, handkerchiefs, blankets, etc. — the offerings or sacrifice of the novice who was about to be initiated into the mysteries of the Me-da-we society. The lodge was full of men and women who sat in a row along both of its sides. None but those who were members of the society and who had regularly been initated, were allowed to enter. They were dressed and painted in their best and most fancy clothing and colors, and each held in his hand the Me-da-wi-aun or medicine sack, which consisted of bird skins, stuffed otter, beaver and snake skins.

The novice in the process of initiation, sat in the centre on a clean mat facing the Me-da-wautig, a cedar post planted in the centre of the lodge, daubed with vermilion and ornamented with tufts of birds' down. The four old and grave-looking We-kauns, or initiating priests, stood around him with their medicine sacks, drums, and rattles.

As I partially understood, and could therefore appreciate, the meaning and objects of their strange ceremonies, and could partially understand their peculiar religious idiom, I stood, watched, and listened with a far deeper interest than could be felt in the mind of a mere casual observer, who is both unacquainted with the objects of the rites or language of these simple children of nature, and who, in his greater wisdom, deems it but the unmeaning mummery and superstitious rites of an ignorant race, buried in heathenish darkness.

One of the four We-kauns, after addressing a few remarks to the novice in a low voice, took from his medicine sack, the Me-da-me-gis, a small white sea-shell, which is the chief emblem of the Me-da-we rite. Holding this on the palm of his hand he ran slowly around the inside of the lodge, displaying it to the inmates, and followed by his fellow We-kauns swinging their rattles, and exclaiming in a deep gutteral tone, "whe, whe, whe." Circling the lodge in this impressive manner, on coming again to the novice, they stopped running, uttering a deep sonorous, "Whay-ho-ho-ho-." They then quietly walked off, and taking their stand at the western end of the lodge, the leader still displaying the shell on the palm of his hand, delivered a loud and spirited harangue.

The language and phrases used were so obscure to a common listener, that it would be impossible to give a literal translation of the whole speech. The following passage, however, forcibly struck my attention:

"While our forefathers were living on the great salt water toward the rising sun, the great Megis (sea-shell) showed itself above the surface of the great water, and the rays of the sun for a long period were reflected from its glossy back. It gave warmth and light to the An-ish-in-aub-ag (red race). All at once it sank into the deep, and for a time our ancestors were not blessed with its light. It rose to the surface and appeared again on the great river which drains the waters of the Great Lakes, and again for a long time it gave life to our forefathers, and reflected back the rays of the sun. Again it disappeared from sight and it rose not, till it appeared to the eyes of the An-ish-in-aub-ag on the shores of the first great lake. Again it sank from sight, and death daily visited the wigwams of our forefathers, till it showed its back, and reflected the rays of the sun once more at Bow-e-ting (Sault Ste. Marie). Here it remained for a long time, but once more, and for the last time, it disappeared, and the An-ish-in-aub-ag was left in darkness and misery, till it floated and once more showed its bright back at Mo-ning-wun-a-kaun-ing (La Pointe Island), where it has ever since reflected back the rays of the sun, and blessed our ancestors with life, light, and wisdom. Its rays reach the remote village of the wide spread Ojibways." As the old man delivered this talk, he continued to display the shell, which he represented as the emblem of the great megis of which he was speaking.

A few days after, anxious to learn the true meaning of this allegory, I proceeded one evening to the lodge of the old priest, and presenting him with some tobacco and cloth for a pair of leggings (which is an invariable custom when any *genuine* information is wanted of them, connected with their religious beliefs), I requested him to explain to me the meaning of his Me-da-we harangue.

After filling his pipe and smoking of the tobacco I had presented, he proceeded to give me the desired information as follows: –

"My grandson," said he, "the megis I spoke of, means the Me-da-we religion. Our forefathers, many string of lives ago, lived on the shores of the Great Salt Water in the east. Here it was, that while congregated in a great town, and while they were suffering the ravages of sickness and death, the Great Spirit, at the intercession of Man-ab-o-sho, the great common uncle of the An-ish-in-aub-ag, granted them this rite wherewith life is restored and prolonged. Our forefathers moved from the shores of the great water, and proceeded westward. The Me-da-we lodge was pulled down and it was not again erected, till our forefathers again took a stand on the shores of the great river near where Mo-ne-aung (Montreal) now stands.

"In the course of time this town was again deserted, and our forefathers still proceeding westward, lit not their fires till they reached the shores of Lake Huron, where again the rites of the Me-da-we were practised.

"Again these rites were forgotten, and the Me-da-we was not built till the Ojibways found themselves congregated at Bow-e-ting (outlet of Lake Superior), where it remained for many winters. Still the Ojibways moved westward, and for the last time the Me-da-we lodge was erected on the Island of La Pointe, and here, long before the pale face appeared among them, it was practised in its purest and most original form. Many of our fathers lived the full term of life granted to mankind by the Great Spirit, and the forms of many old people were mingled with each rising generation. This, my grandson, is the meaning of the words you did not understand; they have been repeated to us by our fathers for many generations."

Thus was it that I first received particular corroborating testimony to the somewhat mooted point of the direction from which the Ojibways have reached their present geographical position. It is only from such religious and genuine traditions that the fact is to be ascertained. The common class of the tribe who are spread in numerous villages north and west of Lake Superior, when asked where they originally came from, make answer that they originated from Mo-ning-wuna-kaun-ing (La Pointe), and the phrase is often used in their speeches to the whites, that "Mo-ning-wuna-kaun-ing" is the spot on which the Ojibway tribe first grew, and like a tree it has spread its branches in every direction, in the bands that now occupy the vast extent of the Ojibway earth; and also that "it is the root from which all the far scattered villages of the tribe have sprung."

A superficial inquirer would be easily misled by these assertions, and it is only through such vague and figurative traditions as the one we have related, that any degree of certainty can be arrived at, respecting their position and movements prior to the time when the tribe first lit their central fire, and built the Me-da-we lodge on the Island of La Pointe.

There is another tradition told by the old men of the Ojibway village of Fond du Lac – Lake Superior, which tells of their former residence on the shores of the great salt water. It is, however, so similar in character to the one I have related, that its introduction here would occupy unnecessary space. The only difference between the two traditions, is that the otter, which is emblematical of one of the four Medicine spirits, who are believed to preside over the Me-da-we rites, is used in one, in the same figurative manner as the seashell is used in the other; first appearing to the ancient An-ish-in-aub-ag from the depths of the great salt water, again on the river St. Lawrence, then on Lake Huron at Sault Ste. Marie, again at La Pointe, but lastly at Fond du Lac, or end of Lake Superior, where it is said to have forced the sand bank at the mouth of the St. Louis River. The place is still pointed out by the Indians where they believe the great otter broke through.

It is comparatively but a few generations back, that this tribe have been known by their present distinctive name of Ojibway. It is certainly not more than three centuries, and in all probability much less. It is only within this term of time, that they have been disconnected as a distinct or separate tribe from the Ottaways and Potta-wat-um-ees. The name by which they were known when incorporated in one body, is at the present time uncertain.

The final separation of these three tribes took place at the Straits of Michili-macinac from natural causes, and the partition has been more and more distinctly defined, and perpetuated through locality, and by each of the three divided sections assuming or receiving distinctive appelations: —

The Ottaways remaining about the spot of their final separation, and being thereby the most easterly section, were first discovered by the white race, who bartered with them their merchandise for furs. They for many years acted as a medium between the white traders and their more remote western brethen, providing them in turn at advanced prices, with their much desired commodities. They thus obtained the name of Ot-tah-way, "trader," which they have retained as their tribal name to the present day. The Potta-wat-um-ees moved up Lake Michigan, and by taking with them, or for a time perpetuating the national fire, which according to tradition was sacredly kept alive in their more primitive days, they have obtained the name of "those who make or keep the fire," which is the literal meaning of their tribal cognomen.

The Ojibways, pressing northward and westward, were soon known as an important and distinctive body or tribe, and meeting with fierce and inveterate enemies, the name of Ojibway, "to roast till puckered up," they soon obtained through practising the old custom of torturing prisoners of war by fire, as has already been mentioned more fully in a previous chapter. The original cause of their emigration from the shores of the Atlantic westward to the area of Lake Superior, is buried in uncertainty. If pressed or driven back by more powerful tribes, which is a most probable conjecture, they are not willing to acknowledge it.

From the earliest period that their historical traditions treat of, they tell of having carried on an exterminating war with the Iroquois, of Six Nations of New York, whom they term Naud-o-waig, or Adders. The name indicates the deadly nature of these, their old and powerful antagonists, whose concentrated strength and numbers, and first acquaintance with the use of the white man's murderous firearms, caused them to leave their ancient village sites and seek westward for new homes.

Sufficient has been seen and written since their discovery by the white race, of the antagonistical position of these two different families, or groups of tribes, to prove the certainty of the above surmise. The name of Naud-o-wa-se-wug, which is sometimes applied to the Dakotas by the Ojibways, is derived from the name by which they have ever known the Iroquois. — Naud-o-waig; it implies "our enemies," but literally, means "like unto the adders." Various definitions have been given to this name by different writers; the above is now presented as the only true one.

It is a well-authenticated fact traditionally, that at the Falls of Sault Ste. Marie, the outlet of Lake Superior, the Ojibways, after separating from the Ottaways and Pottawatumees, made a long and protracted stay. Their village occupied a large extent of ground, and their war-parties numbered many warriors who marched eastward against the Naudoways, and westward against the Dakotas, with whom at this point they first came into collision.

At this point the Ojibway tribe again separated into two divisions, which we will designate as the Northern and Southern. The Northern division formed the least numerous body, and consisted chiefly of the families claiming as Totems the reindeer, lynx, and pike. They proceeded gradually to occupy the north coast of Lake Superior, till they arrived at the mouth of Pigeon River (Kah-mau-a-tig-wa-aug). From this point they have spread over the country they occupy at the present day along the British and United States line, and north, far into the British possessions. A large band early occupied and formed a village at Rainy Lake. Here they first came in contact with the Assineboins (a tribe of seceding Dakotas), and from this point, after entering into a firm and lasting peace with the Assineboins and Knis-te-nos, they first joined their brethen of the Southern division of their wars against the fierce Dakotas. This band have to this day retained the cognomen of Ko-je-je-win-in-e-wug, from the numerous straits, bends, and turnings of the lakes and rivers which they occupy.

A large body of this Northern division residing immediately on the north shores of the Great Lake, at Grand Portage and Thunder Bay, and claiming the Totem of the Ke-nouzhay or Pike, were formerly denominated O-mush-kas-ug. Tradition says that at one time their fellow-Ojibways made war on them. This war was brought about by persons belonging to the Pike family murdering some members of the Marten Totem family. It was but the carrying out of their custom of "blood for blood." It was neither very deadly nor of long duration, and to illustrate its character more fully, I will introduce the following traditional anecdotes: —

A party consisting of warriors belonging to the Marten family was at one time collected at Fond du Lac. They proceeded on the war path against the family of the Omushkas, living on the north shore of the Great Lake, for this family had lately spilled their blood. They discovered a single wigwam standing on the sandy shores of the lake, and the Martens, having stealthily approached, raised the war-whoop, and as was the custom in battle (to show their greater manhood), they threw off every article of clothing, and thus, perfectly naked, rushed furiously to the attack. The Omushkas, head of the family occupying the threatened lodge, was busy arranging his fishnet, and not aware that war had been declared, he paid no attention to his yelling visitor, but calmly continued his peaceful occupation.

One of the Martens, rushing into the lodge, and throwing his arms about him, exclaimed, "Ene-ne-nin-duk-o-nah." (a man I hold), meaning that he took him captive.

The simple Omushkas, looking up, merely remarked, "Let me go; you are tangling my net." Still the Marten, keeping his hold, more loudly exclaimed, "Ene-ne-nin-duk-o-nah." The Omushkas, now perceiving his nakedness, grasped a sensitive part of his person, in turn jokingly exclaimed, "Nim-sah-eta-in-ne-ne-nin-duk-o-nah" ("tis only I who truly hold a man"), and the simple man continued to consider the attack as a mere farce. The war-club, however, of the enraged Marten now descended with fearful force on his head, and he died exclaiming, "Verily they are killing me."

A considerable body of the Northern Ojibways are denominated by their fellow-tribesmen Sug-wau-dug-ah-win-in-e-wug (men of the thick firwoods), derived from the interminable forests of balsam, spruce, pine, and tamarac trees which cover their hunting-grounds. Their early French discoverers named them "Bois Forts," or Hardwoods.

Another section forming the most northern branch of this tribe are denominated Omushke-goes (Swamp-people), derived also from the nature of the country they occupy.

The Northern division, which comprises these different sections, having been separated from the main body of the tribe forming the Southern division, now upwards of eight generations, a difference (though not a radical one), has become perceptible in their common language. This consists mostly in the pronunciation, and so slight is the difference in idiom that one good interpreter, speaking the language of each division, may suffice for both.

The characteristics, also of the northern section of the tribe, differ materially in some important respects from those of their southern and western brethen. Not having been opposed by enemies in the course of their northern emigration, they are consequently not warlike, and the name of Waub-ose (Rabbit), is often applied to them by their more warlike fellows, on account of their mild and harmless disposition.

At the partition of the Ojibway tribe into two divisions, at Sault Ste. Marie, the main body pressed their way gradually up along the southern shores of Lake Superior. They made a temporary stand at Grand Island, near the Pictured Rocks, again at L'Anse Bay, or as they more euphoniously name it, We-qua-dong. This grand division consisted principally of the Crane Totem family, the Bear, the Catfish, the Loon, and the allied Marten and Moose clans. These great families with their several branches, form at least eight-tenths of the whole Ojibway tribe.

The Cranes claim the honor of first having pitched their wigwams, and lighted the fire of the Ojibways, at Shaug-ah-waum-ik-ong, a sand point or peninsula lying two miles immediately opposite the Island of La Pointe. This fact is illustrated by the following highly allegorical and characteristic tradition: —

As a preliminary remark, it is necessary to state that there exists quite a variance between three or four of the principal Totems, as to which is hereditarily entitled to the chief place in the tribe.

At a council (in which the writer acted as interpreter), held some years ago at La Pointe, between the principal chiefs of the Ojibways and the United States Government Agent, the following allegory was delivered by an old chief named

Tug-waug-aun-ay, in answer to the mooted question of "who was the hereditary chief of La Pointe?"

Ke-che-wash-keenh (Great Buffalo), the grandson of the celebrated chief Au-daig-we-os (mentioned in Schoolcraft's works), head of the Loon Totem clan, was at this time, though stricken with years, still in the prime of his great oratorical powers.

On this occasion he opened the council by delivering the most eloquent harangue in praise of his own immediate ancestors, and claiming for the Loon family the first place and chieftainship among the Ojibways. After he had finished and again resumed his seat, Tug-waug-aun-ay, the head chief of the Crane family, a very modest and retiring man, seldom induced to speak in council, calmly arose, and gracefully wrapping his blanket about his body, leaving but the right arm free, he pointed toward the eastern skies, and exclaimed: "The Great Spirit once made a bird, and he sent it from the skies to make its abode on earth. The bird came, and when it reached half way down, among the clouds, it sent forth a loud and far sounding cry, which was heard by all who resided on the earth, and even by the spirits who make their abode within its bosom. When the bird reached within sight of the earth, it circled slowly above the Great Fresh Water Lakes, and again it uttered its echoing cry. Nearer and nearer it circled, looking for a resting place, till it lit on a hill overlooking Bow-e-ting (Sault Ste. Marie); here it chose its first resting place, pleased with the numerous white fish that glanced and swam in the clear waters and sparkling foam of the rapids. Satisfied with its chosen seat, again the bird sent forth its loud but solitary cry; and the No-kaig (Bear clan), A-waus-e-wug (Catfish), Ah-auh-wauh-ug (Loon), and Mous-o-neeg (Moose and Marten clan), gathered at his call. A large town was soon congregated, and the bird whom the Great Spirit sent presided over all.

"Once again it took its flight, and the bird flew slowly over the water of Lake Superior. Pleased with the sand point of Shaug-ah-waum-ik-ong, it circled over it, and viewed the numerous fish as they swam about in the clear depths of the Great Lake. It lit on Shaug-ah-waum-ik-ong, and from thence again it uttered its solitary cry. A voice came from the calm bosom of the lake, in answer; the bird pleased with the musical sound of the voice, again sent forth its cry, and the answering bird made its appearance in the wampum-breasted Ah-auh-wauh (loon). The bird spoke to it in a gentler tone, 'Is it thou that gives answer to my cry?' The Loon answered, 'It is I.' The bird then said to him, 'Thy voice is music – it is melody – it sounds sweet in my ear, from henceforth I appoint thee to answer my voice in Council.'

"Thus," continued the chief, "the Loon became the first in council, but he who made him chief was the Bus-in-aus-e (Echo Maker), or Crane. These are the words of my ancestors, who, from generation to generation, have repeated them into the ears of their children. I have done."

The old man took his seat in silence, and not a chief in that stricken and listening crowd arose to gainsay his words. All understood the allegory perfectly well, and as the curling smoke of their pipes arose from the lips and nostrils of the quiet listeners, there ascended with it the universal whisper, "It is true; it is true."

As an explanation of the figures used in the above traditional allegory, we will add, that the crane, commonly named in the Ojibway language Uj-e-jauk, is the symbol or totem of a large section of the tribe. This bird loves to soar among the clouds, and its cry can be heard when flying above, beyond the orbit of human vision. From this "far-sounding cry" the family who claim it as their totem derive their generic name of Bus-in-aus-e-wug (Echo Makers). This family claim, by this allegory, to have been the first discoverers and pioneer settlers at Sault Ste. Marie, and again at Pt. Shaug-ah-waum-ik-ong.

The Loon is the Totem also of a large clan. This bird is denominated by the Ojibways, Mong, but the family who claim it as their badge, are known by the generic name of Ah-auh-wauh, which is derived by imitating its peculiar cry. This family claim the hereditary first chieftainship in the tribe, but they cannot substantiate their pretensions further back than their first intercourse with the old French discoverers and traders, who, on a certain occasion, appointed some of their principal men as chiefs, and endowed them with flags and medals. Strictly confined to their own primitive tribal polity, the allegory of the Cranes cannot be controverted, nor has it ever been gain-said.

To support their pretentions, this family hold in their possession in a circular plate of virgin copper, on which is rudely marked indentations and hieroglyphics denoting the number of generations of the family who have passed away since they first pitched their lodges at Shaug-ah-waum-ik-ong and took possession of the adjacent country, including the Island of La Pointe or Mo-ning-wun-a-kaun-ing.

When I witnessed this curious family register in 1842, it was exhibited by Tug-waug-aun-ay to my father. The old chief kept it carefully buried in the ground, and seldom displayed it. On this occasion he only brought it to view at the entreaty of my mother, whose maternal uncle he was. Father, mother, and the old chief, have all since gone on to the land of spirits, and I am the only one still living who witnessed, on that occasion, this sacred relic of former days.

On this plate of copper was marked eight deep indentations, denoting the number of his ancestors who have passed away since they first lighted their fire at Shaug-ah-waum-ik-ong. They had all lived to a good old age.

By the rude figure of a man with a hat on its head, placed opposite one of these indentations, was denoted the period when the white race first made his appearance among them. This mark occurred in the third generation, leaving five generations which had passed away since that important era in the history.

Tug-waug-aun-ay was about sixty years of age at the time he showed this plate of copper, which he said had descended to him direct through a line of ancestors. He died two years since, and his death has added the ninth indentation thereon; making, at this period, nine generations since the Ojibways first resided at La Pointe, and six generations since their first intercourse with whites.

From the manner in which they estimate their generations, they may be counted as comprising a little over half the full term of years alloted to mankind, which will materially exceed the white man's generation. The Ojibways never count a generation as passed away till the oldest man in the family has died, and the writer assumes from these, and other facts obtained through observation and inquiry, forty years as the term of an Indian generation. It is necessary to state, however, for the benefit of those who may consider this an over-estimate, that, since the introduction of intoxicating drinks and diseases of the whites, the former well-authenticated longevity of the Indians has been materially lessened.

According to this estimate, it is now three hundred and sixty years since the Ojibways first collected in one grand central town on the Island of La Pointe, and two hundred and forty years since they were first discovered by the white race.

Seventy-seven years after, Jacques Cartier, representing the French nation, obtained his "first formal meeting with the Indians of the interior of Canada," and fifty-six years before Father Claude Allouez (as mentioned in Bancroft's History of America), first discovered the Ojibways congregated in the Bay of Shaug-ah-waum-ik-ong, preparing to go on a war excursion against their enemies the Dakotas.

From this period the Ojibways are traditionally well possessed of the most important event which have happened to them as a tribe, and from nine generations back, I am prepared to give, as obtained from their most veracious, reliable, and oldest men, their history, which may be considered as authentic.

In this chapter we have noted the course of their migrations, which, in all likelihood, occupied nearly two centuries prior to their final occupation of the shores of Lake Superior.

These movements were made while they were living in their primitive state, when they possessed nothing but the bow and arrow, sharpened stones, and bones of animals wherewith to kill game and fight their enemies. During this period they were surrounded by inveterate foes, and war was their chief pastime; but so dreamy and confused are their accounts of the battles which their ancestors fought, and the exploits they enacted, that the writer had refrained from dwelling on them with any particularity. One tradition, however, is deemed full worthy of notice, and while offering it as an historical fact, it will at the same time answer as a specimen of the mythological character of their tales which reach as far back as this period.

During their residence in the East, the Ojibways have a distinct tradition of having annihilated a tribe whom they denominate Mun-dua. Their old men, whom I have questioned on this subject, do not all agree in the location nor details. Their disagreements, however, are not very material, and I will proceed to give, verbatim, the version of Kah-nin-dum-a-win-so, the old chief of Sandy Lake:

"There was at one time living on the shores of a great lake, a numerous and powerful tribe of people; they lived congregated in one single town, which was so large that a person standing on a hill which stood in its centre, could not see the limits of it.

"This tribe, whose name was Mun-dua, were fierce and warlike; their hand was against every other tribe, and the captives whom they took in war were burned with fire as offerings to their spirits.

"All the surrounding tribes lived in great fear of them, till their Ojibway brothers called them to council, and sent the wampum and warclub, to collect the warriors of all the tribes with whom they were related. A war party was thus raised, whose line of warriors reached, as they marched in single file, as far as the eye could see. They proceeded against the great town of their common enemy, to put out their fire forever. They surrounded and attacked them from all quarters where their town was not bounded by the lake shore, and though overwhelming in their numbers, yet the Mun-dua had such confidence in their own force and prowess, that on the first day, they sent only their boys to repel the attack. The boys being defeated and driven back, on the second day the young men turned out to beat back their assailants. Still the Ojibways and their allies stood their ground and gradually drove them in, till on the eve of the second day, they found themselves in possession of half the great town. The Mun-duas now became awake to their danger, and on the third day, beginning to consider it a serious business, their old and tired warriors, 'mighty men of valor,' sang their war songs, and putting on their pants and ornaments of battle, they turned out to repel their invaders.

"The fight this day was hand to hand. There is nothing in their traditionary accounts, to equal the fierceness of the struggle described in this battle. The bravest men, probably, in America, had met — one party fighting for vengeance, glory, and renown; and the other for everything dear to man, home, family, for very existence itself!

"The Mun-dua were obliged at last to give way, and hotly pressed by their foes, women and children threw themselves into, and perished in the lake. At this juncture their aged chief, who had witnessed the unavailing defence of his people, and who saw the ground covered with the bodies of his greatest warriors, called with a loud voice on the 'Great Spirit' for help (for besides being chief of the Mun-duas, he was also a great medicine man and juggler).

"Being a wicked people, the Great Spirit did not listen to the prayer of their chief for deliverance. The aged medicine man then called upon the spirits of the water and of the earth, who are the under spirits of the 'Great Spirit of Evil,' and immediately a dark and heavy fog arose from the bosom of the lake, and covered in folds of darkness the site of the vanquished town, and the scene of the bloody battle. The old chieftain by his voice gathered together the remnants of his slaughtered tribe, and under cover of the Evil Spirit's fog, they left their homes forever. The whole day and ensuing night they travelled to escape from their enemies, until a gale of wind, which the medicine men of the Ojibways had asked the Great Spirit to raise, drove away the fog; the surprise of the fleeing Mun-duas was extreme when they found themselves standing on a hill back of their deserted town, and in plain view of their enemies.

"'It is the will of the Great Spirit that we should perish,' exclaimed their old chief; but once more they dragged their wearied limbs in hopeless flight. They ran into an adjacent forest where they buried the women and children in the ground, leaving a small aperture to enable them to breathe. The men then turned back, and once more they met their pursuing foes in a last mortal combat. They fought stoutly for a while, when again overpowered by numbers, they turned and fled, but in a different direction from the spot where they had secreted their families: but a few men escaped, who afterward returned, and disinterred the women and children. This small remnant of a once powerful tribe were the next year attacked by an Ojibway war-party, taken captive, and incorporated in this tribe. Individuals are pointed out to this day who are of Mun-dua descent, and who are members of the respected family whose totem is the Marten."

White Missionaries in Black

The era of their first knowledge of, and intercourse with the white race, is one of most vital importance in the history of the aborigines of this continent.

So far as their own tribe is concerned, the Ojibways have preserved accurate and detailed accounts of this event; and the information which their old men orally give on this subject, is worthy of much consideration, although they may slightly differ from the accounts which standard historians and writers have presented to the world, and which they have gleaned from the writings of the enterprising and fearless old Jesuit missionaries, and from the published narratives of the first adventurers who pierced into the heart of the American wilderness. This source of information may be considered as more reliable and authentic than the oral traditions of the Indians, but as we have undertaken to write their history as they themselves tell it, we will do so without respect to what has already been written by eminant and standard authors. The writer is disposed to consider as true and perfectly reliable, the information which he has obtained and thoroughly investigated, on this subject, and which he will proceed in this chapter to relate in the words of his old Indian informants.

A few preliminary remarks are deemed necessary, before fully entering into the narrative of the Ojibway's first knowledge and intercourse with his white brother.

Those who have carefully examined the writers of the old Jesuit missionaries and early adventurers, who claim to have been the first discoverers of new regions, and new people, in the then dark wilderness of the west, or central America, have found many gross mistakes and exaggerations, and their works as a whole, are only tolerated and their accounts made matters of history, because no other source of information has ever been opened to the public.

It is a fact found generally true, that the first adventurer who is able to give a flaming account of his travels, is handed down to posterity as the first discoverer of the country and people which he describes as having visited, when mayhap, that same region, and those same people had been, long previous, discovered by some obscure and more modest man, who, because he could not blazen forth his achievements in a book of travels, forever loses the credit of what he really has performed.

Many instances of this nature are being daily brought to light, and might be enumerated. Among others, Mr. Catlin claims in his book (and is believed by all who do not know to the contrary), to have been the first white man who visited the Dakota pipestone quarry, when in fact, that same quarry had been known to, and visited by white traders for nearly a century before Catlin saw it and wrote his book.

In the same manner also, Charles Lanman, of later notoriety, claims to have been the first white man who visited the Falls of St. Louis River, when in fact Aitkin, Morrison, Sayer, and a host of others as white as he, had visited, and resided for fifty years within sounds of those same falls. It is thus that a man who travels for the purpose of writing a book to sell, and who, being a man of letters, is able to trumpet forth his own fame, often plucks the laurels due to more modest and unlettered adventurers.

Mr. Bancroft in his standard "History of the United States," mentions that in the year 1665, the enterprising and persevering Jesuit missionary, Claude Allouez, with one companion, pushed his way into Lake Superior and discovered the Ojibways congregated in a large village in the Bay of Shaug-ah-waum-ik-ong, and preparing to go on a war party against the Dakotas; that he resided two years among them, and taught a choir of their youths to chant the *Pater* and *Ave*.

This is the first visit made by white men to this point on Lake Superior, of which we have any reliable *written* testimony. The account as given in Bancroft's "History" is not altogether corroborated by the Ojibways. It is only through minute and repeated inquiry, that I have learned the fact from their own lips, of this early visit of a "black gowned priest," but not of his having resided with them for any length of time. And they assert positively that it was many years after the first visit of the white men to their village in the Bay of Shaug-ah-waum-ik-ong, that the "priest" made his appearance among them. And I am disposed to doubt that as long a stay as two years was made by Father Allouez among their people, or that any of them learned to chant canticles, for the reason that the Ojibways, who are so minute in the relation of the particulars of any important event in their history, comprised within the past eight generations, do not make any mention of these facts. It is probable that the two years stay of this Jesuit in the Bay of Shaug-ah-waum-ik-ong, amounted to an occasional visit from Sault Ste. Marie, or Quebec, which place had already at this period, become the starting and rallying point of Western French avdenturers.

In those days there appears to have been a spirit of competition and rivalry among the different sects of the Catholic priesthood, as to who would pierce farthest into the western wilderness of America to plant the cross.

Imagination in some instances, outstripped their actual progress, and missionary stations are located on Hennepin's old map, in spots where a white man had never set foot. That the Catholic priests appeared amongst their earliest white visitors, the Ojibways readily acknowledge. And the name by which they have ever known the French people is a sufficient testimony to this fact, Wa-me-tigoshe. For many years this name could not be translated by the imperfect interpreters employed by the agents of the French and English, and its literal definition was not given till during the last war, at a council of different tribes, convened by the British at Drummond's Isle. The several Ojibway interpreters present were asked to give its definition. All failed, till John Baptiste Cadotte, acknowledged to be the most perfect interpreter of the Algics in his time, arose and gave it as follows: "Wa-mit-ig-oshe is derived from wa-wa, to wave, and metig, wood or stick, and means literally, people or 'men of the waving stick,' derived from the fact that when the French first appeared among the Algonquins who have given them this name, they came accompanied with priests who waved the Cross over their heads whenever they landed at an Indian village."

The circumstance also is worthy of mention, that a few years ago, an old Indian woman dug up an antique silver crucifux on her garden at Bad River near La Pointe, after it had been deeply ploughed. This discovery was made under my own observation, and I recollect at the time it created quite a little excitement amongst the good Catholics of La Pointe, who insisted that the Great Spirit had given this as a token for the old woman to join the church. The crucifix was found about two feet from the surface of the ground, composed of pure silver, about three inches long and size in proportion. It has long since been buried at Gull Lake, in the grave of a favorite grandchild of the old Indian woman, to whom she had given it as a plaything.

The Ojibways affirm that long before they became aware of the white man's presence on this continent, their coming was prophesied by one of their old men, whose great sanctity and oft-repeated fasts, enabled him to commune with spirits and see far into the future. He prophesied that the white spirits would come in numbers like sand on the lake shore, and would sweep the red race from the hunting grounds which the Great Spirit had given them as an inheritance. It was prophesied that the consequence of the white man's appearance would be, to the Anish-in-aub-ag, an "ending of the world." They acknowledge that at first their ancestors believed not the words of the old prophet foretellng these events; but now as the present generation daily see the foretold events coming to pass in all their details, the more reflective class firmly believe that they are truly a "doomed race." It was through harping on this prophecy, by which Te-cum-seh and his brother, the celebrated Show-a-no prophet, succeeded so well in forming a coalition among the Algic and other tribes, the main and secret object of which, was the final extermination of the white race from America.

The account which the Ojibways give of their first knowledge of the whites is as follows: —

While still living in their large and central town on the Island of La Pointe, a principal and leading Me-da-we priest, whose name was Ma-se-wa-pe-ga (whole ribs), dreamed a dream wherein he beheld spirits in the form of men, but possessing white skins and having their heads covered. They approached him with hands extended and with smiles on their faces. This singular dream he related to the principal men of the Ojibways on the occasion of a grand sacrificial feast to his guardian dream-spirit. He informed them that the white spirits who had thus appeared to him, resided toward the rising sun, and that he would go and search for them. His people tried to dissuade him from undertaking what they termed a foolish journey, but firm in his belief, and strong in his determination, he was occupied a whole year in making preparations for his intended journey. He built a strong canoe of birch bark and cedar wood; he hunted and cured plenty of meat for his provisions; and early in the spring when the ice had left the Great Lakes, and he had completed his preparations, Ma-se-we-pe-ga, with only his wife for a companion, started on his travels in quest of the white spirits whom he had seen in his dream.

He paddled eastward down the Great Lakes in the route of the former migration of his tribe, till he entered into a large river which flowed in the direction of the rising sun. Undiscovered he passed through the hostile tribes of the Naud-o-ways. At last when the river on which he floated, had become wide and like a lake, he discovered on the banks, a hut, made of logs, and he noticed the stumps of large trees which had been cut by sharper instruments than the rude stone axes used by Indians.

The signs were apparently two winters old, but satisfied that it was the work of the spirits, for whom he was in search, Ma-se-wa-pe-ga proceeded on his journey, and he soon came to another hut and clearing, which though deserted, had been built and occupied during the previous winter. Much encouraged, he paddled on down stream till he discoverd another hut from the top of which arose a smoke. It was occupied by the "white spirits," who, on his landing, cordially welcomed him with a shake of the hand.

When about to depart to return home, presents of steel axe, knife, beads, and a small strip of scarlet cloth were given him, which, carefully depositing in his medicine bag, as sacred articles, he brought safely home to his people at La Pointe. Ma-se-wa-pe-ga again collected the principal men of his tribe in council, and displaying his curious presents, he gave a full narrative of his succesful journey and the fulfillment of his dream. The following spring a large number of his people followed him on his second visit to the supposed "white spirits." They carried with them many skins of the beaver, and they returned home late in the fall with the dread fire-arm, which was to give them power over their much feared enemies. It is on this occasion also, that they first procured the fire-water which was to prove the most dreadful scourge and curse of their race.

It is related that on the arrival of this party at La Pointe, with the fire-water, none dare drink it, thinking it a poison which would immediately cause death.

They, however, to test its virtues, made an experimental trial on a very aged woman who – as they reasoned – had but a short time to live at all events, and whose death would be a matter of no account. The old woman drank it, appeared perfectly happy and in ecstasies, got over the effects of it, and begged for more. On which the men took courage, and drank up the remainder themselves. From that time, fire-water became the mammon of the Ojibways, and a journey of hundred of miles to procure a taste of it, was considered but a boy's play.

They tell, also, the effect of the first gun, which they procured from the whites and introduced among the more remote and ignorant Dakotas, with whom at this time they happened to be on terms of peace. A peace party of the Ojibways visited a village of these people on the St. Croix river, and took with them as a curiosity, the dreadful weapons they had procured. While enjoying their peaceful games, the young men of the Ojibways informed the Dakotas of the fearful and deadly effects of the gun; but they, thinking that the Ojibways wished to intimidate them with an imaginary fear, reviled and laughed at the instrument, and in their disbelief they even offered to bet against its deadly effects. The dispute becoming high, the bet was taken, and a Dakota brave in utter derision, insisted on offering the back part of his body as a prominent mark. He was shot dead on the spot. With difficultly the peace-party succeeded in returning safely home, for the wrath of the Dakotas was aroused at the death of their warrior; and the old feud was again renewed, though from this time they evinced a mortal fear of the gun, which their remoteness from the white strangers precluded them from obtaining, till many years after the Ojibways had been fully supplied.

About this time, the old men of the tribe date the sudden evacuation of their town on the island of La Pointe, and the planting of their lodges in the adjoining Bay of Shaug-ah-waum-ik-ong, which occurrence I have fully mentioned in the preceding chapter. The first white men whom they tell of having visited them, came after this dispersion, and while they were congregated on the shores of the Bay.

One clear morning in the early part of winter, soon after the islands which are clustered in this portion of Lake Superior and known as the Apostles, had been locked in ice, a party of young men of the Ojibways started out from their village in the Bay of Shaug-ah-waum-ik-ong, to go, as was customary, and spear fish through holes in the ice, between the island of La Pointe and the main shore, this being considered as the best ground for this mode of fishing. While engaged in their sport, they discovered a smoke arising from a point of the adjacent island, toward its eastern extremity.

The island of La Pointe was then totally unfrequented, from superstitious fears which had but a short time previous led to its total evacuation by the tribe, and it was considered an act of the greatest hardihood for any one to set foot on its shores. The young men returned home at evening and reported the smoke which they had seen arising from the island, and various were the conjectures of the old people respecting the persons who would dare to build a fire on the spirit-haunted isle. They must be strangers, and the young men were directed, should they again see the smoke, to go and find out who made it.

Early the next morning, again proceeding to their fishing ground, the young men once more noticed the smoke arising from the eastern end of the unfrequented island, and led on by curiosity, they ran thither and found a small log cabin in which they discovered two white men in the last stages of starvation. The young Ojibways filled with compassion, carefully conveyed them to their village, where, being nourished with great kindness, their lives were preserved.

These two white men had started from Quebec during the summer with a supply of goods, to go and find the Ojibways who every year had brought rich packs of beaver to the sea-coast, notwithstanding that their road was barred by numerous parties of the watchful and jealous Iroquois. Coasting slowly up the southern shores of the Great Lake late in the fall, they had been driven by the ice on to the unfrequented island, and not discovering the vicinity of the Indian village, they had been for some time enduring the pangs of hunger. At the time they were found by the young Indians, they had been reduced to the extremity of roasting and eating their woollen cloth and blankets as the last means of sustaining life.

Having come provided with goods they remained in the village during the winter, exchanging their commodities for beaver skins. The ensuing spring a large number of the Ojibways accompanied them on their return home.

From close inquiry, and judging from events which are said to have occurred about this period of time, I am disposed to believe that this first visit by the whites took place about two hundred years ago. It is, at any rate, certain that it happened a few years prior to the visit of the "Black gowns" mentioned in Bancroft's History, and it is one hundred and eighty-four years since this well-authenticated occurrence.

If thorough inquiry were to be made, it would be found that the idea which is now generally believed, that the pious missionaries of those olden times, were the first pioneers into the Indian country about the great chain of Lakes, and Upper Mississippi, and were only followed closely by the traders, is a mistaken one. The adventurous, but obsure and unlettered trader, was the first pioneer. He cared only for beaver skins, and his ambition not leading him to secure the name of the first discoverer by publishing his travels, this honor naturally fell to those who were as much actuated by a thirst for fame, as by religious zeal.

The glowing accounts given by these traders on their return with their peltries to Quebec, their tales of large villages of peaceable and docile tribes, caused the eager Jesuit and Franciscan to accompany him back to the scene of his glowing accounts, and to plant the cross amongst the ignorant and simple children of the forest.

In making these remarks, we do not wish to deteriorate from the great praise which is nevertheless due to these pious and perserving fathers, who so early attempted to save the souls of the benighted Indians.

In the separation of the Ojibway tribe into two divisions, upwards of three centuries ago at the outlet of Lake Superior, which has been fully treated of in a previous chapter, a considerable band remained on their ancient village site at Bow-e-ting or Falls of St. Marie; and here, some years prior to the first visit of the white men and "Black Gowns" to the greater village in the Bay of Shaug-ah-waum-ik-ong, traders and priests had established themselves, and this circumstance naturally conduced to draw thither from their more western and dangerously situated villages, many families of this tribe, till they again numbered many wigwams, on this, the site of their ancient town. It was the first discovery of this tribe, at this point, which has given them the name, by the French, of Saulteaux, from the circumstance of their residing at the "Falls."

This band have ever since this period, remained detached by the intervening southern shores of Lake Superior, from the main body of the tribe who have radiated northward, westward and southward, from their central town of La Pointe.

Aided by the French, Ottaways, Potawatumees, and Wyandots, they succeeded in checking the harassing incursions of the war-like Iroquois, and as they became equally possessed of the fire-arm, instead of being pressed westward, as they had been for centuries before, they retraced the eastern track of their ancestor's former emigration, and rejoined the remnants of their race who had been for many years cut off from them by the intervening Iroquois, and who had first greeted the French strangers who landed in the river St. Lawrence, and who termed them Algonquins.

From this period, the communication between the eastern section or rear of the Algic tribes, occupying the lower waters of the River St. Lawrence, and the great western van who occupied the area of Lake Superior, became comparatively free and open, for villages of the Algic tribes lined the shores of the great chain of Lakes and also the banks of the great river which forms the outlet into the "salt water."

In one of their traditions it is stated that "when the white man first came in sight of the 'Great Turtle' island of Mackinaw, they beheld walking on the pebbly shores, a crane and a bear who received them kindly, invited them to their wigwams, and placed food before them." This allegory denotes that Ojibways of the Crane and Bear Totem families first received the white strangers, and extended to them the hand of friendship and rites of hospitality, and in remembrance of this occurrence they are said to have been the favorite clans with the old French discoverers.

Migration and the Fur Trade

We have now come to that period in their history, when the important consequences of their discovery and intercourse with the white race began to work their effects upon the former even, monotonous, and simple course of life, which the Ojibways had pursued for so many generations. Their clay kettles, pots, and dishes were exchanged for copper and brass utensils; their comparatively harmless bow and arrow, knives and spears of bones, were thrown aside, and in their place they procured the fire-arm, steel knife, and tomahawk of the whites. They early became aware of the value of furs to the white strangers, and that the skins of animals, which they before used only for garments, now procured them the coveted commodities of the pale-faced traders, and the consequence was, that an indiscriminate slaughter, from this period commenced, of the beaver and other fur animals, which had grown numerous because molested only on occasions when their warm fur had been needed to cover the nakedness of the wild Indian, or their meat required to satisfy his hunger.

In the early part of the seventeenth century the Ojibways had already commenced the custom of yearly visiting Quebec, and afterwards Montreal, taking with them packs of beaver skins, and returning with the fire-arms, blankets, trinkets, and firewater of the whites. This custom they kept up for many years, gradually curtailing the length of their journeys as the whites advanced toward them step by step, locating their trading posts, first at Detroit, then at Mackinaw, then at Sault Ste. Marie, till at last the smoke of their cabins arose from the island of La Pointe itself, when these periodical journeys came comparatively to an end.

It was many years before the first French traders located a permanent trading post among the Ojibways of Shaug-ah-waum-ik-ong, and in the meantime, as this tribe became supplied with fire-arms, and killed off the beaver, in the vicinity of their ancient seat, they radiated in bands inland, westward and southward towards the beautiful lakes and streams which form the tributaries of the Wisconsin, Chippeway, and St. Croix rivers, and along the south coast of the Great Lake to its utmost extremity, and from thence even inland unto the headwaters of the Mississippi. All this was the country of the Dakotas and Foxes, and bravely did they battle to beat back the encroaching Ojibways from their best hunting grounds, but in vain; for the invaders, besides having increased in numbers, had become possessed of fearful weapons, against which they feared to battle with their primitive bow and arrow.

For a number of years the Ojibways continued to consider the bay of Shaug-ah-waum-ik-ong as their common home, and their hunting parties returned thither at different seasons of the year. Here also, and only here, were their grand medicine rites performed, and their war-parties collected to march against, and drive further back, their numerous foes. The fur trade has been the mainspring and cause which has led the Ojibways westward and more westward, till they have become possessed through conquest, and a persevering, never-relaxing pressure on their enemies, of the vast tracts of country over which they are scattered at the present day. Their present proud positions in this respect they have not gained without an equivalent price in blood and life, and the Ojibway exclaims with truth when asked by the grasping "Long Knife" to sell his country, that "it is strewed with the bones of his fathers, and enriched with their blood."

Their wars at this period were generally carried on by small and desultory parties, and it was only on occasion when smarting under some severe blow or loss, inflicted by their enemies, that the warriors of the tribe would collect under some noted leader, and marching into the Dakota or Fox country, make a bold and effective strike, which would long be remembered, and keep their enemies in fear and check.

A circumstance happened, about this time, which in the regular course of our narrative, we will here relate. A few lodges of Ojibway hunters under the guidance of Bi-aus-wah, a leading man of the tribe, claiming the Loon Totem, was one spring encamped at Kah-puk-wi-e-kah, a bay on the lake shore situated forty miles west of La Pointe.

Early one morning the camp was attacked by a large war-party of Foxes, and the men, women and children all murdered, with the exception of a lad and an old man, who, running into a swamp, and becoming fastened in the bog and mire, were captured and taken in triumph by the Foxes to their village, there to suffer death with all the barbarous tortures which a savage could invent.

Bi-aus-wah, at the time of the attack, was away on a hunt, and he did not return till towards evening. His feelings on finding his wigwams in ashes, and the lifeless, scalpless remains of his beloved family and relatives strewed about on the blood-stained ground, can only be imagined. He had lost all that bound him to life, and perfectly reckless he followed the return trail of the Foxes determined to die, if necessary, in revenging the grievous wrong which they had inflicted on him. He arrived at the village of his enemies, a day after their successful war-party had returned, and he heard men, women, and children screaming and yelling with delight as they danced around the scalps which their warriors had taken.

Secreting himself on the outskirts of the village, the Ojibway chieftain waited for an opportunity to imbrue his hands in the blood of an enemy who might come within reach of his tomahawk. He had not remained long in his ambush, when the Foxes collected a short distance from the village for the purpose of torturing and burning their two captives. The old was first produced, and his body being wrapped in folds of the combustible birch bark, the Foxes set fire to it and caused him to run the gauntlet amid their hellish whoops and screams; covered with a perfect blaze of fire, and receiving withal a shower of blows, the old man soon expired.

The young and tender lad was then brought forward, and his doom was to run backwards and forwards on a long pile of burning fagots, till consumed to death. None but a parent can fully imagine the feeling which wrung the heart of the ambushed Ojibway chieftain, as he now recognized his only surviving child in the young captive who was about to undergo these torments. His single arm could not rescue him, but the brave father determined to die for or with his only son, and as the cruel Foxes were on the point of setting fire to the heap of dry fagots on which the lad had been place, they were surprised to see the Ojibway chief step proudly and boldly into their midst and address them as follows: —

"My little son, whom you are about to burn with fire, has seen but a few winters; his tender feet have never trodden the war path — he has never injured you! But the hairs of my head are white with many winters, and over the graves of my relatives I have hung many scalps which I have taken from the heads of the Foxes; my death is worth something to you, let me therefore take the place of my child that he may return to his people."

Taken totally by surprise, the Foxes silently listened to the chief's proposal, and ever having coveted his death, and now fearing the consequence of his despairing efforts, they accepted his offer, and releasing the son, they bade him to depart, and burnt the brave father in his stead. The young man returned safely to his people at La Pointe, and the tale of his murdered kindred, and father's death, spread like wild fire among the wide scattered bands of the Ojibways.

A war party was gathered and warriors came, even from distant Ste. Marie and Grand Portage, to join in revenging the death of their chief.

They marched toward the headwaters of the St. Croix and Chippeway rivers, and returned not home till they had attacked and destroyed six villages of the Foxes, some of which were composed of earthen wigwams, which now form the mounds which are spread so profusely over this section of country. They reaped a rich harvest of scalps, and made such an effective strike, that from this time the Foxes evacuated the rice lakes and midland country about the St. Croix and Chippeway rivers, and retired south to the Wisconsin.

Soon after the above occurrence, the Ojibways pressed up the lake shore, and Wa-me-gis-ug-o, a daring and fearless hunter, obtained a firm footing and pitched his wigwam permanently at Fond du Lac, or Wi-a-quah-ke-che-gume-eng. He belonged to the Marten Totem family, and the present respected chiefs of that now important village, Shin-goob and Nug-aun-ub, are his direct descendants. Many families of his people followed the example of this pioneer, and erecting their wigwams on the island of the St. Louis River, near its outlet into the lake, for greater security, they manfully held out against the numerous attacks of the fierce Dakotas, whose villages were but two days' march toward the south of the St. Croix River, and the west, at Sandy Lake. During this time, comprised between the years 1612 (at which I date their first knowledge of the white race), and 1671, when the French made their first national treaty of convocation at Sault Ste. Marie with the northwestern tribes, no permanent trading post had as yet been erected on the shores of Lake Superior; the nearest post was the one located at Sault Ste. Marie, which as early as the middle of the seventeenth century, had already become an important depot and outlet to the Lake Superior fur trade. Their intercourse with the whites consisted in yearly visists to their nearest western posts. The trade was partially also carried on through the medium of the intervening kindred tribe of Ottaways, or by adventurous traders who came amongst them with canoes loaded with goods, made a transient stay, sometimes even passing a winter amongst them, following their hunting camps, but returning the spring of the year to Quebec with the proceeds of their traffic. No incidents which the old men related as connected with the whites, is worthy of mention, till a messenger of the "Great French King" visited their village at Shaug-ah-waum-ik-ong, and invited them to a grand council of different tribes to be held at Sault

St. Marie. Some of the words of this messenger are still recollected and minutely related by the Ojibways.

Early the following spring, a large delegation proceeded to Ste. Marie to attend the council, and hear the words of the "Great King of the French." Ke-che-ne-zuh-yauh, head chief of the great Crane family, headed this party, and represented the nation of the Ojibways. It is his descendants in the fourth generation, from whom I have obtained the few detached items which are here given respecting this important event.

Michel Cadotte (son of the Mons. M. Cadotte whom we have already had occasion to mention), who is now the oldest man of mixed Ojibway and French blood in the northwest, states that his great-grandfather, a Mons. Cadeau, on this occasion first came into the Ojibway country in the train of the French envoy Sieur de Lusson. The name has since been spelled Cadotte, and the wide spread family of this name claims their connection with the Ojibway tribe from this period. From this old half-breed, still living at La Pointe, I have obtained much reliable information, corroborating with that obtained from the Indians themselves.

The envoy of the French king asked, in the name of his nation, for permission to trade in the country, and for free passage to and from their villages all times thereafter. He asked that the fires of the French and Ojibway nations might be made one, and everlasting.

He promised the protection of the great French nation against all their enemies, and addressing himself to the Chippeway chieftain from La Pointe, he said: —

"Every morning you will look towards the rising of the sun and you shall see the fire of your French father reflecting towards you, to warm you and your people. If you are in trouble, you, the Crane, must arise in the skies and cry with your 'far sounding' voice, and I will hear you. The fire of your French father shall last forever, and warm his children." At the end of this address a gold medal shaped like a heart was placed on the breast of Ke-che-ne-zuh-yauh, and by this mark of honor he was recognized as the chief of the Lake Superior Ojibways. These words have been handed down from generation to generation, to his present descendants, and it will be readily seen by them that the French had already learned to use the figurative and forcible style of expression of the Ojibways, and understood their division into Totemic clans, with the peculiarities on which each clan prided themselves.

The Ojibways received the "heart" of the French brethren, and accepted their proposals of peace, amity, and mutual support and protection. From this period their country became more free and open to French enterprise, and they learned to term the French king "father."

The Ojibways learned to love the French people, for the Frenchmen, possessing a character of great plasticity, easily assimilated themselves to the customs and mode of life of their red brethren. They respected their religious rites and ceremonies, and they "never laughed" at their superstitious beliefs and ignorance. They fully appreciated, and honored accordingly, the many noble traits and qualities possessed by these bold and wild hunters of the forest. It is an acknowledged fact that no nation of whites have ever succeeded so well in gaining the love and confidence of the red men, as the Franks. It is probable that their character in many respects was more similar, and adapted to the character of the Indian, than any other European nation. The "voyageur du Nord," as were then termed the common class of the French who visited them for the purposes of trade, were nearly as illiterate, ignorant, and superstitious as themselves, and many of them were far beneath the red man in strength of character and morality.

Their aim was not so much that of gain as of pleasure, and the enjoyment of present life, and mainly in this respect will be found the difference between the nature of their intercourse with the natives of America, and that which has since been carried on by the English and Americans, who, as a general truth, have made Mammon their God, and have looked on the Indian but as a tool or means of obtaining riches, and other equally mercenary ends.

In their lack of care for the morrow, which in a measure characterized the French "voyageur," and in their continual effervescence of animal spirits, openheartedness, and joviality, they agreed fully with the like characteristics possessed by the Ojibways. Some of my readers may be surprised at my thus placing the Indian on a par with the laughter-loving Frenchman, for the reason that he has ever been represented as a morose, silent, and uncommunicative being. It is only necessary to state that this is a gross mistake, and but a character (far different from his real one), assumed by the Indian in the presence of strangers, and especially white strangers in whom he has no confidence. Another bond which soon more firmly attached them one to another with strong ties of friendship, was created by the Frenchmen taking the women of the Ojibways as wives, and rearing large families who remained in the country, and to this day, the mixture and bonds of blood between these two people has been perpetuated, and remains unbroken.

The days of the French domination was the Augustan era of the fur trade, and beavers were so plenty and the profits arising from the trade were so large, that the French traders readily afforded to give large presents of their coveted commodities, their beloved tobacco and fire-water to the Indians who visited them at their posts, or on occasions when they visited them at their own villages. In those days along the lake shore villages of the Ojibways, from Mackinaw to Fond du Lac of Lake Superior, there was no music so sweet to the ears of the inhabitants, as the enlivening boat song of the merry French "voyageurs," as they came from the direction of Quebec and Montreal each spring of the year—rapidly looming up from the bosom of the calm lake, laden with the articles so dearly valued among the wild hunters. They recognized in these yearly visits the "rays of the fire of their great French father," which he bade them to "look for each morning (spring) towards the rising of the sun."

No strangers were more welcome to the Ojibways, and warm were the shaking of hands and embraces on these occasions between the dusky son of the forests, and the polite and warm-hearted Frank. The dark-eyed damsels, though they stood bashfully in the rear of those who thronged the beach to welcome the new-comers, yet with their faces partly hidden they darted glances to welcome, and waited in the wigwams impatiently for their white sweethearts to come in the darkness and silence of night, to present the trinkets which they had brought all the way from Quebec, to adorn their persons and please their fancy.

After the Ojibways became possessed with fire-arms and ammunition, the arrival of a French "Bourgeois" with the flag of France flying at the stern of his canoe, was saluted with a volley of musketry, and in turn, when any chief approached the "posts" or "forts" accompanied with the same ensign, discharges of cannons were fired in his honor by the French. Thus, interchanges of goodwill and polite attention were continually kept up between them.

The French early gained the utmost confidence of the Ojibways, and thereby they became more thoroughly acquainted with their true and real character, even during the comparative short season in which they mingled with them as a nation, than the British and Americans are at this present day, after over a century of intercourse. The French understood their division into clans, and treated each clan according to the order of its ascendency in the tribe. They conformed also to their system of governmental polity, of which the totemic division formed the principal ingredient. They were circumspect and careful in bestowing medals, flags, and other marks of honor, and appointing chiefs, and these acts were never done unless being first certain of the approbation of the tribe, and it being in accordance with their civil polity. In this important respect the British, and American government especially, have lacked most woefully. The agents and commissioners, and even traders of these two nations, have appointed chiefs indiscriminately or only in conformity with selfish motives and ends, and there is nothing which has conduced so much to disorganize, confuse, and break up the former simple but well-defined civil polity of these people; and were the matter to be fully investigated, it would be found that this almost utter disorganization has been one of the chief stumbling-blocks which has ever been in the way of doing good to the Indian race. This short-sighted system has created nothing but jealousies and heart-burnings among the Ojibways. It has broken the former commanding influence of their hereditary chiefs, and the consequence is, that the tribe is without a head or government, and it has become infinitely difficult to treat with them as a people. No good has resulted from this bad and thoughtless policy even to the governments who have allowed it to be pursued by its agents. On the contrary, they are punished daily by the evil consequences arising from it, for in this is to be found the true and first cause of the complaints which are continually to this day being poured into the ears of the "Great Father" at Washington, and it is through this that misunderstandings and nonconformity have arisen to treaties which have been made by the United States, not only with the Ojibways, but other tribes, and which are of the same nature that eventually led to the Creek, Seminole and Black Hawk wars.

The Life, History, and Travels
of Kah-ge-ga-gah-bowh

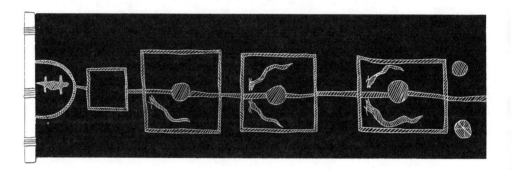

THE LIFE OF KAH-GE-GA-GAH-BOWH

THE CHRISTIAN will no doubt feel for my poor people, when he hears the story of one brought from that unfortunate race called the Indians. The lover of humanity will be glad to see that that once powerful face can be made to enjoy the blessings of life.

What was once impossible – or rather thought to be – is made possible through my experience. I have made many close observations of men, and things around me; but, I regret to say, that I do not think I have made as good use of my opportunities as I might have done. It will be seen that I know but little – yet O how precious *that little!* – I would rather lose my right hand than be deprived of it.

I loved the woods, and the chase. I had the nature for it, and gloried in nothing else. The mind for letters was in me, *but was asleep,* till the dawn of Christianity arose, and awoke the slumbers of the soul into energy and action.

You will see that I served the imaginary gods of my poor blind father. I was out early and late in quest of the favors of the *Mon-e-doos* (spirits), who, it was said, were numerous – who filled the air! At early dawn I watched the rising of the *palace* of the Great Spirit – *the sun* – who, it was said, made the world!

Early as I can recollect, I was taught that it was the gift of the many spirits to be a good hunter and warrior; and much of my time I devoted in search of their favors. On the mountain top, or along the valley, or the water brook, I searched for some kind intimation from the spirits who made their residence in the noise of the waterfalls.

by George Copway

I dreaded to hear the voice of the angry spirit in the gathering clouds. I looked with anxiety to catch a glimpse of the wings of the Great Spirit, who shrouded himself in rolling white and dark clouds – who, with his wings, fanned the earth, and laid low the tall pines and hemlock in his course – who rode in whirlwinds and tornadoes, and plucked the trees from their woven roots – who chased other gods from his course – who drove the Bad Spirit from the surface of the earth, down to the dark caverns of the deep. Yet he was a kind spirit. My father taught me to call that spirit Ke-sha-mon-e-doo – *Benevolent Spirit* – for his ancestors taught him no other name to give to that spirit who made the earth, with all its variety and smiling beauty. His benevolence I saw in the running of the streams, for the animals to quench their thirst and the fishes to live; the fruit of the earth teemed wherever I looked. Every thing I saw smilingly said Ke-sha-mon-e-doo nin-ge-oo-she-ig – *the Benevolent spirit made me.*

Where is he? My father pointed to the sun. What is his will concerning me, and the rest of the Indian race? This was a question that I found no one could answer, until a beam from heaven shone on my pathway, which was very dark, when first I saw that there was a true heaven – not in the far-setting sun, where the Indian anticipated a rest, a home for his spirit – but in the bosom of the Highest.

I view my life like the mariner on the wide ocean, without a compass, in the dark night, as he watches the heavens for the north star, which his eye having discovered, he makes his way amidst surging seas, and tossed by angry billows into the very jaws of death till he arrives safely anchored at port. I have been tossed with hope and fear in this life; no star-light shone on my way, until the men of God pointed me to a Star in the East, as it rose with all its splendor

and glory. It was the Star of Bethlehem. I could now say in the language of
the poet —

"Once on the raging seas I rode,
  The storm was loud, the night was dark;
The ocean yawned, and rudely blowed
  The wind that tossed my foundering bark."

Yes, I hope to sing some day in the realms of bliss —

"It was my guide, my light, my all!
  It bade my dark foreboding cease;
And through the storm and danger's thrall,
  It led me to the port of peace."

I have not the happiness of being able to refer to written records in narrating
the history of my forefathers; but I can reveal to the world what has long been
laid up in my memory; so that when "I go the way of all the earth," the crooked
and singular paths which I have made in the world, may not only be a warning
to others, but may inspire them with a trust in God. And not only a warning
and a trust, but also that the world may learn that there once lived such a man
as Kah-ge-ga-gah-bowh, when they read his griefs and his joys.

My parents were of the Ojebwa nation, who lived on the lake back of Cobourg,
on the shores of Lake Ontario, Canada West. The lake was called Rice Lake, where
there was a quantity of wild rice, and much game of different kinds, before the
whites cleared away the woods, where the deer and the bear then resorted.

My father and mother were taught the religion of their nation. My father
became a medicine man in the early part of his life, and always had by him the
implements of war, which generally distinguish our head men. He was a good
hunter as any in the tribe. Very few brought more furs than he did in the spring.
Every spring they returned from their hunting grounds. The Ojebwas each
claimed, and claim to this day, hunting grounds, rivers, lakes, and whole districts
of country. No one hunted on each other's ground. My father had the northern
fork of the river Trent, above Bellmont Lake.

My great-grandfather was the first who ventured to settle at Rice Lake, after
the Ojebwa nation defeated the Hurons, who once inhabited all the lakes in
Western Canada, and who had a large village just on the top of the hill of the
Anderson farm, (which was afterwards occupied by the Ojebwas), and which
furnished a magnificent view of the lakes and surrounding country. He was of
the *Crane tribe,* i.e. had a crane for totem — *coat of arms* — which now forms the
totem of the villagers, excepting those who have since come amongst us from
other villages by intermarriage, for there was a law that no one was to marry
one of the same totem, for all considered each other as being related. He must
have been a daring adventurer — *a warrior* — for no one would have ventured to
go and settle down on the land from which they had just driven the Hurons,

whom the Ojebwas conquered and reduced, unless he was a great hero. It is said that he lived about the islands of Rice Lake, secreting himself from the enemy for several years, until some others came and joined him, when they formed a settlement on one of the islands. He must have been a great hunter, for this was one of the principal inducements that made him venture there, for there must have been abundance of game of every kind. The Ojebwas are called, here and all around, Massis-suagays, because they came from Me-sey Sah-gieny, at the head of Lake Huron, as you go up to Sault St. Marie falls.

Here he lived in jeopardy – with his life in his hand – enduring the unpleasant idea that he lived in the land of bones – *amidst the gloom*, which shrouded the once happy and populous village of the Hurons; here their bones lay broad-cast around his wigwam; where, among these woods once rang the war cry of the Hurons, echoing along the valley of the river Trent, but whose sinewed arms now laid low, with their badges and arms of war, in one common grave, near the residence of Peter Anderson, Esq. Their graves, forming a hillock, are now all that remain of this once powerful nation. Their bones, gun barrels, tomahawks, war spears, large scalping knives, are yet to be found there. This must have taken place soon after the formation of the settlement in Quebec.

The *Crane tribe* became the sole proprietors of this part of the Ojebwa land; the descendants of this tribe will continue to wear the distinguishing sign; except in a few instances, the chiefs are of this tribe.

My grandfather lived here about this time, and held some friendly intercourse with the whites. My father here learned the manners, customs, and worship of the nation. He, and others, became acquainted with the early settlers, and have ever been friendly with the whites. And I know the day when he used to shake the hand of the white man, and, *very friendly*, the white man would say, "*take some whiskey.*" When he saw any hungering for venison, he gave to eat; and some, in return for his kindness, have repaid him after they became good and great farmers.

My mother was of the *Eagle tribe;* she was a sensible woman; she was as good a hunter as any of the Indians; she could shoot the deer, and the ducks flying, as well as they. Nature had done a great deal for her, for she was active; and she was much more cleanly than the majority of our women in those days. She lived to see the day when most of her children were given up to the Lord in Christian baptism; while she experienced a change of heart, and the fulness of God in man, for she lived daily in the enjoyment of God's favors. I will speak more of her at a proper time, respecting her life and happy death.

My father still lives; he is from sixty-five to seventy years old, and is one of the chiefs of Rice Lake Indian Village. He used to love fire-water before he was converted to God, but now lives in the enjoyment of religion, and he is happy without the devil's spittal – *whiskey.* If Christianity had not come, and the grace of God had not taken possession of his heart, his head would soon have been laid low beneath the fallen leaves of the forest, and I, left, in my youthful days, an orphan. But to God be all the praise for his timely deliverance.

The reader will see that I cannot boast of an exalted parentage, nor trace the past history to some renowned warrior in days of yore; but let the above suffice. My fathers were those who endured much; who first took possession of the conquered lands of the Hurons.

I was born in *nature's wide domain!* The trees were all that sheltered my infant limbs – the blue heavens all that covered me. I am one of Nature's children; I have always admired her; she shall be my glory; her features – her robes, and the wreath about her brow – the seasons – her stately oaks, and the evergreen – her hair – ringlets over the earth, all contribute to my enduring love of her; and wherever I see her, emotions of pleasure roll in my breast, and swell and burst like waves on the shores of the ocean, in prayer and praise to Him who has placed me in her hand. It is thought great to be born in palaces, surrounded with wealth – but to be born in nature's wide domain is greater still!

I was born sometime in the fall of 1818, near the mouth of the river Trent, called in our language, Sah-ge-dah-we-ge-wah-noong, while my father and mother were attending the annual distribution of the presents from the government to the Indians. I was the third of our family; a brother and sister being older, both of whom died. My brother died without the knowledge of the Saviour, but my sister experienced the power of the loving grace of God. One brother, and two step-brothers, are still alive.

I remember the tall trees, and the dark woods – the swamp just by, where the little wren sang so melodiously after the going down of the sun in the west – the current of the broad river Trent – the skipping of the fish, and the noise of the rapids a little above. It was here I first saw the light; a little fallen down shelter, made of evergreens, and a few dead embers, the remains of the last fire that shed its genial warmth around, were all that marked the spot. When I last visited it, nothing but fur poles stuck in the ground, and they were leaning on account of decay. Is this dear spot, made green by the tears of memory, any less enticing and hallowed than the palaces where princes are born? I would much more glory in this birth-place, with the broad canopy of heaven above me, and the giant arms of the forest trees for my shelter, than to be born in palaces of marble, studded with pillars of gold! Nature will be Nature still while palaces shall decay and fall in ruins. Yes Niagara will be Niagara a thousand years hence! the rainbow, a wreath over her brow, shall continue as long as the sun, and the flowing of the river! While the work of art, however impregnable, shall in atoms fall.

Our wigwam we always carried with us wherever we went. It was made in the following manner: Poles were cut about fifteen feet long; three with crotches at the end, which were stuck in the ground some distance apart, the upper ends meeting, and fastened with bark; and then other poles were cut in circular form and bound round the first, and then covered with plaited reeds, or sewed birch bark, leaving an opening on top for the smoke to escape. The skins of animals formed a covering for a gap, which answered for a door. The family all seated tailor-fashion on mats. In the fall and winter they were generally made more secure, for the purpose of keeping out the rain and cold. The covering of our wigwam was always carried by my mother, whenever we went through the woods. In the summer it was easier and pleasanter to move about from place to place, than in the winter. In the summer we had birch bark canoes, and with these we travelled very rapidly and easily. In the winter every thing was carried upon the back. I have known some Indians to carry a whole deer – not a small one, but a buck. If an Indian could lift up his pack off the ground by means of his arms, it was a good load, not too light nor too heavy. I once carried one hundred and ninety-six weight of flour, twelve pounds of shot, five pounds of coffee, and some sugar, about a quarter of a mile, without resting – the flour was in two bags. It was very heavy. This was since I travelled with the missionaries, in going over one of the portages in the west.

Our summer houses were made like those in gardens among the whites, except that the skeleton is covered with bark.

The hunting grounds of the Indians were secured by right, a law and custom among themselves. No one was allowed to hunt on another's land, without invitation or permission. If any person was found trespassing on the ground of another, all his things were taken from him, except a handful of shot, powder sufficient to serve him in going *straight* home, a gun, a tomahawk, and a knife; all the fur, and other things, were taken from him. If he were found a second time trespassing, all his things were taken from him, except food sufficient to subsist on while going home. And should he still come a third time to trespass on the same, or another man's hunting grounds, his nation, or tribe, are then informed of it, who take up his case. If still he disobey, he is banished from his tribe.

My father's hunting ground was at the head of Crow River, a branch of the River Trent, north of the Prince Edward District, Canada West. There are two branches to this river – one belongs to George Poudash, one of the principal chiefs of our nation; the other to my father; and the Crow River belongs to another chief by the name of John Crow. During the last war the Indians did not hunt or fish much for nearly six years, and at the end of that time there were large quantities of beaver, otter, mink, lynx, fishes, &c.

These hunting grounds abound with rivers and lakes; the face of the country is swampy and rocky; the deer and the bear abound in these woods; part of the surrendered territory is included in it. In the year 1818, 1,800,000 acres of it were surrendered to the British government. For how much, do you ask? For $2,960 per annum! What a *great sum* for British generosity!

Much of the back country still remains unsold, and I hope the scales will be removed from the eyes of my poor countrymen, that they may see the robberies perpetrated upon them, before they surrender another foot of territory.

From these lakes and rivers come the best furs that are caught in Western Canada. Buyers of fur get large quantities from here. They are then shipped to

New York City, or to England. Whenever fruit is plenty, ears are also plenty, and there is much bear hunting. Before the whites came amongst us, the skins of these animals served for clothing; they are now sold from three to eight dollars apiece.

My father generally took one or two families with him when he went to hunt; all were to hunt, and place their gains into one common stock till spring, (for they were often out all winter), when a division took place. . . .

The missionaries first visited us on the island called *Be-quah-qua-yong,* in 1837, under the following circumstances. My father and I went to Port Hope, to see our principal trader, John D. Smith, in order to obtain our goods and whiskey, about twelve miles from Rice Lake. After my father had obtained the goods, he asked for whiskey. Mr. Smith said, "John, do you know whiskey will yet kill you, if you do not stop drinking? Why, all the Indians at Credit River, and at Grape Island, have abandoned drinking, and are now Methodists. I cannot give you any whiskey."

"*Tah yah!* (an exclamation of surprise,) *it cannot be,* I *must* have whiskey to carry home; my people expect it," said my father. He wished to buy a barrel, but only obtained, after much pleading, about five gallons. My father *promised* to drink no more when the missionaries should have come to Rice Lake. We reached home the same day about one o'clock, and the Indians were awaiting our arrival, that they might have some fire-water. They assembled themselves together and began to drink and to smoke. Many of them were sitting on the grass when the whiskey began to steal away their brains. One of our number suddenly ran in the crowd, and said, "*the black coats* (missionaries) are coming, and are on the other side of the point." Each looked at the other with perfect astonishment. My father said to our informer, "invite them to come over to us;" and to the one who was dealing whiskey, "cover the keg with your blanket, and don't let the black coats see it." The whiskey was concealed, and then came the messengers of glad tiding and great joy. They were converted Indians, saved by grace, and had been sent to preach to us, and to invite us to attend a camp meeting near Cobourg. After shaking hands all around, one of them delivered a speech to the half drunken Indians. He referred to the day when they were without the good news of *salvation.* He spoke with great earnestness, and the tears fell from his eyes. He said, "*Jesus Christ, Ke-sha-mon-e-doo O-gwe-son,* (i.e., the Benevolent Spirit's son), came down to the world, and died to save the people; all the Indians at the Credit River, and Grape Island, are now on their road to the place where the Saviour has gone. Jesus has left a book containing his commands and saying to all the world; you *will see it, and hear it read,* when you go to Cobourg, for the black coats have it. They wish you to come and hear it. To-morrow is the *Sabbath,* and on that day we do not hunt, or work, for it is the day which the Great Spirit made for himself." He described the way that the Son of God was crucified. I observed some of them crying; my mother heaved deep sighs; the half drunken Indians were struck dumb, and hung their heads. Not a word was uttered. The missionaries said, "We will *sing*, and then we will *kneel down* and *pray* to the Great Spirit." He gave out the following hymn:

"Jesus ish pe ming kah e zhod."
"Jesus, my all, to heaven is gone."

They stood up and sang. O what sweet melody was in their voices! The echo was so great that there appeared to be a great many more singers than we could see. After the hymn, they prayed with the same fervency as they sung.

Peter Wason prayed, and in his prayer said, "O Great Spirit! here are some of my own relatives; open their eyes and save them!" After the prayer, they said they were going to Cobourg that evening; and if any desired to go with them, they would have them do so.

My father arose and took the keg of whiskey, stepped into one of the small canoes, and paddled some thirty feet from the shore; here he poured out the whiskey into the lake and threw the keg away. He then returned and addressed us in the following manner: — "You have all heard what our brothers said to us; I am going with them this evening; if any of you will go, do so this evening; the children can attend the great meeting some other time." Every one ran at once to the paddles and canoes, and in a few minutes we were on the water. The missionaries had a skiff, in which they went from the Island to the opposite side. They sang again, and their very oars seemed to keep time on the still water. O how charming! The scenery of the water; the canoes moving in files, crossing the lake to visit their first camp meeting. When we arrived on the other side, it was about dark, and we bought five candles for a *dollar(!)*, and obtained an old lantern. We marched on a new road the whole of Saturday night, in order to reach the camp ground. During the journey, we had to wade through deep creeks. Just before the dawn, we were about half a mile from the camp ground; here we tarried until day light, and then approached the camp.

When the Indians beheld the fence and gate, and a great number of whites, they began to feel rather timid and suspicious, for the trader had told my father at Rice Lake, and *it was for the purpose of killing all the Indians,* that the black coats had invited them to the meeting. My father told me to keep away from the ground, and hunt birds and squirrels with my bow and arrow; his object was to save my life, in the event of the Indians being killed. After remaining on the camp ground awhile, I departed; but while there, I saw a large number of converted Indians who belonged to Credit River, and Grape Island. Some of them were singing, some praying, and others lying about the ground as if dead. There were a great many preachers present.

On the third day many of our company were converted; among this number was my dear father!

As I entered the ground in the afternoon, I heard many voices, and among them my father's voice. I thought my father was dying; I ran to him, and found him lying partly on one of the seats. My father, said I, what is the matter with you? Are you sick? "Come here, my son, I am not sick, but I am happy in my heart;" he placed his hand upon his breast while he spoke. "I told you you must keep away from the ground, that your life might be spared; but I find that these are good, and not bad, people; kneel down and I will pray for you." I knelt, while he prayed. O, this was *my father's first prayer!* Methinks, that at this time the angels rejoiced in heaven. I became agitated; my bow and arrows had fallen from my hand. The Indians lay about me like dead men. All this was the effect of the power of gospel grace, that had spread amongst them. The shouts, praises, and prayers, of fathers, mothers, sons, and daughters, were heard from every quarter. Those who had just appeared as dead, arose, and shouted the praises of God! They clapped their hands and exclaimed, "*Jesus nin ge shah wa ne mig,*" Jesus has blessed me. The feeling was so general and powerful, that the influence was felt throughout the camp, both by the Indians and the whites. This was one of the happiest seasons I ever witnessed, except the season of my own conversion. Many of my relatives were converted on this occasion. Many of them have since gone to the world of spirits, and are now singing the praises of redeeming love. This *heavenly fire* began to spread from the camp, to Mud, Schoogaug and Balsam Lakes, the homes of the Ojebwas; also to the shores of Lake Simeco, and Lake Huron, and to the vicinity of Lake Superior.

> "Waft, waft, ye winds his story,
>   And you ye waters roll,
> Till like a sea of glory
>   It spreads from pole to pole."

On the camp ground, the Ojebwas sat in squads, giving and receiving in-struction in singing, learning and teaching the Lord's prayer, and other things. Some were singing,

> "Jesus, kuh ba ke zhig
> Ning ee e hug uh moz,
> Uh pa gish kuh ke nuh wahb' dum 'wod
> Ning ee 'nuh da moosh
> A zhe o ne zhe shing,
> O ge che o duh nuh me ah win."

> "Jesus all the day long
> Was my joy and my song;
> O that all, his salvation might see!
> He hath lov'd me, I cried;

He hath suffer'd and died
To redeem such a rebel as me."

The *conversion of my mother* took place during the summer, on Poutash Island, where the Indians had erected a bark chapel. For two years she lived in the enjoyment of religion. Before this chapel was ready she would call us together in the wigwam, and pray with and for us, several times a day, whether our father was home or not. I remember well, at this moment, the language of her prayers.

She was taken sick in the winter of 1829, and was confined to her bed, most of the time, for three months; her disease was consumption. During these three months, she enjoyed much religion; there was not a day, in which she did not speak of Jesus and his promises with the greatest confidence and delight.

When she grew worse, she called for the class leaders to pray with her. She said to her mother, whom she supposed would die first, because her hair was *white*, "you will still live, but I am going to die, and will see Jesus first; soon, however, you will follow me."

The spirit of my dear mother took its flight on the 27th day of February, 1830. Just before her death, she prayed with her children; and advised us to be good Christians, to love Jesus, and meet her in heaven. She then sang her favorite hymn,

"Jesus ish pe ming kah e zhod."
"Jesus, my all, to heaven is gone."

This was the first hymn she had ever heard or learned; and it is on this account that I introduce and sing this sweet hymn whenever I lecture "On the origin, history, traditions, migration, and customs, of the Ojebwa nation." We all knelt again by her bed side, and while clapping her hands, and endeavoring to shout for joy, she swooned away in death. The last words which she feebly uttered, were, "*Jesus, Jesus.*" Her spirit then fled, her lips were cold, and those warm hands that had so often and so faithfully administered comfort and relief, were now stiff. I looked around the wigwam; my father, sister, and brother sat near me, wringing their hands; they were filled with bitter grief, and appeared inconsolable. I then began to understand and appreciate fully her kindness and love. Who, who can, or will, take the place of a *mother?* Who will pray for us when we are sick or in distress? Her body was consigned to the grave without any parade. No church bell was tolled; but the whistling wind sounded through the woods. I have often knelt down, at the head of her grave, and wished that the time would soon arrive when it might please God to relieve me from my troubles and cares, and conduct me to the abode of my beloved parent. My sister Sarah, too, who has since died, is doubtless with my mother. O how glorious the thought, *that both are now in heaven!* There is one spot where none will sigh for home. The flowers that blossom there, will never fade; the crystal waters that wind along those verdant

vales, will never cease to send up their heavenly music; the clusters hanging from
the trees overshadowing its banks, will be immortal clusters; and the friends that
meet, will meet for ever.

Little then did I think that I should have to pass through so many afflictions,
and so many hardships. O my mother, I am still in a *cold, uncharitable miserable
world!* But the thought that thou art happy and blessed, is truly sweet and encouraging! It is this fact, and my own hopes of future bliss, that buoys me up,
and sustains me in the hours of conflict and despondency. Although many years
have elapsed, since her death, still I often weep with mingled joy and grief when
I think of my dear mother. "Blessed are the dead who die in the Lord." "I am
not ashamed of the gospel of Christ, for it is the power of God unto salvation
to every one that believeth." The gospel is the only remedy for the miseries and
sins of the world.

My mother's and sister's cases are not the only ones that I could relate concerning the happy lives and deaths of those once degraded and benighted Indians.
Many have already reached heaven; and many more are now rejoicing on their
road thither. Who will now say that the poor Indians cannot be converted? The
least that Christians could have done, was to send the gospel among them, after
having dispossessed them of their lands; thus preparing them for usefulness here,
and happiness hereafter. Let no one say that I am ungrateful in speaking thus.
It was the *duty* of Christians to send us missionaries; and it is *now* their duty
to send *more* of them. There are still 25,000 of my poor brethren in darkness,
and without the gospel. Let the prayers of all the churches ascend to the Most
High, in their behalf, that He who has power to deliver, may save the poor Indian from misery, ignorance and perdition.

In the summer following my mother's death (1830), *I was converted.* The following are the circumstances connected with my conversion. My father and I attended a camp meeting near the town of Colbourne. On our way from Rice Lake,
to the meeting, my father held me by the hand, as I accompanied him through
the woods. Several times he prayed with me, and encouraged me to seek religion
at this camp meeting. We had to walk thirty miles under a hot sun, in order to
reach that place of destination. Multitudes of Indians, and a large concourse of
whites from various places, were on the ground when we arrived. In the evening,
one of the white preachers (Wright, I believe was his name) spoke; his text was,
"For the great day of His wrath is come, and who shall be able to stand." He
spoke in English, and as he closed each sentence, an Indian preacher gave its interpretation. He spoke of the plain and good road to heaven; of the characters
that were walking in it; he then spoke of the bad place, the judgement, and the
coming of a Saviour. I now began to feel as if I should die; *I felt very sick in my
heart.* Never had I felt so before; I was deeply distressed, and knew not the cause.
I resolved to go and prostate myself at the mourner's bench, as soon as an opportunity offered. We were now invited to approach. I went to the bench and knelt

down by the roots of a large tree. But how could I pray? I did not understand how to pray; and besides, I thought that the Great Spirit was *too great* to listen to the words of a poor Indian boy. What added to my misery was, that it had rained in torrents about three quarters of an hour, and I was soaking wet. The thunder was appalling, and lightning terrific. I then tried again to pray, but I was not able. I did not know what words to use. My father then prayed with and for me. Many were praising God, all around me. The storm now ceased, and nearly all the lights had been extinguished by the rain. I still groaned and agonized over my sins. I was so agitated and alarmed that I knew not which way to turn in order to get relief. I was like a *wounded bird,* fluttering for its life. Presently and suddenly, I saw in my mind, something approaching; it was like a small but brilliant torch; it appeared to pass through the leaves of the trees. My poor body became so enfeebled that I fell; my heart trembled. The small brilliant light came near to me, and fell upon my head, and then ran all over and through me just as if water had been copiously poured out upon me. I knew not how long I had lain after my fall; but when I recovered, my head was in a puddle of water, in a small ditch. I arose; and O! how happy I was! I felt as light as a feather. I clapped my hands, and exclaimed in English, "Glory to Jesus." I looked around for my father, and saw him. I told him that I had found "Jesus." He embraced me and kissed me; I threw myself into his arms. I felt as strong as a lion, yet as humble as a poor Indian boy saved by grace, by grace alone. During that night I did not sleep. The next morning, my cousin, George Shawney, and myself, went out into the woods to sing and pray. As I looked at the trees, the hills, and the vallies, O how beautiful they all appeared! I looked upon them, as it were, with new eyes and new thoughts. Amidst the smiles of creation, the birds sang sweetly, as they flew from tree to tree. We sang

"Jesus the name that charms our fears."

O how sweet the recollections of that day! "Jesus all the day long was my joy and my song." Several hundred were converted during this meeting. Many of the Indians were reluctant to leave the camp ground when the meeting was broken up. When we reached our homes at Rice Lake, every thing seemed to me as if it wore a different aspect; every thing was clothed with beauty. Before this, I had only begun to spell and read. I now resumed my studies with a new and different relish. Often, when alone, I prayed that God would help me to qualify myself to teach others how to read the word of God; this circumstance I had not told to any one. On Sabbath mornings I read a chapter in the New Testament, which had been translated for my father, before we went to meeting.

During this summer, one of our chiefs, John Sunday, with several others, departed from Rice Lake, for the west, with a design to preach to the Ojebwas. When they returned, they told us that the Indians were very eager to hear the word of God, and that many had been converted. John Sunday informed us of a certain Indian, who was so much opposed to the meetings, that he confined his wife and children to one of the islands, to prevent her attending them. But this poor woman was so anxious to obey God in attendance on worship, that she was in the habit of fording the river every night, and carrying her children on her back. Her husband was afterwards converted. He mentioned also an instance of an Indian who brought his medicine sack with him to the meeting, but on being converted, he scattered its contents to the four winds of heaven. These sacks were held very sacred among the Indians. He spoke likewise of the conversion of many chiefs, and of the flocks of children anxious to hear the word of God. He left such an impression on my mind, that often, while alone, I prayed that God might send me to instruct the children in the truths of religion.

The Traditional History and Characteristic Sketches of the Ojibway Nation

by George Copway

Origin Of The Ojibway

IN LISTENING to the traditions of the Indians in their wigwams, the traveller will learn that the chiefs are the repositories of the history of their ancestors. With these traditions there are rules to follow by which to determine whether they are true or false. By these rules I have been governed in my researches.

The first is to inquire particularly into the leading points of every tradition narrated.

The second is to notice whether the traditions are approved by the oldest chiefs and wise men. Such are most likely to be true, and if places or persons are mentioned, additional clue is given to their origin and proof obtained of their truth or falsity.

The chiefs have generally been those who have at all times retained a general history of their nation.

From the year 1834, to the present time, I have been in communication with our nation, with every portion of it. All appear to adopt the belief that most of the Indians came from the west. The present Ojibways, or those now called Messasaugans, settled in Canada West after the years 1634 and 1635. They came over from St. Marie's river to Lake Huron, and relate in their traditions an account of those who came to the Falls of St. Marie from *Pe-quab-qua-wav-ming*, near the Aunce bay, on the south shore of Lake Superior. Others, no doubt in the year 1642, came to this northern shore of the Lake. I have heard that these came from La Pointe, or *Shah-gah-wab-mick*. In this place the Indians lived a long time. Still they trace their own trail to the waters of Red and Sandy Lakes, which places they all, or nearly all, look back to as the home of their forefathers. War came, and in their exercise of it against other nations, they moved eastward from La Point, and towards the south against the *Sioux*.

When they moved from Red and Sandy Lakes, it was the fisheries of Lake Superior that attracted them from their old haunts and induced them to leave the scenes to which, for so many years, they had been accustomed.

The same attraction is supposed to have drawn the Sioux to the south-west end of Lake Superior and to the land bordering all along below *Shah-gah-wab-mick*. In a short time contentions arose between the Ojibways and the Sioux about the right of occupancy. The game of the land and the fish of the waters were probably the first cause of hostility between the two powerful nations, – a hostility which has been marked by many acts of cruelty on both sides. War commenced for the retention of the hunting-lands, and a neutral ground having been between them ever since, the first cause of other wars has been forgotten, and the repeated ravages of death made upon each party have obliterated the remembrance of the cause of the early contention.

DISTRIBUTION OF LAND

I have heard a tradition related to the effect that a general council was once held at some point above the Falls of St. Anthony, and that when the Ojibways came to this general council they wore a peculiar shoe or moccasin, which was gathered on the top from the tip of the toe, and at the ankle. No other Indians wore this style of foot-gear, and it was on account of this peculiarity that they were called *Ojibway*, the signification of which, is *gathering*.

At this council the land was distributed. That part which fell to the lot of the Ojibways is said to have been the surrounding country of Red Lake, and afterwards Sandy and Leach Lakes, which statement coincides with that of the chiefs of the village of La Pointe, or the *Shah-gah-wah-mick*.

The Sauks were once a part of the Chippeway family, as also were the Menomenies and the Ottaways. About the year 1613 the latter began to leave the main body near Lake Superior. When the traders of Champlain began their operations with the Chippeways, the French called them "the trading Indians" (Ottaways). The Sauks fought with the Sioux on the upper waters of those lakes which run down from the southern shores of Lake Superior. They also engaged in combat with the Shawnees of southern Illinois.

Though the Ojibways occupied but a small piece of territory at first, they soon extended their dominions to the very borders of the snow-clad hills of the north, and in the streams of that cold region watched for the beaver, whose furs were wrought by them into warm clothing.

It was at a date just prior to Pontiac's time, that the Ojibways met the Shawnees on the waters of Erie, and united with them in a successful war against the Iroquois in Canada West, after which the two, Ojibways and Shawnees, settled down in the country of the Hurons.

The battle-grounds are yet to be seen, and many marks of the savage warfare are now visible.

1634 and 1635 were years of glorious triumph. The nation had sought intercourse with the French in Montreal, and their communication was carried on by journeys through the lands of an intermediate nation.

The intercession resulted in a long and disastrous war, in which the Ojibways were victorious. After this they enjoyed a free communication with the French, with whom they have had friendly intercourse from that time to the present.

They fought their way through the lands of hostile nations, from the west end of Lake Superior along the entire lake country. The shores of Lake Superior, Lake Huron, and the River St. Lawrence, abound with their battlefields. The dust of many a brave now lies there, friend and foe in one common resting-place.

Exciting stories of the doings of those days have been passed down from mouth to mouth. So the old man related them, the blood of the young Ojibways ran swiftly through his veins, and his eye shone with the fire of enthusiasm.

The war-whoop's shrill notes have now died away. Now the wigwam stands undisturbed, and the hymn of peace is chanted within their thatched walls.

Behold the change! Commerce urged on by the pale-face, strides rapidly and resistlessly into their midst, and orders them back, back, back, to make way for its houses and its merchandise. Scarce is he camped, ere once again he is told to go farther west. When will the last order be given? When will the redman have a home?

THEIR WILD GAME

There is, doubtless, a greater variety of game to be found in the Ojibway country than in any other equal extent of western territory. The northern part is not so well supplied with large game as that district near the head waters of the Wisconsin, Chippeway, St. Croix, Mississippi, and Red Rivers.

Small game is to be found on the northern shores of the Lakes with the hardy reindeer, such as the rabbit, lynx, martin, and fisher. The three latter have been a source of much profit on account of their furs. The rabbit has been the principal game for the northern Indians, who snare them for their food and skins. These latter are made into strings and woven into blankets. They also make their garments of these skins, and are dressed in them from head to foot. The eyes of

a pale-face would considerably extend on beholding a fellow in such accoutre-
ment. These Indians reside in the interior of the shores of Lake Superior, in the
north. We call them (*Nopeming Tah-she-e-ne-neh*) Backwoodmen. The deer are
found in almost all parts of the country, though not as much in the north as
in the south. In the spring they migrate to the north, and return to the south
in the fall, few ever wintering in the north on account of the great depth of snow
in that quarter.

This animal was killed in four different ways before the introduction of
firearms. The first was by a snare formed of a rope of wild hemp, and so placed
that when the deer's neck was caught, the more stir he made the more he could
not stir. At every movement the cord would wind about the neck tighter and
tighter, until he was choked; for at one end of the rope would be fixed a small
rail, which the large end slips off, and in falling it presses upon the deer, who
in a short time dies. When they wished to get through soon, they placed these
snares all around for half a day, then drove the deer all over the snares until some
were caught.

The second was by driving sharp spikes of wood into the ground on the deer
path, just the other side of a log over which they would be expected to jump.
In jumping the logs, they must fall upon these sharp spikes, which would pierce
them through, and thus kill them.

The third way was to drive the deer with dogs into the water, when, being
out of their element, they could be captured. In winter, instead of driving them
into water, a short chase in the deep snow would soon tire them, and they were
soon at the disposal of the hunter.

The fourth and last manner of killing them was by means of bow and arrow.
Bows were made of a power to enable them to shoot through the side of a deer
without any difficulty. The Indian watched at the "Salt Licks," or at the borders
of lakes or rivers, to which the deer often go to feed on the grass. An Indian can
shoot a deer in the woods at a distance of fifty paces.

The bow was generally made of iron-wood or red cedar; sometimes of hickory
well seasoned. The arrows were made like spikes at the end. Before they had iron,
they used bone and shell for the ends: the shells were carved in such a manner
as to admit of being pointed at the end of the arrow. I have no recollection of
killing but one deer with an arrow, as fire-arms came into the field of action as
soon as I did. I remember being at the foot of Rice Lake, Canada West, with others
on a hunting tour in the night. Soon after nine o'clock, we heard the animal feeding
in the grass by the shore. Having a lighted candle, we placed it in a three-sided
lantern; opening one side, the light was thrown upon the deer only. By this con-
trivance we were enabled to approach so near it in our canoe, that it appeared
to be but ten or fifteen paces from us. I drew my bow-string – the arrow winged
its way – the deer made a few short leaps, and died.

During my travels in the east, I have met with individuals whom I found it difficult to convince that the Indian's arrow could execute so much, and doubted me when I told them that with it they killed deer, bears, and such like.

Several years ago, in the state of New York, an elderly gentleman, a farmer and myself were entertained by a kind family to tea. The gentleman monopolized all the time for conversation with questions about the Indian mode of life. I answered them all as well as I could, though some of them were so *very* odd, that it was the exercise of the greatest muscular strength that I could refrain from laughing in the inquisitive person's face. He seemed satisfied with all my answers except those in relation to killing deer with bow and arrow. He doubted. He could not bring his mind to believe such a thing possible. After labouring half an hour to convince him of the fact that we could, he turned aside, firmly resolved not to believe me. I held my tongue, half mad; and made the proposition that the next day I would make a bow and a couple of arrows, and I understood he was a farmer, I should get him to furnish a yearling calf, and if in shooting I did not hit it, I would pay him the price of the calf if he desired it; but if, on the contrary, I should hit it, and kill it, then it should be mine! While our friends at the table could not wait till the morrow to know the result, my friend, the doubting gentleman, coolly declined, saying he *believed* we could kill deer at sixty paces if we hit it at all. I and my friends endeavoured to provoke him to accept my proposition, but failed to accomplish our purpose, his avarice overcoming his unbounded curiosity!

Bears are also taken by means of bow and arrow. – They are very easily captured in winter, for then they are found in hollow logs and in the ground enjoying their winter quarters. The black bear is to be found all over the Ojibway country. They are more numerous in years when fruit and acorns are abundant. Some of the Ojibway people believe the bear to be a transformed being; in other words, that it was once a more intelligent creation, and for this reason they profess a great veneration for its head and paws, but not so much for *its meat,* for they relish that very highly, and seem to forget its former intelligence when indulging their appetites with a savoury steak. The head and paws are festooned with coloured cloth and ribbons, and suspended at the upper end of the Indian's lodge. At the nose they bestow a very liberal quantity of tobacco, as a sort of peace-offering to the dead animal.

In early life I received a lecture from my father upon hunting. He related many cunning stories of the bear, and I remember I got so courageous, that the next day I was all the time in a perfect fright, thinking in every brush heap I met the hiding place of some old Bruin.

In the year 1832, I made my first appearance as a bear hunter. It was in the fall of the year that I with others left our homes with the intention of being absent for three or four weeks. We went down Crook's Rapids below Rice Lake, to hunt. I remember how skittish I felt at first, as I shouldered my gun and followed the six hunters before me into the woods, for just then all the cunning stories

I had heard were fresh in my mind. We came to a halt about three miles distant from our starting place, and the head hunter, my father, gave his companions a brief description of the face of the country and of the places to which the bear would be most likely to resort, for then they were eating acorns. Around us we could see newly-made tracks of the deer and bear; my lips parched, and my whole body fevered with anxiety. When my father had finished his account, he turned to me, and said: – "My son, don't go very far; keep behind the rest as you hear the firing of guns, and when you think it is time to return, you can come round this way and go towards home:" then, waving his hand, off the party started in every direction. I, too, went one way.

When I lost sight of the others of my party, all the "cunning stories" about the bear – of its hiding under rotten logs, of its pretending to die, and its sudden attacks, rushed upon my mind. I was soon roused from my reverie, for in less than twenty minutes I heard the reports of guns from all directions; but for all this I walked along as well as I could, looking out for a bear which I was *afraid of seeing,* and yet *hunting for.*

I would walk along in the open space, so that I might see my bear at a distance, and not come suddenly upon him or he upon me. The guns were fired every few minutes. I could see, occasionally, deer at a distance running at full speed. While I was passing along at the foot of the hills on which the thick foliage concealed the logs, which lay piled one upon another, I heard a tremendous crash near the top. I stood, as if transfixed to the spot, and sure enough, I could see the branches of the young trees waving, and thought I could see objects approaching me. I scarce dare to wink, and trembled in my scarlet leggins, when to my dread astonishment I saw a large bear coming down towards me, like a hogshead rolling down a hill! I jumped behind a pine tree, and prepared for the combat. He came at me at a full gallop, and I feared the worst. When he had approached to within five paces from me, I thought it time to define my position, and make some demonstration of war. I sprang from my hiding-place, and alighted upon the ground. I hallooed at the top of my voice, "Yah!" and at the same time pointed the muzzle of my gun to the white spot on the breast of the animal. I fired, and the smoke enveloped myself and the bear. – As I did so, I fell to the ground, and a bundle of leaves which the bear had scratched up in his "exercises" fell upon my face. This I thought to be the bear, and falling backward, I expected the fellow would get to be quite loving of his new-found companion, and in the transports of his joy, hug me to death. But when I raised my head, I learned my mistake, and beheld a tremendous animal apparently in the agonies of departing life. I arose, picked up my gun, which had fallen from my hand, and immediately reloaded it, in order to be prepared if his actions proved to be a farce instead of a tragedy. I took a long pole, and poked him considerably. He did not show any signs of life. Yet so doubtful was I of his death, that I left him. Thus ended my first adventure on a bear-hunting excursion.

In the immediate vicinity of Lake Superior, Indians trap bears in large "dead falls." Near Red and Lead Lakes, they take them when crossing the water. Some years ago, they were thus captured at the head of Lake Superior.

The Moose and *Deer* are also taken, chiefly, however, in the northern parts of Lake Superior and in the vicinity of Red Lake. The Moose is one of the largest animals found, and the hunters have quite a merry time when three or four are taken at one time. It is considered best to take them before they leave their yard in the winter. If they are not thus taken, it is very difficult to secure them, as they are very fleet.

The Reindeer is taken in all parts of the north-west. It is the hardiest animal in the country. They are often chased for days in succession by the Indians, and a coat of ice is seen to cover them, caused by their perspiration; at the same time a thick steam arises from them. They go in droves, and when they are on the run, the light snow rises in clouds in every direction. – The skin of the deer, as well as the skins of all the animals I have mentioned, are manufactured into clothing, and are oftentimes dressed in a beautiful manner and highly ornamented.

The Elk is to be found in the west, on the neutral ground lying between the Sioux and Ojibway nations, at the head waters of the Wisconsin; in the northern parts of Michigan, and near the Chippeway, St. Croix, Rum and Red rivers. This is one of the noblest looking animals in our country. When on the run, its head is held high, its back curved, on which its large horns appear to rest. At one time, in 1837, I saw a drove of five hundred; and a more animating sight I never beheld. I shot one, and being at that time a prisoner at the foot of Lake Pepin, and wishing to be generous to my enemies, I took it to the chief of the tribe that held me. Soon after I was liberated, and with my cousin Johnson was permitted to depart.

The Buffalo is taken only at the head of Red River, where the Chippeways and the half-breeds kill between eight and ten thousand every year. The Indians form into companies, and take their wagons with them, when they go on a buffalo hunt. The drove of buffalo is very large, and grazing they blacken the prairie as far as the eye can reach.

The tread of the buffalo makes the earth to tremble. The hunters are mounted on ponies, who are so taught, that when a wounded animal falls, they immediately start for an encounter with another. The Indian gathers his arrows from the grass while he is riding at full speed – a feat which is considered very dexterous, but which is quite common on the western prairies.

Before leaving this noble animal, I must indulge my readers with what a recent writer says respecting it: prefacing it with the remark that the bison and the buffalo are one and the same.

"From the species of the ox kind the bison is well distinguished by the following peculiarities. A long shaggy hair clothes the fore parts of the body, forming a well marked beard beneath the lower jaw, and descending behind the knee in a tuft; this hair rises on the top of the head in a dense mass nearly as high as the extremities of the horns. Over the forehead it is closely curled and matted so thickly as to deaden the power of a rifle ball, which either rebounds or lodges in the hair, merely causing the animal to shake his head as he heavily bounds along. The head of the bison is large and ponderous, compared to the size of the body: so that the muscles for its support, necessarily of great size, give great thickness to the neck, and by their origin from the prolonged dorsal vertebrae processes, from the peculiar projection called the hump. This hump is of an oblong form, diminishing in height as it recedes, so as to give considerable obliquity to the line of the neck.

"The eye of the bison is small, black, and brilliant; the horns are black, and very thick near the head, where they curve upwards and outwards, rapidly tapering toward their points.

"The outward line of the face is convexly curved, and the upper lip on each side, being papillons within, dilates and extends downwards, giving a very oblique appearance to the lateral gap of the mouth, in this particular resembling the ancient architectural bas-relief, representing the heads of oxen. The physiognomy of the bison is menacing and ferocious, and no one can see this animal in his native wilds without feeling inclined to attend to his personal safety.

"The summer coat of the bison differs from his winter dress rather by difference of length than by any other particulars.

"In summer from the shoulders backward, the hinder parts of the animal are all covered with a very fine short hair that is as smooth and soft to the touch as velvet.

"The tail is quite short and tufted at the end, and its utility as a fly-brush is very limited. The colour of the hair is uniformly dun; but the long hair on the anterior parts of the body is, to a certain extent, tinged with yellowish or rust colour. These animals, however, present so little variety in regard to colour, that the natives consider any remarkable difference from the common appearance as resulting from the immediate interference of the Great Spirit.

"Some varieties of colour have been observed, though the instances are rare.

"A Missouri trader informed the members of Long's exploring party, that he had seen a greyish-white bison, and a yearling calf, that was distinguished by several white spots on the side, a star or blaze in the forehead, and white forefeet. Mr. I. Doughty, an interpreter to the expedition, saw in an Indian hut a very well prepared bison's head with a star on the front. This was highly prized by the proprietor, who called it his great medicine; for, said he, the herds come every season to the vicinity to seek their white companion.

"In appearance, the bison cow bears the same relation to the bull as is borne by the domestic cow to her mate. Her size is much smaller, and she has much less hair on the fore-part of her body. The horns of the cow are much less than those of the bull, nor are they so much connected by the hair.

"The cow is by no means destitute of beard; but though she possesses the conspicuous appendage, it is quite short when compared with that of her companion.

"From July to the latter part of December, the bison cow continues fat.

"Their breeding season commences towards the latter part of July, and continues until the beginning of September, and often the cows separate from the bulls in distinct herds, and bring forth their calves in April.

"The calves rarely separate from the mother before they are a year old, and cows are often seen accompanied by calves of three seasons.

"The flesh of the bison is somewhat coarser in its fibres than that of the domestic ox, yet travellers are unanimous in considering it equally savoury as an article of food; we must, however, receive the opinions of travellers on this subject with allowance for their peculiar situation, being frequently at a distance from all other food, and having their relish improved by the best of recommendations in favour of the present viands – hunger.

"It is with reason, however, that the flesh is said to be more agreeable, for the grass on which these animals feed is short, firm and nutritious, being very different from the luxurious and less saline grass produced on a more fertile soil.

"The fat of the bison is said to be far sweeter and richer, and generally preferable to that of the common ox.

"The observations made in relation to the bison's flesh when compared to the flesh of the domestic ox, may be extended to almost all wild meat, which has a peculiar flavour and raciness, which renders it decidedly more agreeable than that of tame animals, although much coarser, and the fibre by no means so delicate.

"Of all the parts of the bison that are eaten, the hump is most famed for its peculiar richness and delicacy, because when cooked it is said very much to resemble marrow.

"The tongue and marrow bones are also highly esteemed by the hunters."

Before dismissing the subject of game, I must mention those animals that are taken principally for their fur. I cannot enter into a detailed account of these. The furs brought into the market by the Ojibways, have ever been considered the best. They consist for the most part of beaver, otter, martin, fisher and lynx.

The interior of the Canadian country, between the shores of Ontario, Huron and Lake Superior, was once well hunted for the beaver, but its pelt being here valueless, they are increasing in numbers.

These are some of the animals caught by the Ojibways on land. There is an abundance of fish in all their waters. The best of these is the sweet fish of the lakes, *Sis-ka-way*, which is esteemed a very great delicacy; and many others which I will not mention, lest I should weary my readers, but will allow them to swim from my sight.

Plays And Exercises

I believe all the Indian nations of this continent have amusements among them. Those of the prairie nations are different from those of the Ojibways, suitable to their wide, open fields. The plays I am about to describe are the principal games practised by the people of my nation. There are others; and chance games are considerably in vogue among them.

One of the most popular games is that of ball-playing, which oftentimes engages an entire village. Parties are formed of from ten to several hundred. Before they commence, those who are to take a part in the play must provide each his share of staking, or things which are set apart; and one leader for each party. Each leader then appoints one of each company to be stake-holder.

Each man and each woman (women sometimes engage in the sport) is armed with a stick, one end of which bends somewhat like a small hoop, about four inches in circumference, to which is attached a net work of raw-hide, two inches deep, just large enough to admit the ball which is to be used on the occasion. Two poles are driven in the ground at a distance of four hundred paces from each other, which serves as goals for the two parties. It is the endeavour of each to take the ball to his hole. The party which carries the ball and strikes its pole wins the game.

The warriors, very scantily attired, young and brave fantastically painted – and women, decorated with feathers, assemble around their commanders, who are generally men swift on the race. They are to take the ball either by running with it or throwing it in the air. As the ball falls in the crowd the excitement begins. – The clubs swing and roll from side to side, the players run and shout, fall upon and tread upon each other, and in the struggle some get rather rough treatment.

When the ball is thrown some distance on each side, the party standing near instantly pick it up, and run at full speed with three or four after him. – The others send their shouts of encouragement to their own party. "Ha! ha! yah!" "A-ne-gook!" and these shouts are heard even from the distant lodges, for children and all are deeply interested in the exciting scene. The spoils are not all on which their interest is fixed, but is directed to the falling and rolling of the crowds over and under each other. The loud and merry shouts of the spectators, who crowd the doors of the wigwams, go forth in one continued peal, and testify to their happy state of feeling.

The players are clothed in fur. They receive blows whose marks are plainly visible after the scuffle. The hands and feet are unincumbered, and they exercise them to the extent of their power; and with such dexterity do they strike the ball, that it is sent out of sight. Another strikes it on its descent, and for ten minutes at a time the play is so adroitly managed that the ball does not touch the ground.

No one is heard to complain, though he be bruised severely, or his nose come in close communion with a club. If the last-mentioned catastrophe befall him, he is up in a trice, and sends his laugh forth as loud as the rest, though it be floated at first on a tide of blood.

It is very seldom, if ever, that one is seen to be angry because he has been hurt. If he should get so, they would call him a "coward," which proves a sufficient check to many evils which might result from many seemingly intended injuries.

While I was in La Pointe, Lake Superior, in the summer of 1836, when the interior band of Chippeways, with those of Sandy Lake, Lac Counterville, Lac De Frambou, encamped in the island, the interior bands proposed to play against the Lake Indians. As it would be thought a cowardly act to refuse, the lake Indians were ready at an early hour the next day, when about two hundred and fifty of the best and swiftest feet assembled on a level green, opposite the mansion-house of the Rev. Mr. Hall.

On our side was a thicket of thorns; on the other the lake shore, with a sandy beach of half a mile. Every kind of business was suspended, not only by the Indians, but by the whites of all classes.

There were but two rivals in this group of players. One of these was a small man from Cedar Lake, on the Chippeway river, whose name was "*Nai-nah-aun-gaib*" (Adjusted Feathers), who admitted no rival in bravery, daring or adventure, making the contest more interesting.

The name of the other competitor was "*Mah-koonce*" (Young Bear), of the shore bands.

The first, as I said before, was a small man. His body was a model for sculpture; well proportioned. His hands and feet tapered with all the grace and delicacy of a lady's. His long black hair flowed carelessly upon his shoulders. On the top of the raven locks waved in profusion seventeen signals (with their pointed fingers) of the feathers of that rare bird, the western eagle, being the number of the enemy he had taken with his own hand. A Roman nose with a classic lip, which wore at all times a pleasing smile. Such was *Nai-nah-aun-gaib*. That day he had not the appearance of having used paint of any kind. Before and after the play I counted five bullet-marks around his breast. Three had passed through; two were yet in his body. Besides these, there were innumerable marks of small shot upon his shoulders, and the graze of a bullet on his temple.

His rival on this occasion was a tall muscular man. His person was formed with perfect symmetry. He walked with ease and grace. On his arms were bracelets composed of the claws of grizzly bears. He had been in the field of battle but five times; yet on his head were three signals of trophies.

The parties passed to the field; a beautiful green, as even as a floor. Here they exhibited all the agility and graceful motions. The one was as stately as the proud elk of the plains; while the other possessed all the gracefulness of the antelope of the western mountains.

Shout after shout arose from each party, and from the crowds of spectators. "Yah-hah – yah-hah" were all the words that could be distinguished. After a short contest, the antelope struck the post, and at that moment the applause was absolutely deafening. Thus ended the first day of the play, which was continued for some length of time.

After this day's game was over, the two champions met and indulged in a sort of personal encounter with the ball. This they continued a short time, then parted company, in good humour, and mingled with the crowd.

The Moccasin-play is simple, and can be played by two or three. Three moccasins are used for the purpose of hiding the bullets which are employed in the game. So deeply interesting does this play sometimes become, that an Indian will stake first his gun; next his steel-traps; then his implements of war; then his clothing; and lastly, his tobacco and pipe, leaving him, as we say, "*Nah-bah-wan-yah-ze-yaid*," a piece of cloth with a string around his waist.

The "Tossing-play" is a game seldom seen among the whites. It is played in the wigwam. There is used in it an oblong knot, made of cedar boughs, of length say about seven inches. On the top is fastened a string, about fifteen inches long, by which the knot is swung. On the other end of this string is another stick, two and a half inches long, and sharply pointed. This is held in the hand, and if the player can hit the large stick every time it falls on the sharp one he wins.

"Bone-play," is another in-door amusement, so called, because the articles used are made of the hoof-joint bones of the deer. The ends are hollowed out, and from three to ten are strung together. In playing it they use the same kind of sharp stick, the end of which is thrown into the bones.

Doubtless the most interesting of all games is the "Maiden's Ball Play," in the Ojibway language, *Pah-pah-se-Kah-way*.

The majority of those who take part in this play are young damsels, though married women are not excluded. The ball is made of two deer skin bags, each about five inches long and one in diameter. These are so fastened together as to be at a distance of seven inches each from the other. It is thrown with a stick five feet long.

This play is practiced in summer under the shade of side-spreading trees, beneath which each strives to find their homes, *tahwin*, and to run home with it. These having been appointed in the morning, the young women of the village decorate themselves for the day by painting their cheeks with vermilion, (how civilized, eh!) and disrobe themselves of as much unnecessary clothing as possible, braiding their hair with coloured feathers, which hang profusely down to the feet.

At the set time the whole village assemble, and the young men, whose loved ones are seen in the crowd, twist and turn to send sly glances to them, and receive their bright smiles in return.

The same confusion exists as in the game of ball played by the men. Crowds rush to a given point as the ball is sent flying through the air. None stop to narrate the accidents that befall them, though they tumble about to their no little discomfiture; they rise making a loud noise, something between a laugh and a cry, some limping behind the others, as the women shout. *"Ain goo"* is heard sounding like the notes of a dove, of which it is no bad imitation. Worked garters, moccasins, leggins and vermilion are generally the articles at stake. Sometimes the chief of the village sends a parcel before they commence, the contents of which are to be distributed among the maidens when the play is over. I remember that some winters before the teachers from the pale faces came to the lodge of my father, my mother was very sick. Many thought she would not recover her health. At this critical juncture, she told my father that it was her wish to see the "Maiden's Ball Play," and gave as a reason for her request that were she to see the girls at play, it would so enliven her spirits with the reminiscences of early days as to tend to her recovery.

Our family then resided at the upper end of Belmount Lake, above the Crow River. The next day, at early dawn, the crier of my father was sent round to inform the village damsels that the Ball-game was to be played at the request of the chief's wife.

Two large spruce-trees were transplanted from the woods, to holes in the ice; and in the afternoon the people from the villages were on the shore of the Lake. — Among them was my mother, wrapt up in furs and blankets to protect her from the cold. There was just enough snow upon the ground to make the footing very uncertain. I scarcely recollect any thing equal to the sport of that day. The crowds would fall and roll about, some laughing most heartily at themselves and at the distorted countenances of their companions, whose pain could not be concealed. When it was over, they all stood in a circle, and received the rewards allotted to each, consisting of beads, ribbons, scarlet cloths, &c. In a few moments more I heard them in their wigwams jesting and laughing at their day's sport.

Jumping is an exercise in which my countrymen have always engaged with considerable interest. Trials are made of jumping over a raised stick, or in the sand. — This sport, as well as the use of the bow and arrow, young women are prohibited from engaging in.

Foot Racing is much practiced, mostly however by the young people. Thus in early life they acquire an elasticity of limb as well as health of body, which are of priceless value to them in subsequent years.

The first mortification my pride ever received was on a certain occasion when I engaged in one of these races in the presence of a crowd of warriors. The prize was a piece of scarlet cloth. As I reached forth my hand to grasp the prize, a rope that lay hid in the grass upset me so completely, that I turned half a dozen somersets and finally tumbled into a pool of water. When I got out I had the extreme pleasure of seeing my rival take the cloth, and of hearing him brag that he had actually beaten the chief's son. I wiped my drenched head as best I could, and my eyes of the dirt which adhered to them with all the tenacity of a leech; amid the shouts of laughter which was all the consolation I received in my misfortune. Since then I have walked seventy-five miles a day in the spring of the year, so that I can boast of this, if not of my first pedestrian feat.

I need not say in concluding this chapter, what every one probably knows, that the plays and exercises of the Indians have contributed much towards the formation and preservation of that noble, erect, and manly figure for which they are so remarkable.

Growing up in the daily practice of these has been and is now a sure preventive of disease. Not until recently has the rude and brutish system of wrestling been in vogue among them.

The law of the nation, like that of ancient Greece, has been enacted with a view to the health of its subjects. It obliged the people to engage in these exercises that they might inherit strong constitutions, and be prepared for the cold storms, and the piercing blasts that sweep around the lake shores.

The mildness added to the coldness of the climate conduce to the expansion of the ingenuity of my people. The old saying, "necessity is the mother of invention," finds a verification in them. Did they possess the advantages of education possessed by the whites, many a bright star would shine forth in their ranks to bless and improve mankind. What they want is education. – They have mind, but it requires culture.

A short time since, while on a steamboat on the waters of the upper Mississippi, a gentleman speaking of the Chippeways, said that they were a manly, noble race, that their motto seemed to be, "Suffering before treachery – death before dishonour." It was gratifying to my national pride to hear such an assertion made by an enlightened American.

THEIR LEGENDARY STORIES

The Ojibways have a great number of legends, stories, and historical tales, the relating and hearing of which, form a vast fund of winter evening instruction and amusement.

There is not a lake or mountain that has not connected with it some story of delight or wonder, and nearly every beast and bird is the subject of the storyteller, being said to have transformed itself at some prior time into some mysterious formation – of men going to live in the stars, and of imaginary beings in the air, whose rushing passage roars in the distant whirlwinds.

I have known some Indians who have commenced to narrate legends and stories in the month of October, and not end until quite late in the spring, sometimes not till the month of May, and on every evening of this long term tell a new story.

Some of these stories are most exciting, and so intensely interesting, that I have seen children during their relation, whose tears would flow most plenti-fully, and their breasts heave with thoughts too big for utterance.

Night after night for weeks have I sat and eagerly listened to these stories. The days following, the characters would haunt me at every step, and every mov-ing leaf would seem to be a voice of a spirit. To those days I look back with pleasurable emotions. Many of those fanciful stories have been collected by H. R. Schoolcraft, Esq.

It is not my purpose to unnecessarily extend this work with a large number of these. I will, however, in this connection, narrate a few, in order to give you some idea of the manner in which my people amuse themselves in their wigwams, and promise to send you, at some future day, a good handful from the forest.

These legends have an important bearing on the character of the children of our nation. The fire-blaze is endeared to them in after years by a thousand happy recollections. By mingling thus, social habits are formed and strengthened. When the hour for this recreation arrives, they lay down the bow and arrow, and joyously repair to the wigwam of the aged man of the village, who is always ready to accommodate the young.

Legends are of three distinct classes, namely, the Amusing, the Historical, and the Moral. In the fall we have one class, in the winter another, and in the spring a third. I can at present have only time and space to give specimens of the second of these.

Legend First: The Star And The Lily

An old chieftain sat in his wigwam quietly smoking his favourite pipe, when a crowd of Indian boys and girls suddenly entered, and with numerous offerings of tobacco, begged him to tell them a story. Then the old man began:

"There was once a time when this world was filled with happy people, when all nations were as one, and the crimson tide of war had not begun to roll. Plenty of game was in the forest and on the plains. None were in want, for a full supply was at hand. Sickness was unknown. The beasts of the field were tame, they came and went at the bidding of man. One unending spring gave no place for winter – for its cold blasts or its unhealthy chills. Every tree and bush yielded fruit.

"Flowers carpeted the earth; the air was laden with their fragrance, and redolent with the songs of married warblers, that flew from branch to branch, fearing none, for there were none to harm them. There were birds then of more beautiful song and plumage than now.

"It was at such a time, when earth was a paradise and man worthily its possessor, that the Indians were the lone inhabitants of the American wilderness.

"They numbered millions, and living as Nature designed them to live, en-joyed its many blessings. Instead of amusements in close rooms, the sports of the fields were theirs. At night they met on the wide green fields. They watched the stars; they loved to gaze at them, for they believed them to be the residences of the good who had been taken home by the Great Spirit.

"One night they saw one star that shone brighter than all others. Its location was far away in the south near a mountain peak. For many nights it was seen, till at length it was doubted by many that the star was as far distant in the southern skies as it seemed to be. This doubt led to an examination, which proved the star to be only a short distance, and near the tops of some trees.

"A number of warriors were deputed to go and see what it was. They went, and on their return, said it appeared strange and somewhat like a bird. A committee of the wise men were called to inquire into it, and if possible ascertain the meaning of the strange phenomenon.

"They feared that it might be the omen of some disaster. Some thought it the precursor of good, others of evil, and some supposed it to be the star spoken of by their forefathers, as the forerunner of a dreadful war.

"One moon had nearly gone by, and yet the mystery remained unsolved.

"One night a young warrior had a dream, in which a beautiful maiden came and stood at his side, and thus addressed him:

" 'Young brave! charmed with the land of thy forefathers, its flowers, its birds, its rivers, its beautiful lakes, and its mountains clothed with green, I have left my sisters in yonder world to dwell among you. Young brave! ask your wise and your great men where I can live and see the happy race continually; ask them what form I shall assume in order to be loved.'

"Thus discoursed the bright stranger. The young man awoke. On stepping out of his lodge, he saw the star yet blazing in its accustomed place.

"At early dawn the chief's crier was sent round the camp to call every warrior to the council lodge. When they had met, the young warrior related his dream. They concluded that the star that had been seen in the south had fallen in love with mankind, and that it was desirous to dwell with them.

"The next night five tall, noble-looking, adventurous braves were sent to welcome the stranger to earth. They went and presented to it a pipe of peace, filled with sweet-scented herbs, and were rejoiced to find that it took it from them. As they returned to the village, the star with expanded wing followed, and hovered over their homes till the dawn of day.

"Again it came to the young man in a dream, and desired to know where it should live, and what form it should take.

"Places were named. On the top of giant trees, or in flowers. At length it was told to choose a place itself, and it did so.

"At first, it dwelt in the white rose of the mountains; but there it was so buried that it could not be seen. It went to the prairie, but it feared the hoof of the buffalo. It next sought the rocky cliff, but there it was so high, that the children whom it loved most could not see it.

" 'I know where I shall live,' said the bright fugitive, "where I can see the gliding canoe of the race I most admire. Children! yes, they shall be my playmates, and

I will kiss their brows when they slumber by the side of cool lakes. The nations shall love me wherever I am.'

"These words having been said, she alighted on the waters where she saw herself reflected. The next morning, thousands of white flowers were seen on the surface of the lakes, and the Indians gave them this name, '*Wah-be-gwon-nee*,' (White Lily)."

"Now," continued the old man, "this star lived in the southern skies. Its brethren can be seen far off in the cold north, hunting the great bear, whilst its sisters watch her in the east and west.

"Children! when you see the lily on the waters, take it in your hands, and hold it to the skies, that it may be happy on earth as its two sisters, the morning and evening stars, are happy in heaven."

While tears fell fast from the eyes of all, the old man laid down and was soon silent in sleep.

Since that, I have often plucked the white lily, and garlanded it around my head — have dipped it in its watery bed — but never have I seen it without remembering the legend of the descending star.

Legend Second: Historical: The Long Chase

The Indian warrior of days long past, thought that distance should never be considered when he went forth to war, provided he was certain of winning the applause of his fellows. Fatigue and hunger were alike looked upon as minor matters, and were endured with a murmur.

The long continued wars which once existed between the Ojibways and the Iroquois, gave rise to the following legend, which was originally related to me by an Ojibway chief, whose name was Na-nah-boo-sho.

A party of six Iroquois runners had been sent by their leading chiefs from Ke-wa-we-won, on the southern shore of Lake Superior, to examine the position of the Ojibways, who were supposed to be on the island called Moo-ne-quah-na-kaung-ning. The spies having arrived opposite the island on which their enemies had encamped, (which was about three miles from the main shore), built a war-canoe with the bark of an elm-tree, launched it at the hour of midnight, and having implored the god of war to smile upon them and keep the lake in peace, landed on the island, and were soon prowling through the village of the unconscious Ojibway. They were so cautious in their movements, that their footsteps did not even awaken the sleeping dogs.

It happened, however, that they were discovered, and that too by a young woman, who according to an ancient custom was leading a solitary life previous to becoming a mother. In her wakefulness, she saw them pass near her lodge, and heard them speak, yet could not understand their words, though she thought them to be of the Na-do-way tribe.

When they had passed, she stole out of her own wigwam to that of her aged grandmother, to whom she related what she had seen and heard. The aged woman only reprimanded her daughter for her imprudence and did not heed her words.

"But mother," replied the girl, "I speak the truth; the dreaded Na-do-ways are in our village, and if the warriors of the Buffalo race do not heed the story of a foolish girl, their women and their children must perish."

The words of the girl were finally believed, and the warriors of the Crane and Buffalo tribes prepared themselves for a conflict.

The war-whoop echoed to the sky — and the rattling of bows and arrows was heard in every part of the island. In about one hour the main shore was lined with about eight hundred canoes, the occupants of which were anxiously awaiting the appearance of the spies. These desperate men, however, had made up their mind to ply their oars to the utmost, and as the day was breaking, they launched their canoes from a woody cove, shot round the island, and started in the direction of the Porcupine mountains, which were about sixty miles distant. As soon as they came in sight of the Ojibways, the latter became quite frantic, and giving their accustomed yell, the whole multitude started after them as swift as the flight of birds.

The waters of the mighty lake were without a ripple, other than that made by the swiftly gliding canoe, and the beautiful fish moved among their rocky haunts in perfect peace, unconscious of the chase above.

The Iroquois were some two miles ahead, and while they strained every nerve for life, one voice rose high in the air, bearing an invocation to the spirits of their race for protection. In answer to their prayer, a thick fog fell upon the water and caused great confusion — One of the Ojibway warriors laid down his paddle, seized his mysterious rattle (made of deer's hoof) and in a strange, wild song, implored the spirits of his race to clear away the fog, that they might pursue their enemies. The burden of their song was —

> "Mon-e-doo ne bah bah me tah wah
> Ke shig ne bah bah me tah goon,
> Ne bee ne wah wah goom me goon,
> Ne ke che dah — awas, awas."

Which may be translated as follows: —

> "Spirits! whom we have always obeyed,
> Here cause the sky now to obey;
> Place now the waters all in our power,
> We are warriors — away, away."

As the last strain of music departed, the fog rolled away, and the Iroquois spies were seen hastening to the shore, near Montreal river. Then came the fog again and then departed, in answer to the conflicting prayers of the two nations. Long and exciting was the race. But the Great Spirit was the friend of the

Ojibways – and just as the Iroquois were landing on the beach, four of them were pierced with arrows, and the remaining two taken prisoners. A council was then called for the purpose of determining what should be done with them, and it was determined that they should be tortured at the stake. They were, accordingly, fastened to a tree, and surrounded with wood, when just as the flaming torch was to be applied, an aged warrior stepped forth from the crowd of spectators, and thus addressed the assembly: –

"Why are you to destroy these men? They are brave warriors, but not more distinguished than we are. We can gain no benefit from their death. Why not let them live, that they may go and tell their people of our power, and that our warriors are as numerous as the stars of the northern sky?"

The council pondered upon the old man's advice, and in the breasts of each there was a struggle between their love of revenge and their love of glory. Both were victorious.

One of the spies was released, and as he ascended a narrow valley, leading to the Porcupine mountains, the fire was applied to the dry wood piled around the form of the other, and in the darkness of midnight, and amid the shouting of his cruel enemies, the body of the Iroquois prisoner was reduced to ashes.

The spot where the sacrifice took place has been riven by many a thunder-bolt since that eventful hour, for the god of war was displeased with the faint-heartedness of the Ojibways for valuing a man more highly than the privilege of revenge; and the summer of the next year that saw the remains of the humane Ojibway buried on the shore of Lake Superior, saw also the remains of the pardoned spy consigned to the earth on the shore of Michigan.

Thus ends the legend of Shah-gah-wah-mik, one of the Apostle Islands, which the French named La Pointe, and which was originally known as Mo-ne-quon-a-kon-ing. The village stood where the old trading establishment was located, and among the greenest of the graves now seen in the hamlet of La Pointe is that of the Indian girl who exposed herself to reproach for the purpose of saving her people.

LEGEND THIRD: THE THUNDER'S NEST

The following legend will impart some instruction relative to the Indian idea of thunder.

Once upon a time when no wars existed among men, the only thing they feared was a great bird seen flying through the air during moonlight nights. When it was seen in the day-time its presence was usually followed by the visitation of some great misfortune upon any one who should chance to see it.

These monstrous birds were supposed to have their nests somewhere, and great curiosity existed to know the location, as well as to know somewhat of the nature of the bird; but no one seemed fortunate enough to discover the resort of these great birds, which were called *Ah-ne-me-keeg,* (Thunders).

There lived on the northern shore of Lake Superior, an Indian warrior, who from his childhood had been noted for being a wise and sedate man; it was supposed by many that he would some day go on a great exploit, as none were like him for courage, wisdom, and prudence. As he was returning from one of his hunting expeditions, the night came on sooner than he expected it would, and darkness gathered around him while he was a great distance from his home. On his way he was obliged to traverse the ice on lake and river. The moon shone as clear and perfect as it had ever shone to light a traveller's path. On the warrior's back was a beaver, and in his hand the tried and trusty spear, with which he had captured it. As he was crossing the last lake, the shadow of some great object passed before him, and he soon saw approaching a great bird, which in a moment caught him and all he had, and arose. The bird carried him westward, far above the earth, yet not so far as to prevent him from seeing it, and the doings upon it. After travelling a great distance they came in view of a high hill, which was barren of trees, but bore one bold barren rock. As they neared it, the bird endeavoured to dash him upon its side, but the old Indian so placed his spear that he was not injured in the least degree. At length he was thrown upon the place where the young birds were. He heard fierce muttering thunder overhead, and found himself left to the mercy of the wild birds.

Soon after, they began to peck his head, when he, thinking them helpless, ventured to make battle with them. The Indian arose, and soon found that they were too much for him. Whenever they winked, a flash of lightning would pass from their eyes, and scorch him so severely as to burn his hands and face.

The birds were very small, and not able to execute much, and therefore by perseverance he gained the mastery over them with his spear. He dragged one of them to the edge, rolled it over the precipice, and took the skin from the other.

On looking round, he discovered that he was near the northwest end of Lake Superior; he then threw the other carcase from him, and after filling his pipe with Ke-ne-ke-nik (bark), taking one or two whiffs, he held it in his hand, and pointing with its stem to the four corners of the heaven, he offered up a prayer, which he believed was heard. He then got inside of the young thunder skin, sewed himself in it, and rolled down the rocks. As he tumbled from rock to rock, the feathers of the skin would flash with fire. After descending about half way to the bottom of the precipice, the skin in which he was bound bore him on its wings, and after a long flight, alighted with him near the spot from whence he was taken ten days before. His wife and children were in mourning for his loss, for they had seen him taken from the ice, and were convinced that he had been taken by some mysterious spirit. As might be supposed, when he returned he surprised them by bringing to his children the hearts of the young thunders. He broiled them, and as he did so, the fire made a crackling noise. (Indian children are now told that when the fire makes a noise, the hearts of young thunders are broiling in it.)

The next summer, the mountains west of the Me-she-be-goo-toong, on the borders of Lake Superior were continually enveloped in flames and heavy clouds, for it is there that the remainder of the thunder birds rested.

Since mankind have gone in great crowds, these birds are seldom seen, but are often heard in the skies, where they fly higher than they once did. Once they lived on human flesh, but now they subsist on the wild game of the forest. They wink, and the fire flashes from their eyes. Their nests are now built on the *Ah-sen-wah-ge-wing* (Rocky Mountains), in the far west, and at times they are heard passing through the air towards the east, on their way to the sea, for they live upon fish and serpents, since they have been subdued by man.

LEGEND FOURTH: THE TWO COUSINS

There lived amongst the hills of the north, two most intimate friends, who had appeared to have loved each other from the years of their earliest childhood. In summer they lived by a beautiful lake, in autumn on the banks of a noble river. In personal appearance they were very near alike; they were of the same age and stature. In their early days a good old Indian woman attended to their wants, and cared for their wigwams; together they strolled among the green woods, and shared the results of their ramblings. Years flitted by. Manhood came, when they used large bows and arrows.

One day the old lady took them by her side, and told them that the nation to which they belonged held a fast, and that she wanted them to fast that they might become great hunters. And they did fast.

As spring advanced, they killed a great many wild ducks, and kept the old woman of the wigwam busy in taking care of their game.

In the latter part of the year they killed a great number of beaver, with the furs of which they clothed their grandmother and themselves.

In their journey one day, they made an agreement to this effect, that if the gods should make known any manifest favour to the one he should inform the other.

In the fall, they were far from the rivers, but yet moved towards the north, where they knew the bears most resorted. During that winter they killed a great many, as also during the ensuing March.

At the close of one of their hunting expeditions, they turned their feet towards home, at which they arrived at a late hour. As they approached, they heard the sound of several voices beside that of their grandmother. They listened, and discovered that strangers were in their wigwam. They entered, and beheld two young and beautiful damsels seated in that part of the room in which they generally rested during the night. The hunters and the young women appeared very strange and modest. At length the old lady said to the young men:

"Noo-se-se-took! My children, I have called these two young women from the south, that they may aid me in taking care of all the meat and venison you may bring home, for I am getting old and weak, and cannot do as much as I used to. I have put them by your sides that they may be your companions."

When the last words were spoken, they looked upon each other, and soon left, to wander by themselves in the forest.

They there consulted together as to whether they should comply with her request. One said he should leave the wigwam. The other said that if they left, there would be no one to supply their aged grandmother, and they finally agreed to remain in the wigwam and pay no regard to the new comers.

They slept side by side every night, and agreed that if either should wish to love one of the young strangers he would inform the other, and that they would then separate for ever. In February they obtained a vast amount of game, the bears having returned to their winter quarters were easily found and captured.

It was observed that one of the young men gazed very intently at one of the strangers, and the next morning, as they went out, he asked the other whether he did not begin to love the young damsel who sat on his side of the birchen fire. He replied negatively. It was true one of the cousins appeared to be deeply absorbed in thought every evening, and that his manner was very reserved.

After a fortunate hunting-day, as they were wending their way home with their heavy burden of bear and deer, one accused the other of loving the young woman. "Tell me," said he, "and if you do, I will leave you to yourselves. If you have a wife, I cannot enjoy your company, or take the same delight with you as I do when we follow the chase."

His cousin sighed, and said — "I will tell you to-night as we lie side by side."

At night they conversed together, and agreed to hunt, and if they did not meet with success, they would separate. The next morning they went to the woods, — they were not a great distance from each other during the hunt. The one who was in love shot only five, while the other returned with the tongues of twenty bears. The former was all the time thinking of the damsel at home, while the latter thought only of his game, having nothing else to divert his mind.

On their return, the lucky man informed the grandmother that he should leave the next morning, and that what he should kill on the morrow must be searched after, as he should not return to tell them where he had killed the game. His cousin was grieved to find that his mind was made up to leave, and began to expostulate with him to change his determination; but he would not be per-suaded to do so.

The next day came. The young man who was to leave bound a rabbit-skin about his neck to keep it warm, and having used on himself red and yellow paints, left. His cousin followed close in his rear, entreating him not to leave him.

"I will go," said he, "and live in the north, where I shall see but few persons, and when you come that way, you will see me."

They walked side by side, until the departing cousin began to ascend – and as he did so, the other wept the more bitterly, and entreated him most persever-ingly not to go.

The cousin ascended to the skies, and is seen in the north, *Ke-wa-den-ah-mung* (north star), still hunting the bear; while the other wept himself to nought before he could arrive home, and now he answers and mocks everybody. He lives in the craggy rocks and deep woods, and his name is *Bah-swa-way* (Echo). The young maidens lived for a long time in the south, under ambrosial bowers, awaiting the return of their lovers, until one fell in love with mankind, and the other is waiting for the return of her lover, where

> "She looks as clear as morning roses,
> Newly washed in dew."

Their Language and Writings

The Ojibway language, or the language of the Algonquin stock, is perhaps the most widely spoken of any in North America. The Atlantic tribes partook of this idiom when they were first discovered.

The snows of the north bounded the people who spoke this language on that side, while in the south as far as the Potomac and the mountains of Virginia, down the Ohio, over the plains of Illinois to the east of the upper waters of the Father of River, nations resided three or four hundred years ago who could speak so as to be understood by each other. A person might have travelled nearly one thousand miles from the head of Lake Superior, and yet not journey from the sound of this dialect.

In consequence of this universality of their language; the nation has had a wide-spreading influence. Many of the nation have travelled from the main body to other lands: thus passing in contact with other nations they have adopted their customs, and have so intermixed the two languages, that the original Ojibway is not now so generally spoken, within a thousand miles of the Ojibway or Great Lake, as formerly.

Mr. H. R. Schoolcraft, who has studied the language more than any other person, and to some purpose, has often said through the press, as well in private conversation, that there is in it that which few other languages possess; a force of expression, with music in its words and poetry in their meaning. I cannot ex-press fully the beauty of the language, I can only refer to those who have studied it as well as other languages, and quote their own writing in saying, "every word has its appropriate meaning, and with additional syllables give additional force to the meaning of most words." After reading the English language, I have found words in the Indian combining more expressiveness. There are many Indian words which when translated into English lose their force, and do not convey so much meaning in one sentence as the original does in one word.

It would require an almost infinitude of English words to describe a thunderstorm, and after all you would have but a feeble idea of it. In the Ojibway language, we say "Be-wah-sam-moog." In this we convey the idea of a continual glare of lightning, noise, confusion — an awful whirl of clouds, and much more. Observe the smoothness of its words: —

Ah-nung-o-kah . . . . The starry heavens.
Bah-bah-me-tum . . . . Obedience.
Che-baum . . . . Soul.
De goo wah shak . . . . The rippling wave.
E-nah-kay-yah . . . . The way.
Gah-gah-geeh . . . . Raven.
How-wah-do-seh . . . . Stone carrier (fish).
Ish peming . . . . Heaven.
Jeen quon . . . . Earthquake.
Kah-ke-nah . . . . All.
Mah-nah-ta-nis . . . . Sheep.
Nah-nah-gum-moo . . . . Singing.
O-nah-ne quod . . . . Pleasant weather.
Pah-pah-say . . . . Woodpecker.
Quah-nauge . . . . Pretty.
Sah-se-je-won . . . . Rapids.
Tah-que-shin . . . . He or she comes.
Wah-be-goo-ne . . . . Lily.
Yah-no-tum . . . . Unbelief.
Ze-bee-won . . . . Streams.

Upon examination it will be found that there are several letters not sounded, to wit: F, L, R, V, X, though Carver mentions in his vocabulary the use of the letter L in several instances. This no doubt he did because he lacked a perfect understanding of the language. The same may be said of the letter R. We have none of the mouthing as of the thick sound of the letter L, nor any of gutteral accompaniments of the letter R. To the contrary, all the softness of the vowels are sounded without many of the harsh notes of the consonants, and this produces that musical flow of words for which the language is distinguished.

It is a natural language. The pronunciation of the names of animals, birds and trees are the very sounds these produce; for instance, hoot owl, *o-o-me-seh;* owl, *koo-koo-ko-ooh;* river, *see-be;* rapids, *sah se-je-won.* "See" is the sound of the waters on the rocks. — "*Sah-see*" the commotion of waters, and from its sound occurs its name.

The softness of the language is caused, as I have before said, by the peculiar sounding of all the vowels; though there is but little poetic precision in the formation of verse, owing to the want of a fine discriminating taste by those who speak it.

A language, derived, as this is, from the peculiarities of the country in which it is spoken, must, necessarily, partake of its nature. Our orators have filled the forest with the music of their voices, loud as the roar of a waterfall, yet soft and wooing as the gentle murmur of a mountain stream. We have had warriors who have stood on the banks of lakes and rivers, and addressed with words of irresistible and persuasive eloquence their companions in arms.

The Ojibway language has not yet been reduced to a perfect written form. An attempt to do this was made by the lamented Summerfield, who in his degree of usefulness would not have dishonoured his name had he lived. Close study was followed by a consumptive disease, which terminated his life before his contemplated work was finished. In his attempt he followed too much the English idiom in forming a grammar of the Ojibway language.

The records of the Ojibways have a two-fold meaning; the hieroglyphic symbols of material objects represent the transmission of a tradition from one generation to another. This refers more particularly to their religion, which is itself founded on tradition. Picture writing is more prevalent, and is used altogether in their medicine and hunting songs. Here are figures which suggest sentences to be sung:

This is one of their war songs, which might read in English thus: —

1.
I will haste to the land of the foe,
With warriors clad with the bow.

2.
I will drink the blood of their very heart;
I will change their joy into sorrow's smart;
Their braves, their sires will I defy,
And a nation's vengeance satisfy.

3.
They are in their homes, now happy and free;
No frowning cloud o'er their camp they see;
Yet the youngest of mine shall see the tall
Braves, scattered, wandering, and fall.

The warrior is represented by the figure of a man with a bow about him and arrows in his hand; with the plume of the eagle waving over his head, indicative of his acquaintance with war life. The next figure represents a watching warrior, equally brave, but the heart is represented as dead. The curve of his mouth shows that he is shouting. The next figure represents a person with long hair, an indication that the best of the enemy's warriors were to fall, and their wail must be hard like the wail of a woman. The wigwam with its smoke curling upwards indicates a council fire, and the defiance of an attack. The other wigwams are seen without fire; and the black one signifies silence and death.

When I was young I was taught this, and while singing I could, in imagination, see the enemy, though none were within a hundred miles.

In their war-songs, animals are likewise represented in various attitudes. A rattle is made of deer's hoofs which is shook during the singing.

This rattle was sometimes used for the purpose of transmitting news from one nation to another; but in most cases shells were used for his purpose. I have been present in Canada when a string of beads has been received from the head waters of Lake Superior. A profound silence ensued, then followed a revelation of the message, and at its close a prolonged grunting sound from the vast assembly signified the people's assent.

There is a place where the sacred records are deposited in the Indian country. These records are made on one side of bark and board plates, and are examined once in fifteen years, at which time the decaying ones are replaced by new plates.

This secrecy is not generally known by those people who have searched with interest the Indian, and traced him in all his wanderings to get an idea of his religion and his worship, which however absurd they may have seemed, have nevertheless been held in so rigid respect that he has formed for it a cloak of almost impenetrable mystery. He concluded that all Nature around him was clothed in mystery – that innumerable spirits were ever near to forward a good object and retard a bad one, and that they existed as a chain connecting heaven with earth. His medicine bag contained all those native things of the forest around which, in his opinion, the greatest mystery gathered; as the more of mystery, the more the Great Spirit seemed to be attached to them. A whale was an object of much importance, because it was dedicated to the Supreme Being, and to approach it, or look upon it irreverently, would offend him and his children. They therefore never drew near it but with the most profound silence and veneration. With this great awe of spiritual things in his mind, he feels reluctant to reveal all that he knows of his worship and the objects and rites which perpetuate it.

Most Indian nations of the west have places in which they deposit the records which are said to have originated their worship. The Ojibways have three such depositories near the waters of Lake Superior. Ten of the wisest and most venerable of the nation dwell near these, and are appointed guardians over them.

Fifteen years intervene between each opening. At the end of this time, if any vacancies have been caused by death, others are chosen in the spring of the year, who, about the month of August, are called to witness the opening of the depositories. As they are being opened, all the information known respecting them is given to the new members; then the articles are placed before them. After this, the plates are closely examined, and if any have begun to decay they are taken out; an exact facsimile is made and placed in its stead. – The old one is divided equally among the wise men. It is very highly valued for having been deposited; as a sacred article, every fibre of it is considered sacred, and whoever uses it may be made wise. It is considered efficacious for any good purpose it may be put to.

These records are written on slate-rock, copper, lead, and on the bark of birch-trees. The record is said to be a transcript of what the Great Spirit gave to the Indian after the flood, and by the hands of wise men has been transmitted to other parts of the country ever since. Here is a code of moral laws which, the Indian calls "a path made by the Great Spirit." They believe that a long and prosperous life will be the result of obeying that law. The records contain certain emblems which transmit the ancient form of worship, and the clues for the dedication of four priests who alone are to expound them. In them is represented how man lived happy in his wigwam, before death was in the world and the path he then followed marked out an example for those of the present time.

During my travels over the whole extent of the nation, I have been informed of a great many facts representing these sacred depositories of which most of my brethren are ignorant.

The chief of Lac Coart, Oreille, ("Moose Tail"), in the spring of 1836, related to my uncle John Taunchey, of Rice Lake, C. W., an account of one of these depositories near the mouth of "Round Lake."

He said he had been chosen as one of the guardians about five years previous, and that the guardians had for a long time selected as the places of deposit the most unsuspected spot, where they dug fifteen feet, and sunk large cedar trees around the excavation. In the centre was placed a large hollow cedar log, besmeared at one end with gum. The open end is uppermost, and in it are placed the records, after being enveloped in the down of geese or swan, which are changed at each examination. These feathers are afterwards used in war, being supposed to have a protective power. When camping, a few of these feathers are left near each place where the warriors dance.

These are some of the figures used by us in writing. With these, and from others of a similar class, the Ojibways can write their war and hunting songs.

An Indian well versed in these can send a communication to another Indian, and by them make himself as well understood as a pale face can by letter.

There are over two hundred figures in general use for all the purposes of correspondence. Material things are represented by pictures of them.

The Characters Used in Picture Writing

| Man. | Sunrise. | Sun. | Sea Water. | Moon. | Sunset |

| Death. | Life. | River, stream. | Woman. | Bear. | Sky, heaven. | Fish. |

| Smooth water, Clear Day | Sickness. | Stars. | Land. | Great. | Night. |

| Noon. | Bad spirit, water god. | Great Spirit, every where. | Fight-man, bad spirit. |

| Spirit. | Tree. | Old tree. | Rain, cloudy. | Worship, medicine, pure. | War. |

| Medicine Lodge. | Trees, woods. | Storm, windy. | Animals under ground. |

| Bear killed. | Spirits under water. | Stand. |

Wounded water god.   Mountains.   Bad Spirit, Medicine.   Scalps, number.   Young warrior.

See.   Speak   Sea Monster, eat man.   Ran.   Walked, passed.   Hand did so.

Bad spirit under earth.   Islands.   Duck, water birds.   Deer, Moose.

Spirits above.   Cold, snow.   Fire.   Bad.   Hemlock.

Dream.

Invitations to Indians to come and worship in the spring are made in following form:

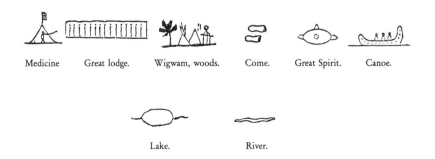

Medicine   Great lodge.   Wigwam, woods.   Come.   Great Spirit.   Canoe.

Lake.   River.

The whole story would thus read—

> "Hark to the words of the Sa-ge-mah."
>
> "The Great Medicine Lodge will be ready in eight days."
>
> "Ye who live in the woods and near the lakes and by streams of water, come with your canoes or by land to the worship of the Great Spirit."

In the above, the wigwam and the medicine pale or worship, represent the depositories of medicine, record and work. The lodge is represented with men in it; the dots above indicate the number of days.

These picture representations were used by the Ojibways until the introduction of European manners among them. When this occurred, they neglected in a great degree their correspondence with other nations, except by special messengers, and became very cautious in giving information respecting their religious worship to the whites, because they, the whites, ridiculed it. It is not kind of the people, who have been among us to do this, which has resulted in much evil. *First,* they have kept to themselves many an important tradition which, if known, would have greatly aided the eye and ear of research in bringing out all the traditions of the Indians with respect to their origin and civilization. However absurd their ideas may have been, it would have been more to the credit of civilized people to have said nothing at all about the falsity of such, for when they see the light of education on them, they have left off these absurdities, without having to laugh down their nation.

In the *second* place. This laughing at their absurd worship or belief, has prejudiced their minds in proportion to the amount of abuse they received from the pale face, and the benefits of Christian education.

Many think we cannot keep the words or tradition longer than one hundred years. We have the tradition of the flood; the organization of the medicine worship of the Indians, originating as it did by the introduction of disease in the earth, in the disobedience of a woman. Why do we have these traditions represented in picture records, and transmitted from one generation to another? And how long since the flood?

The present dependence of the pale face on letters, for the past is too much of a marvel for the history of those times, entirely forgetting that the whole of the old and New Testaments has been handed down in the same form in years back, until letters became the representation of such traditions.

We could communicate by drawings made on bark and on boards to be understood by each of us. Runners have always been sent on such errands of communication.

When William Penn arrived in the Delaware river, the news was sent on to the west by the Delaware native, and such communications was sent in this way to the Shawnees in Sandusky, Lake Erie; and they to the Ojibways in Superior and Huron.

This mode was practised by Pontiac in his appeals to the Indians of Michigan, Huron, and the prairies of the west, during the wars. The Indians say that these beads cannot give false stories, for it is not possible for the man who takes it to alter or to add to them, during his journey.

Red World and White

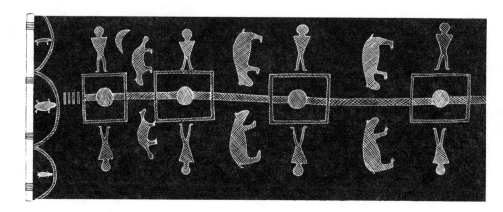

A Chippewa Speaks

I, WAY QUAH GISHIG, was six years old when my two sisters, Bishiu and Min di, accompanied me to Flanreau, South Dakota to attend an Indian boarding school.

It was very difficult for me at first, for students at the school were not allowed to speak the language of the Indians. At that time I understood nothing else.

Neither did I like to be forced to remain with my sisters in the girls' building instead of being assigned to the quarters occupied by the boys.

I was as shy and timid as the young buck in the forest and clung very closely to my sister. But soon I learned to speak and understand a little of the white man's language; and gradually the boys began coaxing me to play with them.

At first I wore my hair in two braids, Indian fashion, but at last my sisters gave in and allowed it to be cut so that I would be like the other boys.

My many happy years at the school have no place in this volume, so I will begin at the time Min di, Bishiu, and I took the train to return home.

Min di, who at school was given the name of Caroline, was tall and slender as the sapling pine. Her eyes as soft and innocent as a doe's. She wore her raven black hair loose, hanging down her back, and tied with a buckskin string.

We got off the puffing, snorting train at Mahnomen. There was a man named John Carr met us. He put us in his light wagon. Min di sat on the seat beside him, and Bishiu and I alternately stood or lay down in the rear.

With ever widening interest we stared off at the passing landscape. The road wound along ahead of us, turning and curling like a slithering serpent.

I was anxious to see my mother and be home again, but even this strong

by John Rogers

desire could not keep me awake for many hours, and finally Weeng, the sleep spirit, settled down over me.

We stopped briefly at the town of Beaulieu, where we got out and stretched our legs and had lunch. When we started out again, the scene was changed. We came into wooded places, where trees seem to tower upward to the sky and cast deep dark shadows on the fallen leaves encircling them.

Finally Min di turned and exclaimed, "Look, Way quah!" She pointed toward the north.

There in the distance I saw the sparkle of water and the ripple of waves as the sun was reflected back through the trees. This I knew was home!

Coming to a halt near a wigwam, the driver got down and helped us out. "Here we are children. Over there is your mother."

He did not mention my father, and I wondered about him.

Mother was seated on the ground, working on some fish nets. She was heavy and broad, but her hands and feet were small. Her hair, straight and black, was tied with a red string. She wore a full-skirted blue calico dress, with long blousey sleeves, a low neck, and tight-fitting waist. Her waist was encircled by a fringed belt with red, yellow green, and blue figures in it.

I learned later that mother had to keep very busy making linen-thread fish nets to sell — for now she had extra mouths to feed.

She looked up from her work, and we children made a mad scramble toward her. As she stood up with outstretched arms her eyes sparkled as does the sun on laughing waters.

What a reunion that was! She endeavored to gather us all into her arms at once. She started talking joyously, but we couldn't understand very well what she said, for we had forgotten much of the Indian language during our six years away from home.

But all that mattered was we were welcome here in mother's wigwam – the home of our birth.

After supper that evening Mother took us back to where the nets were, and there was our baby brother, Ahmeek (meaning "beaver").

I had known nothing about him until then. But there he was, lying in his cradle, which looked something like a white man's hammock strung between two trees. It was situated conveniently so that Mother could reach out as she sat making nets and swing him back and forth, and croon to him to the accompaniment of the wind that rustled in the towering pines.

I stood staring down at my baby brother, and suddenly he looked up at me with his pretty dark eyes, raised his chubby little hands, and gurgled happily. To me he was saying, "Aren't you proud of your new little brother?"

His hair was straight and dark. He wore a little red and white checked calico dress.

Bishiu, now fourteen years of age, came up to me. She was tall for her age, but shorter and heavier than Min di. She had teasing brown eyes and was very pretty. She still wore the uniform of the school – a white blouse and blue skirt, with high-buttoned shoes and black stockings. She always liked the dress of the white people.

Bishiu bent over the cradle and held out her arms to her new baby brother.

"Min di said I should bring him to the wigwam," she said "and you are to help Mother straighten out her nets."

Mother, who sat nearby, shook her head.

"No, we will go into the wigwam now."

She picked up her pipe and kinnikinic (Indian tobacco), and we all went into the wigwam. It was about the size of a large room in a white man's dwelling. In the center was a fireplace, and above in the middle of the roof was an opening for light and for the smoke to escape. Suspended from a framework over the fire were two kettles almost full of water.

On one side of this large room I saw a bedframe made of poles. Over these were laid boughs to make a smooth, springy couch about the size of a double bed. The bedding consisted of deer pelts and, when not in use, could be folded back to the wall and serve as a back-rest.

Along the east wall was mother's workshop, and opposite the door the kitchen equipment was kept. On the west side was a place for the man's workshop. Over at the opposite wall was the pit used for storing and the wood pile. The storage pit was a hole dug in the ground, and this was overlaid with hay, on top of which was some birch bark. Here were potatoes, carrots, corn, onions, and many canned or dried fruits that had accumulated from the gather of fruits and berries.

I wondered where I was to sleep during that first night at home, for I could see but one bed. After awhile I questioned Min di, and she answered in Indian fashion:

"For the time, while our earth mother is still warm, you will sleep outside under the trees. But later, when the thunder clouds bring the rains, you will have another bed on the opposite side of the room."

I was then instructed what to do to prepare the outside bed. They told me to get four poles and place them upright in the ground. From the four corners thus formed a netting was draped down over the sides to protect me from mosquitoes and other insects during the time when darkness reigned and man dwelt under the spell of the sleep spirit.

During the days that followed we had a happy time getting acquainted after those long years of separation. Mother kept saying what a big help I was going to be. She asked whether I thought I would be happy gathering birch bark, tobacco, and wood? I was pleased to feel that I would grow into a strong young brave, and so I tried very hard to please her and to learn once more the Chippewa language. Min di was the only one who could speak both the Chippewa and English tongues, so for a time she interpreted all that mother said to Bishiu and me.

Mother promised to teach me the ways of the forest, rivers, and lakes – how to set rabbit snares and deadfalls, how to trap for wolves and other wild animals that roamed this land of the Chippewas.

While we sat around the fire talking and planning, Mother told my oldest sister to explain that she wanted us to be called by our Indian names. She insisted that we start at once to use them. So Min di told us not ever to use our school names any more. And so we became Min di and Bishiu, my two sisters, and Ahmeek, which meant "beaver" (the baby). My own Indian name, Way quah, meant "dawn of day" and at school I was known as John.

At the time of my homecoming I was twelve years old and quite tall for my age. I was straight as a pine. My hair was black and wavy, and my eyes sharp and brown.

I generally kept very quiet when in the presence of people.

Mother was very clever and direct in teaching me the Indian way of things. One day she called out abruptly: "Way quah, get those rocks and floats out by the tree. They are tied with wegoob."

Wegoob is the green inner bark from the basswood tree. This I got immediately, as mother watched me. I picked the rocks she wanted, which were about the size of a wild-duck egg, and the floats, which were made of cedar. I carried them into the wigwam and Mother and Min di arranged them on the nets.

"And now," said Mother approvingly, "get a hatchet and come with me down the beach to our nearest neighbor. There we will borrow a canoe to use for setting the nets."

As we walked along, she pointed to some red willow. She cut some of this to show me how, and took it along with us.

I shall never forget the experience in the borrowed canoe. This was my first ride in a boat made of birch bark. Mother put me in front, and we paddled back to our landing.

Mother frequently smoked a pipe, and I wondered where she got it and whether I could make one like it. So I asked her, and she explained that when a young girl she had gone with Chief Bay mi chig gah nany (meaning "Long Lake"), and he it was who had given the pipe to her. It had been handed down from chief to chief, until it finally came to him and he then told her that it was now hers.

"And so, Way quah," she said, "when you have grown to be a strong young brave, this pipe shall be yours." And to this day I have it among my prized possessions.

The peace pipe is made of black stone, and has a round bowl on a square base. It is inlaid with red stone and lead. The stem is made from the ash tree that grows in the swamps.

Often when Mother and all of us would sit around the fire, she would tell us stories of the Chippewas and about our brother and sister who were away at school in Morris, Minnesota; a brother and sister I would see again after the robin returned and the sun began once more to melt the snows and warm the earth.

This was the first time I knew I had two brothers and three sisters. I envisioned the fun we would all have playing on the shores of the lake and swimming in its smiling, rippling waters.

In Mother's stories were many interesting facts about our Grandmother. Mother promised we would go to her for a visit before many more suns. She hadn't seen us since we left for school.

It was early morning of a day in the following week that we started on this visit.

We took with us some mosquito netting and enough food to last for a few days. This was quite a load for us to pack, for we also had little Ahmeek to carry, and Grandmother's house was some six miles distant on a different trail.

We traveled slowly, but enjoyed every step of the way. The call of the birds and the voices of other wild things were like music to my ears. It seemed that the trees and shrubs were whispering messages and that the Great Spirit hovered very near on this trail where the shadows were deep. Now and then we would see a deer or a rabbit, or perhaps, it would be a squirrel that would scamper up the tree and scold us for intruding upon his peaceful domain.

Coming at last to the house, we dropped our packs outside. Mother's sister came to the door and greeted us with open arms. Grandma's face lighted up when she saw who it was. She seemed to be a very happy person, and she had been blessed with a very long life. She opened her heart to us instantly and made us feel at home while we remained in her dwelling.

When at last we were ready for the return trip through the forest trail, mother's sister offered to drive us home. Mother and Min di were never idle. They fashioned many useful articles with strips of birch bark peeled from nearby trees. From the sweet grass various roots and bulrushes were obtained. Then there were mats, baskets, and little birch-bark canoes.

In the gathering of rushes, Mother made us go out into the deep water where we would dive for the longer rushes. The longer the better, she told us; for the longer ones made larger and finer mats. Articles she made this way could be traded for flour, sugar, and other food supplies.

Now the time of the melting snows had come and gone. Soft, gentle winds warmed the earth. Summer was well along. We gathered birch bark for Mother, and with this she would make containers and dishes for our winter supplies. To remove this bark from the trees required skill in order not to harm the bark. It we cut too deeply it would leave a scar, for the new bark would not again grow out smooth.

Mother was careful to teach us just how it was done. With a sharp knife we would cut through the inner bark only. Indeed, it seemed that the Great Spirit had placed it there to let us know just how deeply to cut. It was our code never to destroy any thing that Nature had given us. If we took care in stripping the bark, more would be provided on the same tree.

At the coming of the robin was the best season for getting the bark, but since Mother had time now, in the fall, to teach us, she felt there was no need to wait.

While the leaf was still brown on the forest trees and the cold north wind had yet to bring the snow to our village, a young brave named Wa goosh came to our wigwam and asked Mother to come to the church of the white man, for a prayer meeting.

Mother looked upon Wa goosh with favor. He seemed to be always about when needed and always willing to help.

When Wa goosh first saw my sister Min di, it was plain that he liked her and it was the beginning of a beautiful friendship.

Wa goosh (meaning "fox") was tall and strong. He was the typical Chippewa brave. His shirt was tan and of buckskin, open at the throat with long sleeves and beautifully beaded cuffs. His trousers were dark and soft as the forest moss. Knotted about his throat he wore a colored silk handkerchief. But he wore no hat and no earrings. Usually there was just a band about his forehead and his hair hung in two braids.

I learned that Wa goosh was a hunter, a farmer, and a blacksmith, and would gather herbs beneficial to the sick. For these he would never accept pay, saying that those who were helped in their sickness could pay him with gifts if they chose to do so.

One morning Wa goosh asked Mother:

"Have the children ever seen a squaw dance?"

"No, Wa goosh, they haven't," she answered.

"Then at the time of the next dance you are all to go with me."

"We will come," Mother promised.

Thus it was when the Indians next gathered for this great occasion of the dance, we went with Wa goosh. We had heard that he was counted as one of the best solo dancers on the White Earth reservation. In his beautiful costume the young brave made the heart of every Indian maiden beat with desire to win his favor. But apparently he was most pleased when Min di joined him in the dance.

It is the custom at the squaw dance for the male to offer a gift to the girl with whom he wishes to perform, such as a handkerchief or goods for a new dress or maybe an article of food she would like. If she accepts, then she dances with him; and if she desires another dance with him, she gives him something in return. This might be a pair of beaded gloves or beaded cuffs. Or perhaps any beaded article that she owns and believes may please the young brave of her choice.

Here at the dance it was also the custom to exchange articles. If one wanted a pony that would pair with one he owned, he would offer his costume in exchange. This arrangement is made through one of his people, and they too join in the dance.

After a time they sit at the edge of the circle. Next comes the solo dance — without partners. Single dancers weave in and out and around one another, always circling the drummers, who are in the center. Only the men take part in this, and it is very rhythmic and beautiful. Then, after a time, he who has received the costume arises to announce that he will give his pony for it.

I shall never forget that first squaw dance that I attended. Thereafter, I never missed another one.

And so the long white winter passed. The snows melted from field and forest. Birds appeared in the budding trees and their song gladdened the hearts of all who heard.

While playing with Ahmeek one morning, Bishiu and I were swinging him in his cradle when we heard a wagon deep in the forest. A little later it came into view, bringing a man, a woman, and two children. We ran into the wigwam to our sister, Min di, and asked her who it could be. She and mother came out.

"Why, it's your brother and sister — Mah ni do mi naince and Osh kin nah way!" exclaimed Mother.

They were back from school. We boys stood there and admired each other's coats. Boylike, we compared them and found them very much alike, both having brass buttons and buttoned right up to the neck. The rest of Osh kin nah way's costume was a lot like mine too – blue-gray short trousers, high shoes, and black stockings.

He was ten years old, short and chubby, with black hair and brown eyes. He was very bashful. We called him Osh kin for short.

Mah ni do mi naince was twelve, tall and slender, but not very strong. She had long dark hair, braided to fall in front and tied with a red ribbon. Her eyes were brown. Her uniform was a jumper skirt of blue and a white blouse, high shoes, and black stockings. We called her Mah ni.

Neither could talk Indian. So I felt sorry for them. They would have to learn the Indian tongue all over again, the same as Bishiu and I had to do. I felt I could be of much help to them.

The four of us children would make birchbark baskets and take them out to fill with berries. There were strawberries, raspberries, high bush cranberries, wild grapes, and blueberries, for it was the time of their ripening.

If we had more than we could eat, Mother would dry them out in the sun, then put them away for use when the cold, icy days of the winter came.

Soon came the time for the leaves to turn brown and yellow and gold. The forest was beautiful and the wind rustled the dry leaves. We just couldn't resist the temptation to gather those beautiful colored leaves and the empty birds' nests.

At school, if we brought in a nest or a pretty leaf, we were given much credit, and we thought we would also please Mother by bringing some to her. But she did not like our doing this. She would scold and correct us and tell us we were destroying something – that the nests were the homes of the birds and the leaves were the beauty of the forest.

I loved to lie on my back under the trees and watch the clouds forming and moving. Sometimes it seemed they were so swift in their movements I would wonder where they were going. And then at other times they would just hang there, like great white doves.

With the coming of night, Mother would teach us how to make dishes out of birch bark. When we went on camping trips, having no horses, we were able to take only the necessary pots and supplies, so it was urgent that we understood how to make our own dishes.

These we fashioned as we needed them, for always did we carry birch bark with us. Sometimes we had soup, and this would call for deeper dishes. The dishes were always burned after each meal — no washing and nothing left around to attract bugs or flies.

We had so much to learn. Mother taught us how to get larger strips of birch bark, up to eighteen or thirty-six inches. This had to be taken from a tree about six inches through making a strip some eighteen inches wide and as long as we wanted to strip them. They were sewed together to make a strip about twelve to eighteen feet long and thirty-six inches wide. The raw edges were in thirty-six-inch-widths and bound with cedar and sewed with basswood bark. This prevented breaking and tearing when rolled. Ten or twelve sheets like this were sufficient to cover a wigwam.

The rolls were very light in weight. The wigwam frame was made by pushing long poles into the ground about sixteen inches apart and bending and tying them together at the top with basswood bark. These were covered with birch-bark strips, starting at the bottom by the door opening and working around the bottom and upwards.

There is always an opening about three by five feet right in the center of the top, as we were taught that light which came directly down from the abode of the Great Spirit was better for us. It served as an outlet for the smoke from our fires also.

In order to keep the fires burning with the least trouble, Mother taught us the kind of wood to gather that would not throw off sparks and set our clothing or bedding on fire while we slept. The logs were cut larger and greener for the base of the fire, to keep the ashes and hot coals together. The night fire was always made with hardwood limbs, oak or ash, as these burned slower and had no flame and not much smoke. We never expected the fire to last all night, but it would keep the base of the fireplace warm so it wouldn't take long to heat up and allowed a good hearth of coals for baking a fish or fowl for the noonday meal.

The way we prepared fish for baking in the ashes of an open fire was to clean and dress them, cutting out the gills and slitting down the back from the head, leaving the head and scales on and taking out the insides. The fish were then carefully packed in clay, about the thickness of a child's hand, and buried quite deep near the base of the coals. The fire must not be too hot.

It required about half a morning or more to bake them. But when they were taken from the fire and clay, the scales would cling to the clay, so the fish were all ready to eat. And, oh, how delicious they were!

The manner of cooking partridges and ducks was a little different. After cleaning and dressing them, they were packed in clay and buried in the ashes head down, with rocks between them and the fire, so the feet would not burn off. When the feet, if jerked gently, would pull away, the fowl was done.

Mother had accepted the kind offer of Wa goosh to take us to the rice beds. So she made for Osh kin and me "rice moccasins." These were made to fit higher and snugger around the foot and ankle, to prevent the rice husks from getting in.

Finally we were ready to go. It was quite a job getting everything from the wigwam down to the lake shore, a job for us children.

It was decided that Mother and Wa goosh would first take all of the supplies in the canoe, heading towards the river, up the river, across the lake, up another river, and then into the rice bed.

They found the place where Mother wanted to camp and then came back for us. This took from sun to sun.

The first night we slept under the stars, for we had no time to make a wigwam before darkness fell. We thought this was a lot of fun.

With the first morning light Wa goosh took us two boys out to cut down about thirty long poles for the wigwam. We dragged them to the location of the camp. Min di, Mother, and Wa goosh set them up. Then Mother and Min di took the birch bark, which was light, and covered the poles. They tied the bark firmly around the poles so the wind could not easily blow it off.

Our next chore was to get wood for the fires. We gathered enough to last three or four days.

It was the dark of the moon, so Wa goosh suggested that Mother and he go on a fire hunt. This meant he would have to return to his home and get the canoe to be used for the hunt. It was smaller and would be much better for the rice beds too, for the smaller the canoe the less parting in the rice grains. Four could sit in it easily, but even six could ride.

Like all children we begged to go along, and finally Wa goosh consented. We had made little paddles of our own and were dying to use them. Running to get these, we came back and sat in the middle of the canoe and in our rather futile way helped to paddle.

Back over the lake we glided, then down the river into another lake, the waters of which were like glass. But it was beautiful, and we could see the reflection of the shoreline all around. It seemed that we actually skimmed over the water, it was so smooth.

At last we arrived at the lake near Wa goosh's home. He pulled the big canoe up on shore and covered it with twigs and boughs. He told us he wanted us to come up to meet his Mother and Father. This we did as well as snooping around his place. We discovered many interesting things and were astonished at the different kinds of tools he had. I decided with a workshop like this I could build a canoe as graceful as a swan — and some time I would!

We came down again to the shore where Wa goosh uncovered the smaller canoe and pushed it into the water. The difference in size was as that of a mother swan and her young.

By this time the wind had risen and the lake was getting rough, as though the water manito were displeased. Min di and Wa goosh went to the shore.

"Maybe it won't be too bad," they said, "for the wind is blowing in the right direction to be in our backs."

As they came down to get in the canoe, Wa goosh had a box on a pole. It looked like a reflector. This he put in the canoe with us. Sister told us this was what he was going to use in his fire hunt.

Wa goosh and Min di were well trained at the paddles and so the water's roughness did not bother us. We crossed the lake in good time, then into the river again. While paddling along, Wa goosh told Sister that he would teach us how to make bows and arrows – and might one day take us out for a hunt.

When we got back to the wigwam, Mother's face was like storm cloud. She didn't like to have us always wanting to do everything Wa goosh planned. He was a man and we were still little fellows.

After our evening meal around the fire, Mother told Min di she wanted to relate a story about our father. This was in the Indian language, and Min di had to translate it to us in English. We were much excited. Mother started off:

"Your Father was a very brave hunter and a good provider. He knew the woods and lakes, and the habits of different animals. We made our canoe ready by placing a box like a reflector on a pole four feet long. This was placed in the bow of the canoe, so he could sight the game. A lantern was set in the box-like structure throwing the light forward.

"He rowed over to the location where we might sight some deer, and then I took over the paddle. My task was to keep the canoe headed toward shore, so the light would attract the deer. Then he would be prepared to shoot when he saw the two fiery eyes.

"I guess I'm very good at this, for the least ripple from a paddle or the scraping of the paddle on the canoe would scare the animals and cause them to dart into the safety of the forest.

"Suddenly we heard a strange noise. It didn't sound like a deer or a large animal. I stopped paddling. Never had we heard anything like it, and Father turned his head quickly. Neither one of us spoke – just listened, wondering what it was.

"Finally Father motioned for me to pull closer to the shore. I obeyed, and as we advanced I saw that the object was a porcupine – probably just coming down to drink. Father and I looked at one another. We both knew that meeting a porcupine at night was not a good omen. Should we catch him or let him go? Finally Father whispered; 'Let's get him and put him in the canoe. I want to get some venison. We'll take a chance on our good luck.'

"Your Father got out on the shore, seized a club and prepared to kill the porcupine. This accomplished, he loaded it into the canoe, and we continued paddling around looking for a deer.

"Before long we heard a splashing sound. Your Father looked at me. I shook my head and nodded. He pointed out the direction toward which I should paddle the canoe. As we approached I had to be very careful the light didn't move from side to side nor flicker. We both sat very still. He had put his paddle in the bottom of the canoe and was ready with his gun. Then we saw that it was a great moose."

As Mother talked, we children forgot all about what we were so eager to hear, about the trouble that had made Mother and Father forget the love that had once brought them together. We listened eagerly to know what would happen next in the story.

"I wondered why your father didn't shoot," continued Mother. "Then he whispered that he must get close enough to kill it with one shot, for the gun was loaded with buckshot.

"Finally we got close enough, and he took a shot at the moose and almost at the same instant put out the light. He thought at first he had killed the moose with one shot, but now we heard it coming our way. We realized we were in for a fight.

"I turned the canoe around quickly and headed it out to deeper water. But the beast, being wounded, made a lunge and came right out after us. He lashed the canoe to pieces, and we were both thrown into the lake. Luckily the beast didn't mangle us. We swam to shore while the moose turned to go back. But he bled to death before he could make it.

"We returned home, but the next day we borrowed a canoe and went back to where the moose had died. The lake was like glass and at the bottom of it we could see the gun, the sack of cartridges, and the lantern. We pulled the moose from the water and dressed him, then loaded him into the canoe. Father retrieved the gun and dried it out and as he looked at the shells, he saw that instead of buckshot the gun was loaded with fine shot, suitable for smaller game.

"'No wonder we met the porcupine,' he said to me. 'We were not prepared with the right shot. Surely the Great Spirit was watching over us.'"

Mother stopped in her story to be sure that we understood if anything out of the ordinary ever happened, like a porcupine, we must be sure to take warning.

Mother went on to tell how they got the meat home, but before she had finished, sleep had made our eyes heavy.

The next morning we awoke to see a deer strung up in a tree. It was then that Wa goosh told us how, in the dead of the night, he and Mother had gone out on the fire hunt. He had used his box, and when they got to the location, Mother kept the canoe pointed to shore, sliding along until the light attracted the deer. It was then Wa goosh had a chance to shoot. By good luck he had killed a big buck. Mother and he loaded it into the canoe and rowed it home. It was two o'clock in the morning by then, and before going to sleep they had been forced to skin it and dress it.

Later that day we built a fire out of doors. Over this we fashioned a rack to hang the rice kettles on. Higher over this was another rack on which the deer meat could be dried.

While Wa goosh was cutting the venison, Osh Kin and I were very alert, watching him. We noticed how he cut it up into long strips, as thick as a good steak and as long as he could cut them. The smoke kept the flies away. These strips were hung over the poles to dry in the sun and to absorb the heat from the fire and sun. The meat shrank a lot. This worried me, because I thought it would become tough. But Mother explained:

"It will be good for your teeth, having to chew the food well. It will make your teeth stronger and you can use them longer."

Love Medicine   by Louise Erdrich

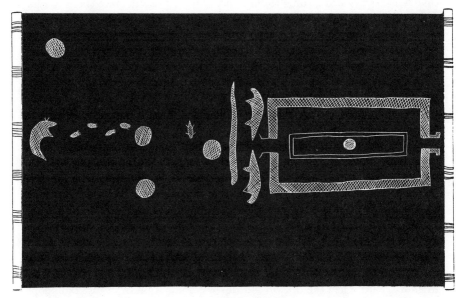

Lipsha Morrissey

I NEVER REALLY done much with my life, I suppose. I never had a television. Grandma Kashpaw had one inside her apartment at the Senior Citizens, so I used to go there and watch my favorite shows. For a while she used to call me the biggest waste on the reservation and hark back to how she saved me from my own mother, who wanted to tie me in a potato sack and throw me in a slough. Sure, I was grateful to Grandma Kashpaw for saving me like that, for raising me, but gratitude gets old. After a while, stale. I had to stop thanking her. One day I told her I had paid her back in full by staying at her beck and call. I'd do anything for Grandma. She knew that. Besides, I took care of Grandpa like nobody else could, on account of what a handful he'd gotten to be.

But that was nothing. I know the tricks of mind and body inside out without ever having trained for it, because I got the touch. It's a thing you got to be born with. I got secrets in my hands that nobody ever knew to ask. Take Grandma Kashpaw with her tired veins all knotted up in her legs like clumps of blue snails. I take my fingers and I snap them on the knots. The medicine flows out of me. The touch. I run my fingers up the maps of those rivers of veins or I knock very gentle above their hearts or I make a circling motion on their stomachs, and it helps them. They feel much better. Some women pay me five dollars.

I couldn't do the touch for Grandpa, though. He was a hard nut. You know, some people fall right through the hole in their lives. It's invisible, but they come to it after time, never knowing where. There is this woman here, Lulu Lamartine, who always had a thing for Grandpa. She loved him since she was a girl and always said he was a genius. Now she says that his mind got so full it exploded.

How can I doubt that? I know the feeling when your mental power builds up too far. I always used to say that's why the Indians got drunk. Even statistically we're the smartest people on the earth. Anyhow with Grandpa I couldn't hardly believe it, because all my youth he stood out as a hero to me. When he started getting toward the second childhood he went through different moods. He would stand in the woods and cry at the top of his shirt. It scared me, scared everyone, Grandma worst of all.

Yet he was so smart – do you believe it? – that he *knew* he was getting foolish.

He said so. He told me that December I failed school and come back on the train to Hoopdance. I didn't have nowhere else to go. He picked me up there and he said it straight out: "I'm getting into my second childhood." And then he said something else I still remember: "I been chosen for it. I couldn't say no." So I figure that a man so smart all his life – tribal chairman and the star of movies and even pictured in the statehouse and on cans of snuff – would know what he's doing by saying yes. I think he was called to the second childhood like anybody else gets a call for the priesthood or the army or whatever. So I really did not listen too hard when the doctor said this was some kind of disease old people got eating too much sugar. You just can't tell me that a man who went to Washington and gave them bureaucrats what for could lose his mind from eating too much Milky Way. No, he put second childhood on himself.

Behind those songs he sings out in the middle of Mass, and back of those stories that everybody knows by heart, Grandpa is thinking hard about life. I know the feeling. Sometimes I'll throw up a smokescreen to think behind. I'll hitch up to Winnipeg and play the Space Invaders for six hours, but all the time there and back I will be thinking some fairly deep thoughts that surprise even me, and I'm used to it. As for him, if it was just the thoughts there wouldn't be no problem. Smokescreen is what irritates the social structure, see, and Grandpa has done things that just distract people to the point they want to throw him in the cookie jar where they keep the mentally insane. He's far from that, I know for sure, but even Grandma had trouble keeping her patience once he started sneaking off to Lamartine's place. He's not supposed to have his candy, and Lulu feeds it to him. That's *one* of the reasons why he goes.

Grandma tried to get me to put the touch on Grandpa soon after he began stepping out. I didn't want to, but before Grandma started telling me again what a bad state my bare behind was in when she first took me home, I thought I should at least pretend.

I put my hands on either side of Grandpa's head. You wouldn't look at him and say he's crazy. He's a fine figure of a man, as Lamartine would say, with all his hair and half his teeth, a beak like a hawk, and cheeks like the blades of a hatchet. They put his picture on all the tourist guides to North Dakota and even copied his face for artistic paintings. I guess you could call him a monument all of himself. He started grinning when I put my hands on his templates, and I knew right then he knew how come I touched him. I knew the smokescreen was going to fall.

And I was right: just for a moment it fell.

"Let's pitch whoopee," he said across my shoulder to Grandma.

They don't use that expression much around here anymore, but for damn sure it must have meant something. It got her goat right quick.

She threw my hands off his head herself and stood in front of him, over-matching him pound for pound, and taller too for she had a growth spurt in middle age while he had shrunk, so now the length and breadth of her surpassed him. She glared up and spoke her piece into his face about how he was off at all hours tomcatting and chasing Lamartine again and making a damn old fool of himself.

"And you got no more whoopee to pitch anymore anyhow!" she yelled at last, surprising me so my jaw just dropped, for us kids all had pretended for so long that those rustling sounds we heard from their side of the room at night never happened. She sure had pretended it, up till now, anyway. I saw tears were in her eyes. And that's when I saw how much grief and love she felt for him. And it gave me a real shock to the system. You see I thought love got easier over the years so it didn't hurt so bad when it hurt, or feel so good when it felt good. I thought it smoothed out and old people hardly noticed it. I thought it curled up and died, I guess. Now I saw it rear up like a whip and lash.

She loved him. She was jealous. She mourned him like the dead.

And he just smiled into the air, trapped in the seams of his mind.

So I didn't know what to do. I was in a quaundry then. They was like parents to me, the way they had took me home and reared me. I could see her point for wanting to get him back the way he was so at least she could argue with him, sleep with him, not be shamed out by Lamartine. She'd always love him. That hit me like a ton of bricks. For one whole day I felt this odd feeling that cramped my hands. When you have the touch, that's where longing gets you. I never loved like that. It made me feel all inspired to see them fight, and I wanted to go out and find a woman who I would love until one of us died or went crazy. But I'm not like that really. From time to time I heal a person all up good inside, however when it comes to the long shot I doubt that I got staying power.

And you need that, staying power, going out to love somebody. I knew this quality was not going to jump on me with no effort. So I turned my thoughts back to Grandma and Grandpa. I felt her side of it with my hands and my tangled guts, and I felt his side of it within the stretch of my mentality. He had gone out to lunch one day and never came back. He was fishing in the middle of Lake Turcot. And there was big thoughts on his line, and he kept throwing them back for even bigger ones that would explain to him, say, the meaning of how we got here and why we have to leave so soon. All in all, I could not see myself treating Grandpa with the touch, bringing him back, when the real part of him had chose to be off thinking somewhere. It was only the rest of him that stayed around causing trouble, after all, and we could handle most of it without any problem.

Besides, it was hard to argue with his reasons for doing some things. Take Holy Mass. I used to go there just every so often, when I got frustrated mostly, because even though I know the Higher Power dwells everyplace, there's something very calming about the cool greenish inside of our mission. Or so I thought, anyway. Grandpa was the one who stripped off my delusions in this matter, for it was he who busted right through what Father Upsala calls the sacred serenity of the place.

We filed in that time. Me and Grandpa. We sat down in our pews. Then the rosary got started up pre-Mass and that's when Grandpa filled up his chest and opened his mouth and belted out them words.

HAIL MARIE FULL OF GRACE.

He had a powerful set of lungs.

And he kept on like that. He did not let up. He hollered and he yelled them prayers, and I guess people was used to him by now, because they only muttered theirs and did not quit and gawk like I did. I was getting red-faced, I admit. I give him the elbow once or twice, but that wasn't nothing to him. He kept on. He shrieked to heaven and he pleaded like a movie actor and he pounded his chest like Tarzan in the Lord I Am Not Worthies. I thought he might hurt himself. Then after a while I guess I got used to it, and that's when I wondered: how come?

So afterwards I out and asked him. "How come? How come you yelled?"

"God don't hear me otherwise," said Grandpa Kashpaw.

I sweat. I broke right into a little cold sweat at my hairline because I knew this was perfectly right and for years not one damn other person had noticed it. God's been going deaf. Since the Old Testament, God's been deafening up on us. I read, see. Besides the dictionary, which I'm constantly in use of, I had this Bible once. I read it. I found there was discrepancies between then and now. It struck me. Here God used to raineth bread from clouds, smite the Phillipines, sling fire down on red-light districts where people got stabbed. He even appeared in person every once in a while. God used to pay attention, is what I'm saying.

Now there's your God in the Old Testament and there is Chippewa Gods as well. Indian Gods, good and bad, like tricky Nanabozho or the water monster, Missepeshu, who lives over in Lake Turcot. That water monster was the last God I ever heard to appear. It had a weakness for young girls and grabbed one of the Blues off her rowboat. She got to shore all right, but only after this monster had its way with her. She's an old lady now. Old Lady Blue. She still won't let her family fish that lake.

Our Gods aren't perfect, is what I'm saying, but at least they come around.

They'll do a favor if you ask them right. You don't have to yell. But you do have to know, like I said, how to ask in the right way. That makes problems, because to ask proper was an art that was lost to the Chippewas once the Catholics gained ground. Even now, I have to wonder if Higher Power turned its back, if we got to yell, or if we just don't speak its language.

I looked around me. How else could I explain what all I had seen in my short life – King smashing his fist in things, Gordie drinking himself down to the Bismarck hospitals, or Aunt June left by a white man to wander off in the snow. How else to explain the times my touch don't work, and farther back, to the old-time Indians who was swept away in the outright germ warfare and dirty-dog killing of the whites. In those times, us Indians was so much kindlier than now.

We took them in.

Oh yes, I'm bitter as an old cutworm just thinking of how they done to us and doing still.

So Grandpa Kashpaw just opened my eyes a little there. Was there any sense relying on a God whose ears was stopped? Just like the government? I says then, right off, maybe we got nothing but ourselves. And that's not much, just personally speaking. I know I don't got the cold hard potatoes it takes to understand everything. Still, there's things I'd like to do. For instance, I'd like to help some people like my Grandpa and Grandma Kashpaw get back some happiness within the tail ends of their lives.

I told you once before I couldn't see my way clear to putting the direct touch on Grandpa's mind, and I kept my moral there, but something soon happened to make me think a little bit of mental adjustment wouldn't do him and the rest of us no harm.

It was after we saw him one afternoon in the sunshine courtyard of the Senior Citizens with Lulu Lamartine. Grandpa used to like to dig there. He had his little dandelion fork out, and he was prying up them dandelions right and left while Lamartine watched him.

"He's scratching up the dirt, all right," said Grandma, watching Lamartine watch Grandpa out the window.

Now Lamartine was about half the considerable size of Grandma, but you would never think of sizes anyway. They were different in an even more noticeable way. It was the difference between a house fixed up with paint and picky fence, and a house left to weather away into the soft earth, is what I'm saying. Lamartine was jacked up, latticed, shuttered, and vinyl sided, while Grandma sagged and bulged on her slipped foundations and let her hair go the silver gray of rain-dried lumber. Right now, she eyed the Lamartine's pert flowery dress with such a look it despaired me. I knew what this could lead to with Grandma. Alternating tongue storms and rock-hard silences was hard on a man, even one who didn't notice, like Grandpa. So I went fetching him.

But he was gone when I popped through the little screen door that led out on the courtyard. There was nobody out there either, to point which way they went. Just the dandelion fork quibbling upright in the ground. That gave me an idea. I snookered over to the Lamartine's door and I listened in first, then knocked. But nobody. So I went walking through the lounges and around the card tables. Still nobody. Finally it was my touch that led me to the laundry room. I cracked the door. I went in. There they were. And he was really loving her up good, boy, and she was going hell for leather. Sheets was flapping on the lines above, and washcloths, pillowcases, shirts was also flying through the air, for they was trying to clear out a place for themselves in a highheaped but shallow laundry cart. The washers and the dryers was all on, chock full of quarters, shaking and moaning. I couldn't hear what Grandpa and the Lamartine was billing and cooing, and they couldn't hear me.

I didn't know what to do, so I went inside and shut the door.

The Lamartine wore a big curly light-brown wig. Looked like one of them squeaky little white-people dogs. Poodles they call them. Anyway, that wig is what saved us from the worse. For I could hardly shout and tell them I was in there, no more could I try and grab him. I was trapped where I was. There was nothing I could really do but hold the door shut. I was scared of somebody else upsetting in and really getting an eyeful. Turned out though, in the heat of the clinch, as I was trying to avert my eyes you see, the Lamartine's curly wig jumped off her head. And if you ever been in the midst of something and had a big change like that occur in the someone, you can't help know how it devastates your basic urges. Not only that, but her wig was almost with a life of its own. Grandpa's eyes were bugging at the change already, and swear to God if the thing didn't rear up and pop him in the face like it was going to start something. He scrambled up, Grandpa did, and the Lamartine jumped up after him all addled looking. They just stared at each other, huffing and puffing, with quizzical expression. The surprise seemed to drive all sense completely out of Grandpa's mind.

"The letter was what started the fire," he said. "I never would have done it."

"What letter?" said the Lamartine. She was stiff-necked now, and elegant, even bald, like some alien queen. I gave her back the wig. The Lamartine replaced it on her head, and whenever I saw her after that, I couldn't help thinking of her bald, with special powers, as if from another planet.

"That was a close call," I said to Grandpa after she had left.

But I think he had already forgot the incident. He just stood there all quiet and thoughtful. You really wouldn't think he was crazy. He looked like he was just about to say something important, explaining himself. He said something, all right, but it didn't have nothing to do with anything that made sense.

He wondered where the heck he put his dandelion fork. That's when I decided about the mental adjustment.

Now what was mostly our problem was not so much that he was not all there, but that what was there of him often hankered after Lamartine. If we could put a stop to that, I thought, we might be getting someplace. But here, see, my touch was of no use. For what could I snap my fingers at to make him faithful to Grandma? Like the quality of staying power, this faithfulness was invisible. I know it's something that you got to acquire, but I never known where from. Maybe there's no rhyme or reason to it, like my getting the touch, and then again maybe it's a kind of magic.

It was Grandma Kashpaw who thought of it in the end. She knows things. Although she will not admit she has a scrap of Indian blood in her, there's no doubt in my mind she's got some Chippewa. How else would you explain the way she'll be sitting there, in front of her TV story, rocking in her armchair and suddenly she turns on me, her brown eyes hard as lake-bed flint.

"Lipsha Morrissey," she'll say, "you went out last night and got drunk."

How did she know that? I'll hardly remember it myself. Then she'll say she just had a feeling or ache in the scar of her hand or a creak in her shoulder. She is constantly being told things by little aggravations in her joints or by her household appliances. One time she told Gordie never to ride with a crazy Lamartine boy. She had seen something in the polished-up tin of her bread toaster. So he didn't. Sure enough, the time came we heard how Lyman and Henry went out of control in their car, ending up in the river. Lyman swam to the top, but Henry never made it.

Thanks to Grandma's toaster, Gordie was probably spared.

Someplace in the blood Grandma Kashpaw knows things. She also remembers things, I found. She keeps things filed away. She's got a memory like them video games that don't forget your score. One reason she remembers so many details about the trouble I gave her in early life is so she can flash back her total when she needs to.

Like now. Take the love medicine. I don't know where she remembered that from. It came tumbling from her mind like an asteroid off the corner of the screen.

Of course she starts out by mentioning the time I had this accident in church and did she leave me there with wet overalls? No she didn't. And ain't I glad? Yes I am. Now what you want now, Grandma?

But when she mentions them love medicines, I feel my back prickle at the danger. These love medicines is something of an old Chippewa specialty. No other tribe has got them down so well. But love medicines is not for the layman to handle. You don't just go out and get one without paying for it. Before you get one, even, you should go through one hell of a lot of mental condensation. You got to think it over. Choose the right one. You could really mess up your life grinding up the wrong little thing.

So anyhow, I said to Grandma I'd give this love medicine some thought. I knew the best thing was to go ask a specialist like Old Man Pillager, who lives up in a tangle of bush and never shows himself. But the truth is I was afraid of him, like everyone else. He was known for putting the twisted mouth on people, seizing up their hearts. Old Man Pillager was serious business, and I have always thought it best to steer clear of that whenever I could. That's why I took the powers in my own hands. That's why I did what I could.

I put my whole mentality to it, nothing held back. After a while I started to remember things I'd heard gossiped over.

I heard of this person once who carried a charm of seeds that looked like baby pearls. They was attracted to a metal knife, which made them powerful. But I didn't know where them seeds grew. Another love charm I heard about I couldn't go along with, because how was I suppose to catch frogs in the act, which it required. Them little creatures is slippery and fast. And then the powerfullest of all, the most extreme, involved nail clips and such. I wasn't anywhere near asking Grandma to provide me all the little body bits that this last love recipe called for. I went walking around for days just trying to think up something that would work.

Well I got it. If it hadn't been the early fall of the year, I never would have got it. But I was sitting underneath a tree one day down near the school just watching people's feet go by when something tells me, look up! Look up! So I look up, and I see two honkers, Canada geese, the kind with little masks on their faces, a bird that mates for life. I see them flying right over my head naturally preparing to land in some slough on the reservation, which they certainly wouldn't get off of alive.

It hits me, anyway. Them geese, they mate for life. And I think to myself, just what if I went out a got a pair? And just what if I fed some part – say the goose heart – of the female to Grandma and Grandpa ate the other heart? Wouldn't that work? Maybe it's all invisible, and then maybe again it's magic. Love is a stony road. We know that for sure. If it's true that the higher feelings of devotion get lodged in the heart like people say, then we'd be home free. If not, eating goose heart couldn't harm nobody anyway. I thought it was worth my effort, and Grandma Kashpaw thought so, too. She had always known a good idea when she heard one. She borrowed me Grandpa's gun.

So I went out to this particular slough, maybe the exact same slough I never got thrown in by my mother, thanks to Grandma Kashpaw, and I hunched down in a good comfortable pile of rushes. I got my gun loaded up. I ate a few of these soft baloney sandwiches Grandma made me for lunch. And then I waited. The cattails blown back and forth above my head. Them stringy blue herons was spearing up their prey. The thing I know how to do best in this world, the thing I been training for all my life, is to wait. Sitting there and sitting there was no hardship on me. I got to thinking about some funny things that happened. There was this one time that Lulu Lamartine's little blue tweety bird, a paraclete, I guess you'd call it, flown up inside her dress and got lost within there. I recalled her running out into the hallway trying to yell something, shaking. She was doing a right good jig there, cutting the rug for sure, and the thing is it *never* flown out. To this day people speculate where it went. They fear she might perhaps of crushed it in her corsets. Is sure hasn't ever yet been seen alive. I thought of funny things for a while, but then I used them up, and strange things that happened started weaseling their way into my mind.

I got to thinking quite naturally of the Lamartine's cousin named Wristwatch. I never knew what his real name was. They called him Wristwatch because he got his father's broken wristwatch as a young boy when his father passed on. Never in his whole life did Wristwatch take his father's watch off. He didn't care if it worked, although after a while he got sensitive when people asked what time it was, teasing him. He often put it to his ear like he was listening to the tick. But it was broken for good and forever, people said so, at least that's what they thought.

Well I saw Wristwatch smoking in his pickup one afternoon and by nine that evening he was dead.

He died sitting at the Lamartine's table, too. As she told it, Wristwatch had just eaten himself a good-size dinner and she said would he take seconds on the hot dish when he fell over to the floor. They turnt him over. He was gone. But here's the strange thing: when the Senior Citizen's orderly took the pulse he noticed that the wristwatch Wristwatch wore was now working. The moment he died the wristwatch started keeping perfect time. They buried him with the watch still ticking on his arm.

I got to thinking. What if some gravediggers dug up Wristwatch's casket in two hundred years and that watch was still going? I thought what question they would ask and it was this: Whose hand wound it?

I started shaking like a piece of grass at just the thought.

Not to get off the subject or nothing. I was still hunkered in the slough. It was passing late into the afternoon and still no honkers had touched down. Now I don't need to tell you that the waiting did not get to me, it was the chill. The rushes was very soft, but damp. I was getting cold and debating to leave, when they landed. Two geese swimming here and there as big as life, looking deep into each other's little pinhole eyes. Just the ones I was looking for. So I lifted Grandpa's gun to my shoulder and I aimed perfectly, and *blam! Blam!* I delivered two accurate shots. But the thing is, them shots missed. I couldn't hardly believe it. Whether it was that the stock had warped or the barrel got bent someways, I don't quite know, but anyway them geese flown off into the dim sky, and Lipsha Morrissey was left there in the rushes with evening fallen and his two cold hands empty. He has before him just the prospect of another day of bone-cracking chill in them rushes, and the thought of it got him depressed.

Now it isn't my style, in no way, to get depressed.

So I said to myself, Lipsha Morrissey, you're a happy S.O.B. who could be covered up with weeds by now down at the bottom of this slough, but instead you're alive to tell the tale. You might have problems in life, but you still got the touch. You got the power, Lipsha Morrissey. Can't argue that. So put your mind to it and figure out how not to be depressed.

I took my advice. I put my mind to it. But I never saw at the time how my thoughts led me astray toward a tragic outcome none could have known. I ignored all the danger, all the limits, for I was tired of sitting in the slough and my feet were numb. My face was aching. I was chilled, so I played with fire. I told myself love medicine was simple. I told myself the old superstitions was just that – strange beliefs. I told myself to take the ten dollars Mary MacDonald had paid me for putting the touch on her arthritis joint, and the other five I hadn't spent yet from winning bingo last Thursday. I told myself to go down to the Red Owl store.

And here is what I did that made the medicine backfire. I took an evil short-cut. I looked at birds that was dead and froze.

All right. So now I guess you will say, "Slap a malpractice suit on Lipsha Morrissey."

I heard of those suits. I used to think it was a color clothing quack doctors had to wear so you could tell them from the good ones. Now I know better that it's law.

As I walked back from the Red Owl with the rock-hard, heavy turkeys, I argued to myself about malpractice. I thought of faith. I thought to myself that faith could be called belief against the odds and whether or not there's any proof. How does that sound? I thought how we might have to yell to be heard by Higher Power, but that's not saying it's not *there*. And that is faith for you. It's belief even when the goods don't deliver. Higher Power makes promises we all know they can't back up, but anybody ever go and slap an old malpractice suit on God? Or the U.S. government? No they don't. Faith might be stupid, but it gets us through. So what I'm heading at is this. I finally convinced myself that the real actual power to the love medicine was not the goose heart itself but the faith in the cure.

I didn't believe it, I knew it was wrong, but by then I had waded so far into my lie I was stuck there. And then I went one step further.

The next day, I cleaned the hearts away from the paper packages of gizzards inside the turkeys. Then I wrapped them hearts with a clean hankie and brung them both to get blessed up at the mission. I wanted to get official blessings from the priest, but when Father answered the door to the rectory, wiping his hands on a little towel, I could tell he was a busy man.

"Booshoo, Father," I said. "I got a slight request to make of you this afternoon."

"What is it?" he said.

"Would you bless this package?" I held out the hankie with the hearts tied inside it.

He looked at the package, questioning it.

"It's turkey hearts," I honestly had to reply.

A look of annoyance crossed his face.

"Why don't you bring this matter over to Sister Martin," he said. "I have duties."

And so, although the blessing wouldn't be as powerful, I went over to the Sisters with the package.

I rung the bell, and they brought Sister Martin to the door. I had her as a music teacher, but I was always so shy then. I never talked out loud. Now, I had grown taller than Sister Martin. Looking, down, I saw that she was not feeling up to snuff. Brown circles hung under her eyes.

"What's the matter?" she said, not noticing who I was.

"Remember me, Sister?"

She squinted up at me.

"Oh yes," she said after a moment. "I'm sorry, you're the youngest of the Kashpaws. Gordie's brother."

Her face warmed up.

"Lipsha," I said, "that's my name."

"Well, Lipsha," she said, smiling broad at me now, "what can I do for you?"

They always said she was the kindest-hearted of the Sisters up the hill, and she was. She brought me back into their kitchen and made me take a big yellow wedge of cake and a glass of milk.

"Now tell me," she said, nodding at my package. "What have you got wrapped up so carefully in those handkerchiefs?"

Like before, I answered honestly.

"Ah," said Sister Martin. "Turkey hearts." She waited.

"I hoped you could bless them."

She waited some more, smiling with her eyes. Kindhearted though she was, I began to sweat. A person could not pull the wool down over Sister Martin. I stumbled through my mind for an explanation, quick, that wouldn't scare her off.

"They're a present," I said, "for Saint Kateri's statue."

"She's not a saint yet."

"I know," I stuttered on, "in hopes they will crown her."

"Lipsha," she said, "I never heard of such a thing."

So I told her. "Well the truth is," I said, "it's a kind of medicine."

"For what?"

"Love."

"Oh Lipsha," she said after a moment, "you don't need any medicine. I'm sure any girl would like you exactly the way you are."

I just sat there. I felt miserable, caught in my pack of lies.

"Tell you what," she said, seeing how bad I felt, "my blessing won't make any difference anyway. But there is something you can do."

I looked up at her, hopeless.

"Just be yourself."

I looked down at my plate. I knew I wasn't much to brag about right then, and I shortly became even less. For as I walked out the door I stuck my fingers in the cup of holy water that was sacred from their touches. I put my fingers in and blessed the hearts, quick, with my own hand.

I went back to Grandma and sat down in her little kitchen at the Senior Citizens. I unwrapped them hearts on the table, and her hard agate eyes went soft. She said she wasn't even going to cook those hearts up but eat them raw so their power would go down strong as possible.

I couldn't hardly watch when she munched hers. Now that's true love. I was worried about how she would get Grandpa to eat his, but she told me she'd think of something and don't worry. So I did not. I was supposed to hide off in her bedroom while she put dinner on a plate for Grandpa and fixed up the heart so he'd eat it. I caught a glint of the plate she was making for him. She put that heart smack on a piece of lettuce like in a restaurant and then attached to it a little heap of boiled peas.

He sat down. I was listening in the next room.

She said, "Why don't you have some mash potato?" So he had some mash potato. Then she gave him a little piece of boiled meat. He ate that. Then she said, "Why you didn't never touch your salad yet. See that heart? I'm feeding you it because the doctor said your blood needs building up."

I couldn't help it, at that point I peeked through a crack in the door.

I saw Grandpa picking at that heart on his plate with a certain look. He didn't look appetized at all, is what I'm saying. I doubted our plan was going to work. Grandma was getting worried, too. She told him one more time, loudly, that he had to eat that heart.

"Swallow it down," she said. "You'll hardly notice it."

He just looked at her straight on. The way he looked at her made me think I was going to see the smokescreen drop a second time, and sure enough it happened.

"What you want me to eat this for so bad?" he asked her uncannily.

Now Grandma knew the jig was up. She knew that he knew she was working medicine. He put his fork down. He rolled the heart around his saucer plate.

"I don't want to eat this," he said to Grandma. "It don't look good."

"Why it's fresh grade-A," she told him. "One hundred percent."

He didn't ask percent what, but his eyes took on an even more warier look.

"Just go on and try it," she said, taking the salt shaker up in her hand. She was getting annoyed. "Not tasty enough? You want me to salt it for you?" She waved the shaker over his plate.

"All right, skinny white girl!" She had got Grandpa mad. Oopsy-daisy, he popped the heart into his mouth. I was about to yawn loudly and come out of the bedroom. I was about ready for this crash of wills to be over, when I saw he was still up to his old tricks. First he rolled it into one side of his cheek. "Mmmmm," he said. Then he rolled it into the other side of his cheek. "Mmmmmmm," again. Then he stuck his tongue out with the heart on it and put it back, and there was no time to react. He had pulled Grandma's leg once too far. Her goat was got. She was so mad she hopped up quick as a wink and slugged him between the shoulderblades to make him swallow.

Only thing is, he choked.

He choked real bad. A person can choke to death. You ever sit down at a restaurant table and up above you there is a list of instructions what to do if something slides down the wrong pipe? It sure makes you chew slow, that's for damn sure. When Grandpa fell off his chair better believe me that little graphic illustrated poster fled into my mind. I jumped out the bedroom. I done everything within my power that I could do to unlodge what was choking him. I squeezed underneath his ribcage I socked him in the back. I was desperate. But here's the factor of decision: he wasn't choking on the heart alone. There was more to it than that. It was other things that choked him as well. It didn't seem like he wanted to struggle or fight. Death came and tapped his chest, so he went just like that. I'm sorry all through my body at what I done to him with that heart, and there's those who will say Lipsha Morrissey is just excusing himself off the hook by giving song and dance about how Grandpa gave up.

Maybe I can't admit what I did. My touch had gone worthless, that is true. But here is what I seen while he lay in my arms.

You hear a person's life will flash before their eyes when they're in danger. It was him in danger, not me, but it was *his* life come over me. I saw him dying, and it was like someone pulled the shade down in a room. His eyes clouded over and squeezed shut, but just before that I looked in. He was still fishing in the middle of Lake Turcot. Big thoughts was on his line and he had half a case of beer in the boat. He waved at me, grinned, and then the bobber went under.

Grandma had gone out of the room crying for help. I bunched my force up in my hands and I held him. I was so wound up I couldn't even breathe. All the moments he had spent with me, all the times he had hoisted me on his shoulders or pointed into the leaves was concentrated in that moment. Time was flashing back and forth like a pinball machine. Lights blinked and balls hopped and rubber bands chirped, until suddenly I realized the last ball had gone down the drain and there was nothing. I felt his force leaving him, flowing out of Grandpa never to return. I felt his mind weakening. The bobber going under in the lake. And I felt the touch retreat back into the darkness inside my body, from where it came.

One time, long ago, both of us were fishing together. We caught a big old snapper that started towing us around like it was a motor. "This here fishline is pretty damn good," Grandpa said. "Let's keep this turtle on and see where he takes us." So we rode along behind that turtle, watching as from time to time it surfaced. The thing was just about the size of a washtub. It took us all around the lake twice, and as it was traveling, Grandpa said something as a joke. "Lipsha," he said, "we are glad your mother didn't want you because we was always looking for a boy like you who would tow us around the lake."

"I ain't no snapper. Snappers is so stupid they stay alive when their head's chopped off," I said.

"That ain't stupidity," said Grandpa. "Their brain's just in their heart, like yours is."

When I looked up, I knew the fuse had blown between my heart and my mind and that a terrible understanding was to be given.

Grandma got back into the room and I saw her stumble. And then she went down too. It was like a house you can't hardly believe has stood so long, through years of record weather, suddenly goes down in the worst yet. It makes sense, is what I'm saying, but you still can't hardly believe it. You think a person you know has got through death and illness and being broke and living on commodity rice will get through anything. Then they fold and you see how fragile were the stones that underpinned them. You see how instantly the ground can shift you thought was solid. You see the stop signs and the yellow dividing markers of roads you traveled and all the instructions you had played according to vanish. You see how all the everyday things you counted on was just a dream you had been having by which you run your whole life. She had been over me, like a sheer overhang of rock dividing Lipsha Morrissey from outer space. And now she went underneath. It was as though the banks gave way on the shores of Lake Turcot, and where Grandpa's passing was just the bobber swallowed under by his biggest thought, her fall was the house and the rock under it sliding after, sending half the lake splashing up to the clouds.

Where there was nothing.

You play them games never knowing what you see. When I fell into the dream alongside of both of them I saw that the dominions I had defended myself from anciently was but delusions of the screen. Blips of light. And I was scot-free now, whistling through space.

I don't know how I come back. I don't know from where. They was slapping my face when I arrived back at Senior Citizens and they was oxygenating her. I saw her chest move, almost unwilling. She sighed the way she would when somebody bothered her in the middle of a row of beads she was counting. I think it irritated her to no end that they brought her back. I knew from the way she looked after they took the mask off, she was not going to forgive them disturbing her restful peace. Nor was she forgiving Lipsha Morrissey. She had been stepping out onto the road of death, she told the children later at the funeral. I asked was there any stop signs or dividing markers on that road, but she clamped her lips in a vise the way she always done when she was mad.

Which didn't bother me. I knew when things had cleared out she wouldn't have no choice. I was not going to speculate where the blame was put for Grandpa's death. We was in it together. She had slugged him between the shoulders. My touch had failed him, never to return.

All the blood children and the took-ins, like me, came home from Minneapolis and Chicago, where they had relocated years ago. They stayed with friends on the reservation or with Aurelia or slept on Grandma's floor. They were struck down with grief and bereavement to be sure, every one of them. At the funeral I sat down in the back of the church with Albertine. She had gotten all skinny and ragged haired from cramming all her years of study into two or three. She had decided that to be a nurse was not enough for her so she was going to be a doctor. But the way she was straining her mind didn't look too hopeful. Her eyes were bloodshot from driving and crying. She took my hand. From the back we watched all the children and the mourners as they hunched over their prayers, their hands stuffed full of Kleenex. It was someplace in that long sad service that my vision shifted. I began to see things different, more clear. The family kneeling down turned to rocks in a field. It struck me how strong and reliable grief was, and death. Until the end of time, death would be our rock.

So I had perspective of it all, for death gives you that. All the Kashpaw children had done various things to me in their lives — shared their folks with me, loaned me cash, beat me up in secret — and I decided, because of death, then and there I'd call it quits. If I ever saw King again, I'd shake his hand. Forgiving somebody else made the whole thing easier to bear.

Everybody saw Grandpa off into the next world. And then the Kashpaws had to get back to their jobs, which was numerous and impressive. I had a few beers with them and I went back to Grandma, who had sort of got lost in the shuffle of everybody being sad about Grandpa and glad to see one another.

Zelda had sat beside her the whole time and was sitting with her now. I wanted to talk to Grandma, say how sorry I was, that it wasn't her fault, but only mine. I would have, but Zelda gave me one of her looks of strict warning as if to say, "I'll take care of Grandma. Don't horn in on the women."

If only Zelda knew, I thought, the sad realities would change her. But of course I couldn't tell the dark truth.

It was evening, late. Grandma's light was on underneath a crack in the door. About a week had passed since we buried Grandpa. I knocked first but there wasn't no answer, so I went right in. The door was unlocked. She was there but she didn't notice me at first. Her hands were tied up in her rosary, and her gaze was fully absorbed in the easy chair opposite her, the one that had always been Grandpa's favorite. I stood there, staring with her, at the little green nubs in the cloth and plastic armrest covers and the sad little hair-tonic stain he had made on the white doily where he laid his head. For the life of me, I couldn't figure what she was staring at. Thin space. Then she turned.

"He ain't gone yet," she said.

Remember that chill I luckily didn't get from waiting in the slough? I got it now. I felt it start from the very center of me, where fear hides, waiting to attack. It spiraled outward so that in minutes my fingers and teeth were shaking and clattering. I knew she told the truth. She seen Grandpa. Whether or not he had been there is not the point. She had *seen* and that meant anybody else could see him, too. Not only that, but as is usually the case with these here ghosts, he had a certain uneasy reason to come back. And of course Grandma Kashpaw had scanned it out.

I sat down. We sat together on the couch watching in his chair out of the corner of our eyes. She found him sitting in his chair when she walked in the door. "It's the love medicine, my Lipsha," she said. "It was stronger than we thought. He came back even after death to claim me to his side."

I was afraid. "We shouldn't have tampered with it," I said. She agreed. For a while we sat still. I don't know what she thought, but my head felt screwed on backward. I couldn't accurately consider the situation, so I told Grandma to go to bed. I would sleep on the couch keeping my eye on Grandpa's chair. Maybe he would come back and maybe he wouldn't. I guess I feared the one as much as the other, but I got to thinking, see, as I lay there in darkness, that perhaps even through my terrible mistakes some good might come. If Grandpa did come back, I thought he'd return in his right mind. I could talk with him. I could tell him it was all my fault for playing with power I did not understand. Maybe he'd forgive me and rest in peace. I hoped this. I calmed myself and waited for him all night.

He fooled me though. He knew what I was waiting for, and it wasn't what he was looking to hear. Come dawn I heard a blood-splitting cry from the bedroom and I rushed in there. Grandma turnt the lights on. She was sitting on the edge of the bed and her face looked harsh, pinched-up, gray.

"He was here," she said. "He came and laid down next to me in bed. And he touched me."

Her heart broke down. She cried. His touch was so cold. She laid back in bed after a while, as it was morning, and I went to the couch. As I lay there, falling asleep, I suddenly felt Grandpa's presence and the barrier between us like a swollen river. I felt how I had wronged him. How awful was the place where I had sent him. Behind the wall of death, he'd watched the living eat and cry and get drunk. He was lonesome, but I understood he meant no harm.

"Go back," I said to the dark, afraid and yet full of pity. "You got to be with your own kind now," I said. I felt him retreating, like a sigh, growing less. I felt his spirit as it shrunk back through the walls, the blinds, the brick courtyard of Senior Citizens. "Look up Aunt June," I whispered as he left.

I slept late the next morning, a good hard sleep allowing the sun to rise and warm the earth. It was past noon when I awoke. There is nothing, to my mind, like a long sleep to make those hard decisions that you neglect under stress of wakefulness. Soon as I woke up that morning, I saw exactly what I'd say to Grandma. I had gotten humble in the past week, not just losing the touch but getting jolted into the understanding that would prey on me from here on out. Your life feels different on you, once you greet death and understand your heart's position. You wear your life like a garment from the mission bundle sale ever after – lightly because you realize you never paid nothing for it, cherishing because you know you won't ever come by such a bargain again. Also you have the feeling someone wore it before you and someone will after. I can't explain that, not yet, but I'm putting my mind to it.

"Grandma," I said, "I got to be honest about the love medicine."

She listened. I knew from then on she would be listening to me the way I had listened to her before. I told her about the turkey hearts and how I had them blessed. I told her what I used as love medicine was purely a fake, and then I said to her what my understanding brought me.

"Love medicine ain't what brings him back to you, Grandma. No, it's something else. He loved you over time and distance, but he went off so quick he never got the chance to tell you how he loves you, how he doesn't blame you, how he understands. It's true feeling, not no magic. No supermarket heart could have brung him back."

She looked at me. She was seeing the years and days I had no way of knowing, and she didn't believe me. I could tell this. Yet a look came on her face. It was like the look of mothers drinking sweetness from their children's eyes. It was tenderness.

"Lipsha," she said, "you was always my favorite."

She took the beads off the bedpost, where she kept them to say at night, and she told me to put out my hand. When I did this, she shut the beads inside of my fist and held them there a long minute, tight, so my hand hurt. I almost cried when she did this. I don't really know why. Tears shot up behind my eyelids, and yet it was nothing. I didn't understand, except her hand was so strong, squeezing mine.

The earth was full of life and there were dandelions growing out the window, thick as thieves, already seeded, fat as big yellow plungers. She let my hand go. I got up. "I'll go out and dig a few dandelions," I told her.

Outside, the sun was hot and heavy as a hand on my back. I felt it flow down my arms, out my fingers, arrowing through the ends of the fork into the earth. With every root I prized up there was return, as if I was kin to its secret lesson. The touch got stronger as I worked through the grassy afternoon. Uncurling from me like a seed out of the blackness where I was lost, the touch spread. The spiked leaves full of bitter mother's milk. A buried root. A nuisance people dig up and throw in the sun to wither. A globe of frail seeds that's indestructible.

Shadows at La Pointe

THIS MORNING the lake is clear and calm.

Last night a cold wind washed slivers of ice clear over the beach, the end of a winter to remember. Now, the pale green becomes blue on the horizon. Spring opens in the birch, a meadow moves in the wind. The trees thicken down to the water, an invitation to follow the sun over the old fur trade post to a new world of adventures.

We are late for school.

The slivers of ice that marked the first cattails melt. The sun is warmer on our cheeks. We turn from side to side, new wild flowers. In the distance a thin banner of smoke rises from the first steamer of the season.

We wait on the beach near the dock.

The sand is smooth and cold under our fingers.

MARGARET CADOTTE

ANGELICK FRONSWA

In large block letters we print our names down to the cold water rim, our last names hold back the flood. We are certain that the people who came here on the steamer to visit this island will notice our names and remember that we were here first and late for school. We will be remembered in the future because we boarded the first steamer that followed the sun in our dream. Someone will tell stories that we were the first mixedbloods on the island, a new people on the earth, and that our names would last forever because we learned how to read and write in a mission school.

by Gerald Vizenor

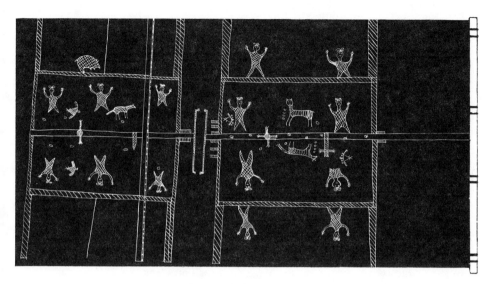

Last week when we were late for school, we heard the old men tell stories about the hard winters on the island in the past, a sure message that one more winter had ended. We sat near the old woodstove in the American Fur Company Store, painted bright red outside, and listened to the men catch their words in their wrinkled hands. We listened to stories about hard times, adventure on the trail, white men in the bush, and disasters on the lake. The fur trade had changed from the old days remembered in the stories when there were more animals. The market and the animals moved to a new place on the earth; the animals in tribal dreams were weakened by white politics, diseases, competition, and new fashions, but there are hundreds of barrels of corn stored from the last season to feed a population of more than six hundred people. The men in the fur business, the missionaries and their wives, about fifteen people on the island, were white. The rest were tribal people, and more than half were mixedblood families.

We remember the stories:

Elizabeth Morrison, mixedblood wife of the hunter and trader John Morrison, was born in November 1837 at La Pointe on Madeline Island. "As I remember," she writes in an autobiographical letter, "there used to be thirty-seven houses on the flats, all of them made of round logs roofed with cedar bark.

"My uncle built a house alongside ours. For a period of thirty years he was one of those who traded with the Chippewas off to the north and west. They used to get goods from the Company and go out and establish their posts during the winter. They would be gone eight months from home each year and would return quite late in the spring. They used dogs, when they had them. My uncle told me that the Indians would not sell dogs, but they would hire them out to those who were trading with the Indians. The dogs were very large. I used to see some of them brought in. They were yellow, had long hair, and looked like wolves.

"When I was a girl the Chippewas used to come to La Pointe to be paid off by the government. To my knowledge the largest payment made was eighteen dollars a head. Thousands of Indians came to the island at one time for pay. I used to be very afraid of them. Our folks used to keep us from school while payments were made."

Later, she and her husband moved to Spider Lake near Iron River, Wisconsin, deep in the woodland. She wrote about the hard winters and construction of the first railroad in the area. "My husband feared that we would have to go without bread before spring. . . . " Her husband and eldest son had to leave to find food. "I made up my mind that if they were not back by the time our provisions were consumed I would first kill the chickens to keep my children from starving. . . . When I thought about those hard times my grandmother had, I wondered what would happen to my children and me should my husband and boy fail to get through to Ashland. . . . We had only enough grub for two more meals, small ones at that," when they returned with provisions.

"When the snow got too deep for hunting, my husband began tanning deerskins to have them ready to sell. We both took time to teach our boys to read. We had some friends who would send us books.

"I would say it is hard for me to write a history of my forest life in English. My husband and I would talk to one another in Chippewa, but to our children we spoke in English as much as we could. My husband had a chance to go to school to learn to read and write. He can write in English and Chippewa if necessary, and he can also talk French when it comes to that. . . . Thirty years ago, about two out of every ten Indians could speak English. Now three-fourths of them can speak English," she remembers from the turn of the century, when she first wrote about her experiences, "but when I see their complexion I feel like using my native language to talk with them. They are pretty well civilized, but there are some who still follow the medicine dance, the pen names, and other old habits.

The Indians in this vicinity are selling the timber off their allotments. This enables them to live in good houses. Not one family lives in a wigwam anymore. There is a big sawmill here where they can buy lumber. Some have large gardens and sell vegetables to the whites. They hunt in the fall and gather wild rice. And it is a great place for hunting ducks in the spring and in the fall.

"I have nothing more to write. I might say that I have almost consumed the history of my life. Well, I believe this is the end of my story." Eliza died at age eighty-three.

Provident people were seldom without food on the island, we were told time and time again in school. The old tribal mixedbloods remembered that gospel, the one about being civilized, in their slowest stories at the fire. The men turned one to the other, like ceremonial birds around the stove, and winked, pulled at their ears, winked more, smiled some, and then looked down in silence at the stove. The stove seemed human, a listener: the fire cracked on, a wind-checked side of white pine inside, while the old men waited for the first steamer of the season to reach the dock.

We listened to more stories.

One man pulled at his beard and told about the little people on the island. He crouched forward in his chair and measured with his slender hands, floor to nose, "those little fellows were no more than three feet, not one of them could see over the packs they carried with a tumpline across their foreheads.

"These little people were covered with tattoos, one mark for all the fur posts between Montreal and Fort Pierre, and they drank dark rum mixed with wine on the trail," the old man said as he leaned back in his chair and aimed his long finger past his ear, behind him, toward the east. The visitors followed the direction of his finger. "Back there, clear across the widest angle of the lake you can smell those little pork eaters coming upwind a week ahead in a rain storm. . . . The smell of pork moves quicker than the eye of a crow."

A stout mixedblood under a wide fur hat told about the time when government agents from the east sent saddles to the woodland, because they thought that all tribal people must ride horses. "A thumb rider in a wild east show shipped us a dozen saddles, so as, no doubt, we could catch rabbits from above.

"One of the missionaries found two horses and tried to teach us to ride," said the old trapper. He never changed his focus from the base of the stove as he spoke. He seemed to growl when he spoke, and between phrases, even single words at times, he ground his front teeth together. "The best we could do was cut four holes in a canoe and teach the horses to paddle."

Then a wizened old mixedblood with a smart smile, like a mongrel on a trap line, clapped his hands, pulled up his sleeves to reveal dozens of tattoos dedicated to his wives. "And then some," he added, and all the old men laughed around the stove in the American Fur Company Store. When he turned down his sleeves his face turned sallow. He looked into the fire and told about the time he was mentioned in a printed book.

"Thomas Loraine McKenney came through these parts on his tour to the lakes," the mixedblood said as he leaned forward in his chair. The hard wooden chair creaked. The old men and visitors were silent. The fire snapped. "We called the place Michael's Island then, and this McKenny was a demanding fellow with swift eyes and a nervous hand, he must have come from a place where people salute too much. . . . Anyway, he wrote about an old fisherman on the island, sixty-nine years of age, and active as a boy," the old man remembered. He reached into his inside shirt pocket and removed a folded sheet of paper, a page from a book. "Here is what he wrote," the old man said as he began to read. The visitors who had arrived that morning on the steamer shifted their feet on the rough wooden floor, impressed that the old mixed-blood could read, and fine print at that.

"His pulse beats only twenty-five strokes in a minute. On his legs, and arms, and breast are tattooed the marks of superiority in his profession, which had been that of a voyageur, and it seems he excelled in carrying packages across the portages, both on account of their weight and the celerity of his movement. . . . On questioning him as to his former life, he said with a slap of the hands, 'he had been the greatest man in the northwest.'"

"That man," said the old mixedblood as he folded with care the book page and returned it to his pocket, "is me, the greatest man in the northwest." He opened his shirt and there beneath the thin strands of white hair on his chest, like the sleet storm, was a faded sunset scene on a lake with two crude loons and a canoe.

The third old mixedblood at the American Fur Company Store that morning told true stories about the tall people who came from the east. The tall people, he explained to the visitors, never trusted the little people because some of the little people pretended to be tall people, mocked the tall people in their dances. Tall people never pretend to be little, no matter how far their fortunes fall. Tall people are white, educated, they march and give orders, sweat in dark clothes, and hold pet birds in house cages. The little people are mixedbloods who wear bright colors, dance and dream out of time, trick their friends, animals and birds, in good humor.

"Henry Rowe Schoolcraft was a tall person," the old mixedblood revealed. "He was more than eight feet tall in the cold, even when he slouched. The little people, the pork eaters, had to stand on a trunk or a fence rail to speak in similar space. Schoolcraft was a geologist, a government agent, treaty commissioner, who explored the sacred copper regions of the tribes with Lewis Cass, and territory governor of Michigan.

"Schoolcraft believes he found the sacred copper back on the Ontonogan River but he was mistaken. The shamans planted a chunk of mined copper there; the explorer thought that he had discovered more than the next white man, which made him taller. With the copper find he sprouted an additional inch back east, an inch less in the tribe. He remained the same height when he tried to change the name of this place to Virginia Island. Madeline, the mixedblood wife of Michel Cadotte, remained the favorite name, the place name on the maps.

"He also asked the tribal people, even a few mixedbloods, where to find the source of the Mississippi River. He asked his way and then revealed his discoveries back east. He lost three inches there, gained one back in humor, but he took on six more inches back east for the river find. He was a giant then, and it was time to find a mixedblood wife from the wilderness. He did just that, in the daughter of John Johnson, the fur trader from La Pointe. Johnson, who was Irish, married the daughter of Waubojeeg, or Chief White Fisher.

"Schoolcraft gained back a few inches with his marriage, but lost more than a foot when he became an expert on the 'red race' and when he invented the 'Algic tribes,' as he called us out here. This copper hunter learned all he knew about tribal people from his mixedblood relatives, but he gives them no credit for his discoveries.

"When Schoolcraft was the United States Indian agent at Mackinac he came to the island for another visit. We saw him down at the dock, eight to nine feet tall, white people all stood on stools and stilts to shake his enormous hand, as if his hand was a healing animal from a strange place.

"When the tall man died," said the old man in a loud voice to hold the ears of the visitors, "the tribe made a grave house for him about four feet long and put it out behind the mission in the weeds, but back east, we were told, the tall man was buried in a ten foot coffin. . . . Some tell that his coffin is two feet longer since his death, and still growing. . . . The grave house out here has become a bird nest, and even smaller."

The visitors soon departed from the store, ears filled, to conduct their business with the traders, the coopers, and the brownstone cutters, before the steamer departed from the island. Later, the visitors learned that they left the store too soon and missed the best stories about tall people by the old mixedblood with the tattoos. While he told his stories he did a striptease around the stove, exposed all his tattoos but three.

"The second time we heard that tall man with the nervous hands, Thomas Loraine McKenney, that talk and walk man, was out at the American Fur Company post at Fond du Lac," said the mixedblood as he danced in slow motions around the fire. "McKenney was twelve feet tall there, three feet taller than he was when he discovered and wrote about me on the island, twelve feet tall no less; we knew this because the soldiers packed him there flat in a *canot du nord* with room enough for a brass band. Flags and his wild red hair, red as the outside of this store, waved from shore to shore.

"When a man speaks from three sides of his mouth at once, a special number in the government service," said the mixedblood as he danced, "you know he is twelve feet tall and from the east because the little people are three feet tall and it took two of them, one on top of the other, to even shake his hand.

"That twelve foot red said from one side of his mouth that we were his equals, from another side he told us we were children, and from the third side of his mouth he said we were savages. No telling how a mixedblood would be parted in his mouth.

"We never forgot the old red threat and what he said and wrote about the tribes," said the little mixedblood who had removed his coat and shirt to reveal a second time the scenic tattoo on his chest.

McKenney and Governor Lewis Cass, who was much taller than the red one, told us that we were "the worst clad and the most wretched body of Indians" that he ever met with. . . . He said we were "wandering savages who inhabit the sterile and unhospitable shores of the northern lakes . . . the most miserable and degraded of the native tribes. . . . They have little ambition and few ideas. . . . ," which was what we wanted the tall people in the government to think about us because when the tall ones admire a tribe, the people become pets and lose their land, their shadows, and their humor.

"We laughed and laughed and danced and dreamed about the tall ones in white water, too tall to fit in their canoes," chanted the old mixedblood as he danced. He did not remove his trousers, but he did fold up the legs to reveal several tattoos in honor of his wives and children and fur post encounters with the tall people. "The canoes turn and the tall logs shoot the rapids, turn wide, dam the rivers, and stop the white water . . . for a time."

"The tall red one spoke to us at Fond du Lac, his words rolled like logs in white water, he demanded that we produce the murderers of four white people," said the mixedblood who stopped his dance and stood erect about four feet tall near the stove. "So we did that, we named four tribal people, and hundreds more who had been murdered by white soldiers and settlers . . . we danced in the dark and named the dead until morning.

"McKenney was not pleased with us, and as he spoke he got smaller and smaller, his lips rolled at a great distance when he told us that "this is not a thing to pass away like a cloud,' so we named more dead and danced for all those who died at the hands of the tall people. 'If they are not surrendered then,' the tall red one continued, '*destruction will fall on your women and children.* Your father will put out his strong arm. Go, and think of it. Nothing will satisfy us but this.'

"We danced until he disappeared in the distance, a small animal on the run, too small to notice, then in a swarm of transparent flies he vanished," the old mixedblood concluded as he resumed his dance around the stove. Animals and dream figures, faces from the little people in his past, sagged and shivered on the calves of his thin legs.

Richard Drinnon, in *Facing West: The Metaphysics of Indian-hating and Empire-Building*, writes about the arrival of Colonel Thomas McKenney, who was "tall and had a military carriage and shock of red hair," and the other white commissioners at the American Fur Company post at Fond du Lac on 28 July 1826. The expedition, a squadron of barges and canoes which contained a detachment of soldiers, a company band, and staff assistants, "stretched out over a quarter mile, all in order, and "all with flags flying, and martial music," according to the memoirs of the commissioner. "Ashore the troops drilled each morning and were inspected by General Cass and Colonel McKenney, with the latter in his militia uniform. . . . "

McKenney, with more on his mind than land and treaties, demanded that the tribe "produce the alleged murderers of four whites. 'It is a very serious matter,' he declared, and unless they obeyed 'you will be visited with your great father's heaviest displeasure. No trader shall visit you – not a pound of tobacco, nor a yard of cloth, shall go into your country. This is not a thing to pass away like a cloud.' Spokesmen for the band under suspicion replied it was difficult to speak for their absent tribesmen."

The man who threatened the tribe, Drinnon writes, "is perhaps better described as high-handed rather than high-minded. . . . McKenney confidently expected the destruction of tribal cultures. . . . He severed the family connections of his 'little Indians,' used mission schools to batter tribal relations, and by stripping away native language sought to cut off all ties between generations." McKenney, who was celebrated by some as a champion of tribal reform, was appointed as the head of the new Bureau of Indian Affairs, which was then under the War Department.

We were late for school:

Abigail Spooner was our teacher at the first mission school on Madeline Island. She had a voice that hurt on a spring afternoon, but she worked ever so hard to teach us how to read and to write. We were mixedbloods, halfbreeds, neither here nor there to some. Abba, as she was known to friends and families on the island, promised that we could establish in the wilderness a new civilization with books. We had some books, not many, and an occasional magazine passed from house to house, which we shelved in a special place in the corner of the school room. The other books on the island were owned by Lyman Marcus Warren and Truman Warren. The brothers were married to Mary and Charlotte Cadotte, the mixedblood daughters of Michel Cadotte, who was an educated man and was once the factor at the fur post. These families, educated in the east with the tall people, were important; we did not ask to borrow their books to make *our* civilization.

Abba said, "If not now, then at the right time in heaven, the last and perfect civilization for those who believe and are righteous." We believed her then, but most of the time we found real evidence of the civilized world down at the store and at the American Fur Company dock when the steamers arrived with mail, supplies, and visitors.

"The girls with bead pantalets, porcupine moccasins, new blue broadcloth shawls, plaited hair and clean faces looked almost good enough to kiss," noted Charles Penny, who had accompanied the geologist Douglass Houghton on an expedition in search of copper. He visited the island and admired the mixedblood and tribal women of all ages.

Sherman Hall, the superintendent of the school at La Pointe, wrote a letter to a government agent that the teachers have continued "their labors as usual, endeavoring to instruct all who were willing to receive instruction from us, in the duties and doctrines of the Christian religion, and in letters. . . .

"The school during the year has numbered sixty-five different scholars, forty-three males, and twenty-two females. It has been kept in operation regularly during the year, except the usual vacations. . . . The proficiency of the scholars who have been regular attendants is very satisfactory. The branches taught have been spelling, reading, writing, arithmetic, geography and composition. The scholars are taught in the Ojibwa and English languages. The schools are open and free to all who choose to avail themselves of their privileges, no charge being made for books or other expenses. During the past year the Ojibwa and English spelling book, mentioned in my last report as being nearly ready for use, has been introduced into the schools, and used, it is believed, with good effect."

Sherman Hall was a Presbyterian who dedicated his time to the conversion of the tribes, even the mixedbloods. He arrived on the island with his wife and a tribal woman who was once married to a fur trader. Reverend Hall started the mission and the school, and the tribal woman served as his interpreter.

This was not as simple as it might appear, because most of the mixedblood families and the children in the school, like us, were Roman Catholic. This seemed to trouble Reverend Sherman more than the tribal ceremonial dances on the island. He was, at times, critical of Catholics, and once or twice we were released from school to receive our religious instruction. He complained in a letter to his father, who lived back east, that the boatmen and laborers in the fur trade, who were, for the most part, Canadian French and Catholic, "may be as wicked as they choose; the priest can pardon all their sins when they go to Mackinac next year. He will do it, if they pay him a few shillings. I have more fears that the Catholics will cause us difficulties, than the Indians will."

Reverend Hall and his wife were separated from their culture and families in the east. The two of them seemed to be lost, without shadows, with no humor to throw at the weather. Their isolation turned into a dedication to convert the tribes. Sometimes, we whispered, it was the missionaries who needed to be saved. We lived in a world of comedies, thunderstorms, chances like a flight of passenger pigeons over the lake, and surprises, dreams about whales in a fish barrel. Some of our friends think it is strange to find pale, weak and shadowless, individual church heroes, in the middle of old woodland families. The biblical stories were fun to tell, the old men turned them over in the oral tradition. The moral lessons that end in words end in comedies. These missionaries were never loons, never bears, their wives and mothers were never killdeers on the shoreline. We were animals and birds, even when we were converted, and that was the difference between culture and civilization. We once spoke the language of animals, the missionaries were caught in wordwinds.

Reverend Hall, of course, was proud of his religion but he was disappointed with the tribes. We could all tell when he was displeased with us because two small muscles would twitch on his face. He liked us, he spoke our names from time to time when he visited the schoolroom, and he even called us scholars in his reports. He said our names were in his reports and that we would be known in the government. We knew he cared more for us and other mixedblood families at La Pointe than he did for the tribal families on Chequamegon Point and the Bad River Reservation. He reported to a government agent that the mission school there was "discontinued for want of scholars. . . . We regret to see so little interest taken by these Indians in the subject of education. Most of them attach little or no importance to having their children instructed. I have been informed, that many of the head men have expressed a desire to have their school money divided among them, as their other annuities are, that they might expend it in the same way. . . .

"In some respects these Indians are improving. Many of them are adopting partial habits of civilization. This is more and more apparent every year in their mode of dress, in their efforts to procure houses to live in, and in their enlarging their gardens and small fields. Many are much more industrious than formerly, and are much less disposed to depend on the same precarious modes of obtaining the means of subsistence, which almost universally prevailed among them formerly. These changes are most apparent among the younger portion of them.

"If the right kind of influences are brought to bear upon them, and they can be shielded from the degrading and destroying evils of intoxicating drink, I do not see why they may not eventually become a civilized and happy people. This however must be the work of time, and will require much perseverance on the part of those who are disposed to live among them for the purpose of teaching them letters, the arts, and the Christian religion."

MARGARET CA
ANGELICK FRO

The narrow waves from the wake of the steamer washed over the last few letters of our names printed in the sand. We collect names and words, some are secrets, but we take much more time to remember the clothes that visitors wear, their hats and shoes and coats. The trunks on the dock, unloaded from the steamer, capture our attention for hours. We imagine the contents of the arriving trunks, and we dream we are on an adventure to the cities inside the departing trunks.

When Reverend Hall and his wife first arrived, the content of their trunks and boxes became the talk of the island, but the secrets lasted for a few minutes at the most because they owned little more than their simple clothes. The Warren families gave them some furniture, a washbowl and stand, chairs, tables and a bedstead, for their little house. "It is not the deprivation of the conveniences of life," he wrote to his friend back east, "that makes us feel more sensibly that we are in a heathen land. It is the want of society. There are not more than three or four, besides our own family, with whom we can communicate in our native tongue at this place."

Madeline Island is our tribal home, the place where the earth began, the place that first came back from the flood. Naanabozho, the trickster, was born here, on this island; the old men told us he was the first little person in the world. He stole fire from across the lake. We are little people. This is our place on the earth, this place is in our bodies, in our words and in our dreams. Our new names, there in the sand, hold back the next flood, but nothing holds back the tall people who come from the east. Naanabozho must have stolen fire from them; now the tall white people are here and they want the whole earth back as punishment.

Even so, we love to watch white visitors and the dark trunks that come on the steamer from the east, and to listen to the stories at the American Fur Company Store across from the dock.

Abba Spooner will think that we are late because we were making maple sugar, or something, or we could tell her that we were with the priest for religious instruction.

The Catholic church is located behind the American Fur Company Store and warehouses. A high stockade fence surrounds a fruit and vegetable garden and separates the sacred from the secular commercial world of the tall people. The priest lives near the church in a small house built of hewn logs because frame houses are much too expensive to build on the island. The cemetery is next to the church.

A visitor to the island told about how the little people buried the dead in grave houses. "On the whole, it can be truly said they they have more regard for the dead than many whites have. The pagans used to bury various articles used by the deceased during life, also place tobacco or sugar on the grave, or in the drawer made for that purpose in the little house built over the grave. But these customs are falling into disuse more and more. A peculiar feeling of sadness and pity seizes one in passing a pagan graveyard. . . . "

White children, sons of the missionaries, would raid the grave houses at night and steal the food, a confection with cooked wild rice and maple sugar, the little people placed there.

Right Reverend Frederic Baraga, an Austrian sent by the Leopoldine Society in Vienna, was not welcomed by the lonesome ministers on the island. The first mission resisted encroachment and hoped that Henry Rowe Schoolcraft, the government agent, would refuse the priest a "license of residence." Schoolcraft did not respond; the priest moved to the island and built a church in less than two weeks. During the summer, as if his time there was limited, Father Baraga had baptized more than a hundred mixedbloods and tribal people.

Reverend Sherman Hall wrote to the secretary of the American Board of Commissioners for Foreign Missions in Boston – the little people were considered foreign – that "the Catholics were not prejudiced against the mission school. The priest stationed here encouraged their attendance."

Father Francis Pierz, who had established missions at several fur trade posts in the woodland, visited the island that summer. He admired the garden behind the fur post and, of course, the new church and mission. His neck and back caused him pain as he walked. No one seemed to notice, so eager were they to present their accomplishments in the wilderness. He blessed the children when he passed them and complimented those who worked on the island. Later, in a letter he described his experiences with more candor. "A large trading company has a branch store on this island and it is therefore the rendezvous of many Indians and French-Canadians, all of whom lived like pagans before Father Baraga's arrival.

"At first this pious missionary had to contend with many difficulties and hardships, but with his customary, perservering energy and apostolic zeal he soon formed out of these rude, wild barbarians a very large Christian congregation, which continues to grow daily through new conversions. To his great joy he has completed his beautiful new church and a suitable priest's house with the money he brought with him from Europe. . . .

"As regards my own personal experience, having had many opportunities during my three years' stay among the Indians of several places to watch them, pagans as well as Christians, I can justly assert that they are, as a rule, phlegmatic, good-natured, exceedingly patient and docile, and well disposed to lead a good life. Even in their wild, aboriginal state, when they are removed from bad, scandalous people, they do not live at all wickedly and viciously. They listen eagerly to the priest who comes to them, readily embrace the faith and allow themselves to be soon transformed into good, steadfast Christians.

"But where the poor Indians have been scandalized by the great vices of white Christians, or have been spoiled by intoxicating liquor, and have been seduced by the enemies of religion and prejudiced against our holy faith, they naturally become far harder to convert and civilize. . . . "

Father Baraga was a little man with enormous conversion plans for the tribe. His dark brown hair bounced in long curls as he walked. He was firm, careful in his speech, and when he was out walking on the road, his short legs moved quicker than a shore bird. He was determined to save souls and he warned the teachers at the mission school that "if they meddle with religion I would order all the Catholic children to leave their schools; and I am watching strictly this observance."

The little priest was troubled by tribal manner and woodland culture. He abhorred the wilderness in their lives, and describes cruelties that he relates to savagism. He praised the little people who followed the cross and disapproved of those tribal people who gathered on the island for government payments. The priest even cursed the tribal dances that healed the soul, restored tribal shadows near tall people, and earned a meal. The missionaries rebuked the presentation of bare flesh, rhythmic body movements, and imaginative face paint. Church strictures soon became government policies. The tribes were not permitted to gather to dance.

Julia Spears, the daughter of Lyman Marcus Warren, would have none of this bad talk from the missionaries about tribal dances. She remembers a more peaceful island than did the missionaries. Julia was also known by her tribal nickname Conians, which means "little money" in translation.

Several thousand tribal people came to Madeline Island from various places around the lake to receive government payments according to agreements in treaties. "That year the Indians received ten dollars a head," Julia Spears wrote, "and each family got a very large bundle of goods. . . . They had rations issued out to them during payments. . . . The day before they would start for their homes they had a custom of going to all the stores and houses and dancing for about one hour, expecting food to be given them. . . . They went around in different parties of about twenty-five or thirty. A party came to our house at the old fort. We were prepared for them. The day before, we cooked a lot of bread, a lot of boiled salt pork and cookies to give them. They came dancing and hooting. They were naked with breechcloths, their bodies painted with black, red, yellow, vermilion, with all kinds of strips and figures.

"They were a fierce looking crowd. They were all good dancers. After they were through they sat down on the grass and smoked. We gave them their *wapoo* and they were well pleased. They thanked us and shook hands with us as they left." The word *wapoo*, or *wabo*, from the oral tradition, at the end of some words in *anashinaabemowi* denotes fluid or liquid, as in the word *mashkikiwabo*, a liquid medicine, or *ishkotewabo*, "firewater," or an alcoholic drink according to *A Dictionary of the Otchipwe Language* by Father Baraga. Nichols and Nyholm transcribe the word for liquor as *ishkodewaaboo* in *Ojibwewi-Ikidowinan*.

We waited on the dock near the steamboat until no one was watching and then we climbed into two huge brown trunks with bright brass corners. The sun leaped through thin cracks and seams on the curved trunk cover, enough light inside to read our secret maps, the ones we charted with places from all the stories we had heard in the store: all the mixedblood routes and portage places between land and lakes and fur posts.

We were silent, alone, breathless, counting out rapid heart beats past the island view, past the distant shores of the lake and over the picture mountains to the cities in the east. We smelled smoke and imagined a circus show with acts and clowns, but instead it was the trader and his dock hands, the ones with the little pighead pipes, smoking their strong tobacco.

We traveled to Fond du Lac.

We listened.

Shingabaossin, an orator of the Crane family from Sault Ste. Marie, was the first to speak to the tribal leaders and to the tall white men, Lewis Cass and Thomas McKenney, who were treaty commissioners; and Henry Rowe Schoolcraft, the government agent, and others at Fond du Lac where hundreds of tribal people came together late in the summer to talk about the mixedbloods and minerals.

The tribal orator told about other meetings, and agreed that land should be provided for mixedbloods, and then his voice seemed to disappear on the wind when he said that, "our fathers have come here to embrace their children. Listen to what they say. It will be good for you.

"If you have any copper on your lands," said Shingabaossin in a distant voice as he looked over the commissioners to the western horizon where thunderclouds were blooming, "I advise you to sell it. It is of no advantage to us. They can convert it into articles for our use. If any of you has any knowledge on this subject, I ask you to bring it to light. . . . "

William Whipple Warren, the mixedblood historian, wrote that Shingabaossin did not mean what was attributed to him in translation. When the orator referred to minerals it was "meant more to tickle the ears of the commissioners and to obtain their favor, than as an earnest appeal to his people, for the old chieftain was too much imbued with the superstition prevalent amongst the Indians, which prevents them from discovering their knowledge of miners and copper boulders to the whites."

Tribal leaders, nevertheless, signed a treaty there that provided in part that the "Chippewa tribe grant to the government of the United States the right to search for, and carry away, any metals or minerals from any part of their country. . . ." The leaders must have believed in the spiritual power of secrets, the unspoken in the oral tradition, because what is held in secrets cannot be discovered and removed. Copper was located in sacred places, the metal had not been used in the secular production of material possessions. The elders signed an agreement on paper, through a translator, but did not tell the white men where the copper could be found.

Pezeekee spoke that morning to the white men who sat behind tables, dressed in dark clothes. The elder from La Pointe placed his right hand over his left forearm and looked toward Henry Connor, the government interpreter, and watched him write down in translation the words he heard. Pezeekee remembered the wind in the bullrushes and turned his words with care. "The name of a speaker has come down to me from my fathers," he said to the commissioners.

"I will not lie.

"That sun that looks upon me, and these, you red children around me, are witnesses. . . . Our women and children are very poor. You have heard it. It need not have been said. You see it. . . . I lend those who have put me here, my mouth. . . .

"This was given to us by our forefathers," he said as he spread a map on the table before the commissioners and interpreters. "There are few now here who were then living." He directed the tall men at the table to notice certain places on the map, tribal communities, memories in space. Then he looked up from the map and over the heads of the tall men. He spoke to them but did not look into their faces. Small clouds seemed to speak through the white pine on the horizon. "You have deserted *your* country," he told the commissioners, looking past their faces. "Where your fathers lived, and your mothers first saw the sun, there you are not. I am alone, am the solitary one remaining on our own ground. . . .

"I am no chief," Pezeekee said and then paused to listen. "I am put here as a speaker. The gift has descended to me. . . . It will be long before I open my mouth to you again. Listen therefore, to what I say. I live in one place, I do not move about. I live on an open path, where many walk. The traders know me. None can say I ever looked in his cabin or his canoe. My hands are free from the touch of what does not belong to me. . . . "

Pezeekee recovered his map and there was silence.

Then an old man who did not reveal his tribal name told the commissioners that he did not sell the sacred earth for a peace medal and a flag from the government agents. He was troubled, his voice wavered as he spoke: "You told me to sit still and hold down my head, and if I heard birds singing, to bend it still lower.

"My friends held down their heads when I approached. When I turned, bad words went out of their mouths against me. I could not sit still. I left my cabin, and went out along into the wild woods," the old man said as he looked down from time to time at the weeds. "There had I remained, till I heard of your coming. I am here now, to take you by the hand. . . . "

The commissioners were silent.

Obarguwack moved toward the commissioners at the table. She was in her seventies. Her bones were old, and it took her twice the time to walk and talk than it did when she was younger. She said that she was blessed with her age. To live so long was not a curse, she reminded the commissioners as they watched her slow movements. The wrinkles on her face all seemed to converge at her mouth, and when she spoke, and paused to compose her thoughts, the wrinkles moved from her mouth like ripples expanding from the place a stone skipped on calm water. She told the commissioners seated at the table under the trees that she was representing her husband. "His eyes are shut, but his mouth and ears are still open," she said and then paused a second time to move a few more steps closer to the table. "He has long wished to see the Americans. He hopes now to find something in his cabin.

"He has held you a long time by the hand," she told the tall white men. "He still holds you by the hand. He is poor. His blanket is old and worn out, like the one you see." She paused again and moved a few steps closer to the commissioners behind the table to show the worn blanket she mentioned. "But he now thinks he sees a better one."

The commissioners waited in silence for a few minutes until the old woman moved back from the table and then the meeting was adjourned until the next day when a treaty would be prepared for signatures. The commissioners listened, but what the government wanted had been decided in advance. The experiences of tribal people were translated from the oral tradition, but there was little more than condescension in the manners of the commissioners. The simple needs of the tribes: blankets, a place of peace on the earth, medical assistance, were no match under the trees in the word wars to locate and possess minerals and natural resources.

James Otis Lewis drew pictures of the tribal people who spoke and while the treaty was being read in translation by a government interpreter. The flags in his pictures were all taller than the trees behind the table. Colonel Thomas McKenney bumped his knee on the corner of the table as he sat down, prepared to make histories on paper. He looked toward the eastern horizon, in the opposite direction that tribal people spoke, with a mark of pain on his face while he listened and waited. Then he looked toward the artist, finding more to consider in a face on paper than in tribal events in the oral tradition. He brushed his thick hair back form his forehead, white strands in the red. Even his hand in his own hair seemed unnatural that afternoon at Fond du Lac.

We remember article four of the treaty:

It being deemed important that the half-breeds, scattered through this extensive country, should be stimulated to exertion and improvement by the possession of permanent property and fixed residences, the Chippewa tribe, in consideration of the affection they bear to these persons, and of the interest which they feel in their welfare, grant to each of the persons described . . . six hundred and forty acres of land. . . .

"The objects of the commissioners were easily attained," wrote William Whipple Warren in his book *History of the Ojibway Nation*, "but the Ojibways, who felt a deep love for the offspring of their women who had intermarried with the whites, and cherished them as their own children, insisted on giving them grants of land on the Sault Ste. Marie River, which they wished our government to recognize and make good.

"These stipulations were annexed by the commissioners to the treaty, but were never ratified by the Senate of the United States. It is merely mentioned here to show the great affection with which the Ojibways regarded their half-breeds, and which they have evinced on every occasion when they have had an opportunity of bettering their condition."

Eighty-five tribal leaders from fifteen different woodland communities signed their marks beneath the signature of Lewis Cass and Thomas Mckenney to a treaty at Fond du Lac in the presence of fourteen white men, two of whom were official commissioners. The tribal leaders who were awarded peace medals to remember the occasion, were from La Pointe, Rainy Lake, Lac du Flambeau, Ontonagon, Vermillion Lake, River de Corbeau, and other places. The white men were from the east. John Quincy Adams, then President of the United States, signed the treaty, with the exception of the articles that provided for the mixed-blood people.

We imagined our names on these treaties, we marked these places on our personal dream maps, places the old mixedbloods told about in their stories around the stove at the store. . . . *To each of the children of John Tanner, being of Chippewa descent . . . To Charlotte Louisa Morrison, wife of Allan Morrison . . .*
To Saugemauqua, widow of the late John Baptiste Cadotte, and to her children Louison, Sophia, Archangel, Edward, and Polly, one section each . . . upon the islands and shore of the Saint Mary River wherever good land enough for this purpose can be found. . . . Our places on the dream maps, our shadows in the stories.

Slivers of sunlight shivered inside the trunks as we were loaded from the dock to the steamboat. Dock men commented on the weight of the possessions of the tall people from the east. Inside the trunks we listened to conversations on the dock and on the deck of the steamboat as people boarded. Comments on the weather, how severe had been the last winter, arrival times at the next ports and fur posts on the lake. We listened and counted our heartbeats, faster and faster across the lake and over the mountains, in a horse-drawn carriage, alone in the parlor of a tall frame house, a mansion with double lace curtains and with windows in the doors. In each trunk we found a parasol, high button boots, fine clothes, hat boxes, and a small chest with precious stones. We imagined the world at the end of the lake where the steamboat stopped for the last time.

The steamboat whistle sounded several times, breathless at the dock, the last invitation to those still on shore. The sound of the steam whistle was muffled inside the trunks, and each sound was a new port, a new dock, new faces, places on our dream maps. We walked down each dock beneath new parasols, our shadows traveled across the earth.

The steamboat moved from the dock. We could hear conversations on the side of the deck and we could imagine from the dark interior of the trunks all the people on the dock. Our friends from school were there, the old mixedbloods who would tell stories about us in the store, the little priest, all waving to us as we leave the island for the first time. Our names held back the flood at the first place we know on the earth. We will be remembered forever.

Laurel Hole in the Day

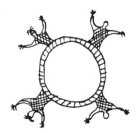

By Gerald Vizenor

I FIRST MET *Laurel Hole in The Day about twenty years ago at the Waite Neighborhood House, an old mansion in Minneapolis. There, Archie Goldman, the director, and several social workers, helped poor and troubled families. I was an advocate for American Indians, determined to change the conditions that made life difficult on the "urban reservation." The experiences of Laurel and Peter Hole in The Day were not uncommon at the time. Their names have been changed to protect their identities.*

Laurel Hole in The Day opened her mouth to speak. Her lips shaped the first words, but she could not tell her impossible dream that cold spring morning. She stood in silence in the kitchen of the Waite Neighborhood House. Tears dripped down her brown cheeks and blotted the small flowers on her print dress.

"Would you like some coffee?" the tribal advocate asked. He tried to ease her emotional burdens in a public place.

Laurel nodded.

The advocate passed her a cup and when he poured the coffee he asked her if she wanted to talk about something that had happened to her family.

Laurel nodded.

Laurel was married and the mother of nine children. The youngest, an infant daughter, was scheduled for surgery to repair a cleft palate. The eldest, a sixteen-year-old daughter was in charge of the other children back on the reservation.

The Hole In The Days, related to the distinguished tribal leader with the same dream name, were practical people with a rich sense of humor to endure their hardships in the world. Their home on the reservation was a three-room, tar-paper covered cabin, perched high on concrete corner blocks. Two automobiles were abandoned behind the cabin: one, with a broken windshield, became a house for two mongrels; the second, a station wagon, was used for storage. The cabin was heated with a wood stove. The windows, covered with sheets of plastic, rattled on the winter wind. Inside, the small rooms were warm and smelled of birch and cedar.

The public health nurse on the reservation made it possible for Laurel and Peter Hole In The Day to live in Minneapolis for one week while their daughter recovered in the hospital.

Laurel sipped coffee in the kitchen of the neighborhood house. She seemed more at ease, but she could not tell her impossible dream – to leave the reservation, move to the city, and to live in an apartment with her husband and children.

The advocate placed two pieces of blank paper on the kitchen table. He asked Laurel to list what she wanted, her dreams, on the first piece of paper, and on the second sheet he told her to list the problems she must overcome to realize her dreams.

The dreams:

We want to live with our children in the city together. We need a place to live and my husband wants to work so to pay the rent on time. This is all we want.

The problems:

My daughter is getting better. She is very sick and she will be able to talk when she grows up because of the operation. Peter is with her now. We do not have money and no work so we could not pay the rent right away. Peter has a bad back from the woods. I hope you can help us, we got to go back next week.

Laurel returned the paper to the advocate. The words were written in a clear and readable hand. She had been educated at a federal boarding school where the teachers had demanded precise handwriting.

The tribal advocate told her to come back in three days with her husband. Meanwhile, he said, he would do what he could to fulfill her impossible dream – an apartment, furniture, a job, and a cash advance.

The dream was impossible on the income from one unskilled worker, unless the couple separated and she applied for welfare assistance. The best employment the advocate could arrange on short notice was with a small firm where Laurel and Peter could work together, at least for a few weeks until a better paying job could be found. The company manufactured plastic caps for glue bottles. The owner, sensitive to the problems of tribal people, agreed that the couple could plan their own hours, but he would not provide a cash advance.

* * *

The advocate located a two-bedroom apartment in a four-unit building two blocks from Franklin Avenue in Minneapolis. The area, where thousands of tribal people lived in run-down housing, was known as the "urban reservation." The owner of the apartment building agreed to a six-month lease and free rent for two weeks on the condition that the tenants paint the apartment at their own expense and repair the windows and locks. Laurel wanted to live there, closer to the people she knew from boarding school and from the reservation where she was born.

Laurel and Peter returned to the neighborhood house three days later. She spoke to the advocate for the first time, in a whisper, when he told her about the jobs and the apartment. She was silent again, however, when the advocate introduced them to their employer who explained the operation of the assembly line in a loud voice, over the sound of machines:

"You put the caps on the mandrils, these moulding pins here, in sequence, going around twice, watch the blue caps on the red pins. If the pin does not function or is not installed then push this reset index button which releases the escape mandrils. Wait, and then when you see red pins coming down around the corner you will know the pins are in where they should be. The pins spiral up by vibration and ten drop through the slot at a time. Notice that if the seam on the cap separates from the mould line, or flashing, it could catch in the feeder slot and pile up. Watch and feel for the voids at the end of the line."

Laurel nodded.

Laurel and Peter worked on the assembly line that night and moved into their apartment the next morning. Friends of the advocate and staff members from the neighborhood house painted the apartment while the couple was at work. Their infant daughter recovered, the other eight children came down from the reservation, and the Hole In The Days were together in the city for the first time. Two months later the advocate found them better work with higher pay, insurance, and other benefits.

Their impossible dream was complete for several months, but then new problems appeared. Other tribal people "borrowed" their food and charged long-distance calls on their phone while Laurel and Peter were at work.

Laurel whispered that she wanted to move. "We work hard for nothing," she pleaded. "When we come home the back door is broken down, even with our oldest children here, and people take everything."

The tribal advocate nodded. He located a small house in a "white neighborhood" on the north side of the city. The rent was less than the apartment, and the house was larger, with closets in each bedroom.

The Hole In The Days were lonesome and soon missed the casual humor on the urban reservation. Laurel and Peter returned at night to drink with old friends in familiar bars on Franklin Avenue. Peter drank too much, missed too much work, and was fired; two weeks later he disappeared with the car.

Laurel applied for welfare assistance. Several months later, in the spring when the juncos returned, she moved with her children back to their tar-paper cabin on the reservation. She found her husband there, alone in the woods. She set aside her dream to live on the urban reservation.

The Waite Neighborhood House was demolished to make room for a hospital parking lot. Popular memories from the kitchen of that old mansion endure in oral and written stories; at the same time, tribal people and their experiences in the world change. Laurel Hole In The Day completed her high school education and then went on to earn a degree from a state university near the reservation. She now works as a counselor in a drug and alcohol treatment program and lives with her children in a larger house on the reservation.

Heathens vs. Christians

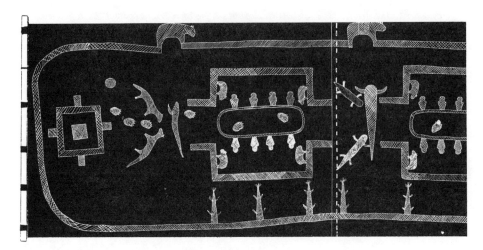

Open Heart with a Grunt

LUKE WARMWATER was doing his part as a grunt in South Vietnam. It was hot and humid. The monsoon was coming just over the mountains. It was getting close to the scary dark time that was also protective.

Luke and a couple other grunts happened to be near the Battalion Aid Station. Somebody, somewhere must have stepped in some shit. The wounded and other Marines were being carried in. They didn't recognize any of them but it was hard to tell because they looked so different when they're dead and wounded.

A TV news crew was at the aid station and was filming the stretchers and ponchoes filled with wounded, dead or dying Marines. The grunts didn't like that. The news crew was easily persuaded not to do that when faced by the three field Marines. They were heavily armed and they had the look in their eyes that indicated they had all used these tools of war recently.

The news crew disappeared as the grunts pitched in to help. The VC decided to liven things up with automatic weapons and mortars. The mortar rounds were walking closer to the Battalion Aid Station. The explosion sound was followed by a dirty cloud of dust and smoke. The green tracers began zipping through the perimeter. The grunts were a little worried when they saw these. They knew there were four rounds in between that you couldn't see. The tracers seemed to be going by mostly overhead but the mortars continued their deadly fifty meter

by Jim Northrup

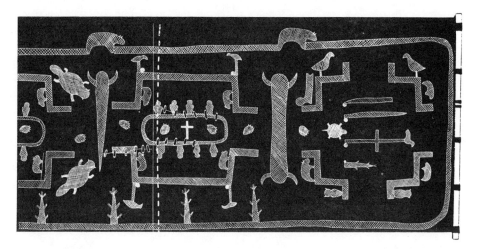

steps through the area. The mortars walked through and then began to come back with their fifty meter steps.

The Marines returned fire with everything they had. This included rifles, machine guns, rocket launchers, 60 and 81mm mortars, and M-79 grenade launchers. The grunts knew that friendly artillery and helicopter gunships were just minutes away. Puff the Magic Dragon was also flying circles overhead.

Luke and the other grunts couldn't return fire because they were inside the perimeter. They were also busy carrying the Marines who couldn't walk or would never walk again. Luke was carrying a Marine who had the grey color of death. He had been hit in the chest with a large projectile. The wound was about the size of a "C" ration can. He had other wounds that were bleeding.

The corpsmen and doctors began working on this guy right away. The medical people crowded the grunts out of the way as they worked. They were done carrying so they stood around and watched. The incoming fire seemed to be lightening up.

The Marine had his shirt cut off and various things were hooked up to the guy on the stretcher. The grunts recognized plasma and a device that pumped air into the shattered chest. A doctor came running up. He seemed oblivious to the small arms fire and mortars. He used a scalpel to cut between the guy's ribs on the left side. He used his hands and a rib spreader to open the grey Marine's chest. They couldn't hear the bones breaking because of the noise. The doctor reached in and began squeezing the guy's heart. There wasn't much blood visible as the procedure went on. The foot wide trail of blood explained the lack of blood coming from the grey Marine.

The medivac choppers began arriving and their noise added to the confusion. The engine noise and the door gunner firing their M-60 machine guns seemed to drown out the noise of the incoming fire. The appearance of the choppers drew the VC fire. A hovering chopper was too big of a target. The choppers were like deadly magnets as the VC mortars and machine guns began hitting near them.

The grunts began loading up the choppers. Only the wounded were being taken. The dead could wait until things settled down. The machine gun bullets hit the choppers with a characteristic sound and it was easy to hear this sound above the noise of the firefight.

The grey Marine was being carried on a stretcher as the doctor walked alongside still squeezing. One grunt was handed the bag that pumped air, another was given the plasma and blood bags. Luke was given something to squeeze. It was the size of a tennis ball and it was connected to the guy somewhere. A corpsman told Luke and the other grunts their duties as the grey Marine and his soggy stretcher were loaded on the chopper. The door gunner helped load the wounded between bursts of his machine gun.

Dark was adding to the confusion as the overloaded chopper tried to lift off with its macabre cargo. The green tracers were searching for the chopper as the pilot used forward momentum to gain altitude. The chopper floor was slippery with blood. The noise inside the chopper was loud. It was semi-dark inside the chopper as they cleared the trees outside the perimeter.

The grunts looked out and down while assisting the doctor. The perimeter was lit up with flares, fires and explosions. Luke saw a chopper struggling to get off the ground. Marines jumped out of the chopper and began carrying the wounded back out.

Luke wanted to fire his rifle at an enemy machine gun that was plainly shooting at them. The tracers were almost pretty as they arched towards them. Luke couldn't shoot and squeeze at the same time so he just tried to make himself as small as possible inside his flak jacket and helmet.

The door gunner began screaming as a round came through the floor. Blood squirted out of his leg as he screamed and fired his machine gun. Luke was able to get a battle dressing on the gunner's leg between squeezes.

Something happened to time. It no longer flowed along. Time slowed down and the grunts were no longer aware. Their eyes, ears and minds kept on absorbing things as the chopper climbed out of rifle range.

Luke looked down at the grey Marine. He didn't know him but Luke realized it very easily could have been him lying on that blood soaked stretcher. Luke prayed for him. The doctor shouted encouraging words as they flew the 25 miles to DaNang. The doctor said the guy was still alive but the grunts doubted it because once someone was that color grey, they never came back.

The chopper landed and the wounded were carried into the operating rooms.

Luke and the other grunts just stood around outside, trapped inside their minds with the memories of what they saw, heard and felt. Time returned to normal as the doctor came out and told them the grey Marine died on the table.

They got back into another chopper for the return to the scene of the firefight. This time they could fire back as the chopper came in.

Luke still sees that grey Marine in his nightmares every couple months.

Heathens vs. Christians

L UKE WARMWATER and his cousin, Dunkin Black Kettle were sitting on a hill overlooking the campus of the Christian boarding school they were either sent or sentenced to.

The school was one of those missionary schools which was supposed to turn the reservation heathens into devout, God-fearing, obedient American citizens. The methods used for this religious mission were based on fear, isolation, and fundamentalist beliefs. The school operated on guilt donations solicited from all over the country. The Christians who thought Indians had gotten a dirty deal assuaged their feelings by donated clothing, money and anything else they could write off their taxes. The school was a self-sufficient enclave located in the Black Hills of South Dakota. It was about 519.3 miles from home.

Luke and Dunkin were two of the five Chippewas from a reservation in Northern Minnesota. The rest of the student converts were from South Dakota and New York. The five Chippewa figured they had their hereditary enemies, the 25 Sioux and the 15 New Yorkers, outnumbered. The Christians preached brotherhood and all that, but the Chippewas knew from the old stories who the enemy really was.

Every Sunday, the student body was rounded up and herded into the bus for the ten-mile trip to town. In town, they marched into a holiness church for a three-hour sermon. When that service was over, they went back to the school to eat. When they were finished eating, it was time for another ride to town for another three-hour sermon. Every Sunday, it was a game to outwit the teachers and preachers to avoid the six-hour lecture on sin, fire and brimstone, and eternally burning lakes of fire. Luke couldn't picture the lake back home burning.

As they sat and watched the campus, they saw the old bus being worked on for the trip to town on Sunday. The ideas began to form as they watched the attempts to get the last miles out of the ancient bus. They thought if the bus were to break down on the way, they wouldn't have to go to church. They might have to walk back to the campus but that was better than sitting in the small church for six hours.

They waited for dark and when the lights went out, they began their offensive directed at the offensive bus. They crawled for about twenty minutes to reach the bus undetected. It would have been easy to disable the bus where it sat but they wanted it to happen on the road.

Luke and Dunkin divided the job up, while Dunkin filed the gas line, Luke was rearranging the spark plug wires. They topped off the gas tank with a couple handfuls of sand. The bus would still run for a while until it hit a bump, then the gas line would break through, maybe.

After crawling back to the dormitory, they began to prepare the innocent faces they would need when the sabotage was discovered. When the quiet laughter died down, they were ready for when the shit hit about the bus.

The Sunday sunrise was nice as it lit up the hills and then the valleys. While marching to breakfast, Luke and Dunkin talked about how much easier it would be to worship the Creator outside rather than inside the confining church. They also saw the bus sitting there, waiting for its meeting with destiny on the road someplace. It was hard to keep a straight face and not brag about their overnight visit to the bus.

The students were dressed in the donated shirts and ties that were necessary for this religion and marched to the bus. Luke and Dunkin took up positions over the filed gas line. They wanted to be ready to shout the alarm about the leaking gasoline. The bus began ascending a long hill to their religious torture. On the way up, the engine died. The driver was able to restart it but the engine had no power. The Indians marched alongside as the bus tried to make the hill. It wasn't necessary to sound the alarm about the leaking gas because the bus gave up the ghost and died for good.

The students roamed back to the campus, church was out for that day. Along the way, Luke and Dunkin noticed the little things the Creator had made. They pointed out the hills, trees, animals, and warm sunshine. They both realized this is the way their elders worshipped. The elders did it every day, not just on Sundays.

When the teachers and preachers dragged the bus back to the campus, evidence of the sabotage was discovered and the hunt for the culprits began. By this time, Luke and Dunkin had plenty of time to work on their most pious and innocent faces. When it was time for their interrogation, they denied everything. The teachers and preachers couldn't prove it but they knew the two Chippewas were involved somehow.

When the staff tried to resurrect the bus, Luke and Dunkin knew that it was a hopeless cause. The school was prepared for this and bought another bus. This bus was kept in a locked garage but this was no problem because the Chippewas had most of the campus keys. The locked garage just gave them a quiet place to disable the new bus. This worked out pretty good. The new bus would run fine all week, but, on Saturday night it would break down and refuse to start for the church run.

The teachers and preachers outwitted the heathen Indians. The school invited a touring revival group to the campus. Church was held every evening for three hours for three weeks.

Luke and Dunkin were watching the Indians who had been converted from their pagan ways and belonged to that new tribe called Christians. The new Christians had life a little easier on the campus. They got extra food, they didn't have to do manual labor and the teachers and preachers didn't watch them as closely.

Just as an experiment, Luke thought he'd give this Christian thing a try. During one of the revival altar calls, Luke ignored the snickers and teasing and marched up to the altar. The teachers and preachers had been trying to get Luke up there since the beginning of the school year. They saw their chance and descended on Luke and began praying around and over him. Luke honestly tried. He prayed for what seemed like a long time. Nothing was happening, no divine light, no new feelings. The only thing Luke felt was sore knees and he began to wonder how to get up. He couldn't just stand up and say it didn't work. The teachers and preachers would have thought he was just playing with them. The answer came in a flash. Fake it. Luke stood up and said that Jesus came down and personally entered his heart. Luke wondered if all Christians felt this way.

He was able to keep the fake going for about three hours. He became a backslider when he and Dunkin spotted some unguarded food. They ate it. Luke decided you couldn't win with these Christians and easily slipped back to his heathen ways. It was a three hour conversion. The heathens were always underfed. Luke and Dunkin had a plan. . . .

Holiday Inndians

LUKE WARMWATER and his cousin were on the road. Butch Storyteller was driving his car. It was a good car, the radio and heater both worked. They had spent the previous day preparing the car for the trip. The problems of gas, oil and tires had been solved. Luke hocked one of his shotguns to buy a tire.

The two Sawyer "skins" were on their way to Minneapolis. The National Indian Education Convention was being held at one of the hotels there. Since they were both college students, they were mildly interested in Indian education. They were more interested in the fancy "snagging" that went on at these conventions.

Indians from all over the United States would be there. Luke and Butch were interested in meeting Indians of the female gender. The two "skins" would become members of the Holiday Inndian tribe for the duration of the convention.

To quote the novelist Snoopy, "it was a dark and stormy night." The snow started before they got to the sweet rolls at Hinckley, Minnesota. In the headlights, the snow seemed to be coming from a point about 20 feet in front of the car. The snow was the kind that fell in a horizontal direction.

As usual they were late getting started. Because of the snow, they had to slow all the way to the speed limit. This made them late for the opening of the convention. Butch said, "When I die, they're going to call me the late Butch Storyteller." Luke laughed and said, "Who did you steal that line from?"

Butch started telling about the snagging he did at the last funeral in Sawyer. "That woman I met there was so pretty, she would have made Miss Indian America look like a boy, an ugly boy."

"She might have been with you, Butch, but she was thinking of me all the time," said Luke.

"Yeah, but, whose relative was that I saw you with, I thought you told me she was a good one, you said she wanted to marry you."

"She might have been 30 or 40 pounds heavier than I first thought and maybe 10, 15 years older when I first saw her in the good light," Luke added defensively.

They laughed and lied their way down the slippery interstate to the Cities. The anticipation started to build more and more as they got closer to the Cities. They took turns telling convention stories. Butch fondly remembered the one in Milwaukee.

"There were 11 floors of partying Indians in that 16 floor hotel, one guy told me he wound up eight floors away from where he registered."

"That was me, don't you remember? I fell in lust with that woman from Tama, Iowa. We would be living together today if her big boyfriend from Arizona hadn't shown up. I'm glad he didn't want to fight me," Luke remembered.

"Sipping, snagging and silliness went on for four days at that one, as I recall," Butch said.

"Uh huh, don't forget the nights either."

"How could I?"

The last big convention that Butch and Luke attended was in Denver. It was a library-related convention. "Remember that librarian I met there?" Butch asked.

"She was from Wisconsin wasn't she?"

"Yeah, she showed me what the last syllable in Wisconsin really means."

"How about the woman I was with, she was from Washington D.C., she explained the Library of Congress classification system to me as we explored each other's systems."

"Do you ever hear from her anymore?"

"I get a postcard now and then."

"Maybe you'll get lucky and see her at this convention."

"Who knows?"

With the memories of that convention still tickling them, they arrived at the hotel. They were late. The evening proceedings were all over with. The snagging was pretty well done by the time they arrived. The bars and restaurants were all closed.

Butch and Luke decided to hang around the lobby to see if anyone else had arrived late. The elevator door quietly opened behind the two "skins" from the Fond du Lac reservation. They heard it and turned to see who was getting off.

Two women got off, one of them was thin and the other was quite large. As the two women prowled the lobby, Butch observed, "They look like the number 10, when they walk together like that."

The women circled around and came up to the two Sawyer skins. The women were out snagging. Butch and Luke became the "snagees" instead of the snaggers.

Before they really knew what was happening, Butch and Luke found themselves in the women's hotel room. They introduced themselves.

"I'm Patty, and I'm from Turtle Mountain," said the thin one. Butch thought she was built like a rice knocker.

"I'm June, I'm from Turtle Mountain too." Butch thought she was so big she could be called June, July and part of August. Butch said, "I'm George and I'm a Seneca from New York."

"I'm Frank and I live in Ohio, I'm a Winnebago," Luke lied.

Trying to make the best of the situation, Butch and Luke sat down and tried to drink the women pretty. Luke suspected the two were trying to drink them handsome. It later turned out there was not enough beer in the room or even in the whole building. Everyone in the room told their life story as they settled into the drinking party. Butch and Luke continued telling lies.

Patty got up and looked out the window, she wondered aloud, "I wonder what I'd look like if I fell out of this window?"

"You'd look like a hamburger, Patty," June told her.

They were out of beer. Butch quit telling funny stories because every time he did, June would laugh and punch him on the arm. His arm was getting sore. Patty's response to Butch's stories was to laugh and stick out her tongue almost to her chin and say "Haaaaaaaa."

It looked like June was trying to edge Butch over to a corner. He was trying to keep a lane open to the door. She outweighed him by 50 pounds and he was getting worried.

Butch eased over by the door, invented an emergency, then left the room to move his car, make a phone call, or something. Luke hung around the room for a few minutes and then left to go check on his cousin.

They weren't drunk enough to wake up any of their relatives at this ungodly hour, so they found a cheap hotel and slept. Tomorrow was the second day of the four day convention.

Ricing Again

LUKE WARMWATER woke up wondering where he was. He remembered being at the party and remembered being one of the last ones awake. It all came crashing back. He was at Mukwa's house and he was supposed to meet that woman who was his new rice partner.

His head hurt and he knew his breath was foul. His ribs hurt and he wondered if he had been in a fight. No, no one had punched him, it must have been the way he slept. The couch was responsible for the rib ache. The alcohol was responsible for his parched throat, queasy stomach and shaking fingers. The headache came from the guilt and the excessive amount of alcohol he drank.

His bloody eyes scanned the room looking for something to put out the fire in his throat and settle his stomach. He knew the guilt feeling would go away on its own. He saw a 12-pack that had been overlooked last night. The twelver still had seven cold ones left. The world didn't look so bad now.

His old car was outside and the cold beer in his belly was making him forget his assorted aches. He drained the bottle as he stood outside and drained his bladder.

The canoe was still on the car, and under a quilt in the back seat was his new partner, Dolly. She looked a little tough as she snored away her share of the party.

Dolly came from the other side of the rez. He knew he wasn't related to her but had heard of her family. He also remembered her laugh from last night as she playfully punched him on the arm. He was trying to tell her how pretty she was when the punch stopped the chain of compliments. He looked forward to getting to know her better as soon as they straightened up a bit. As he was trying to remember everything he knew about her, he decided it wasn't important. What was important was to make rice.

Today was the first day of the opening of the "committee" lakes. Luke had a car, canoe, knockers, pole and a new partner. He only had to find lunch and sacks for the green rice. They were signed up for Dead Fish Lake and he didn't want to miss that first run through the ripe, untouched rice.

As he drove to the store to score the sacks and lunch, Dolly woke up and asked for a smoke. His crushed pack still had some left. As they lit up he noticed, she really is pretty. He shared his beer with her as she began to pull herself together. She took his rearview mirror to comb her hair, inspect her teeth, cough and blow her nose. She could complete her toilet at the bathroom in the store.

His headache was subsiding down to a dull throb as they pulled into the store parking lot. He saw a couple of cars he recognized and his cousin's truck. He reached for his wallet and suddenly realized he had been jackrolled as he slept on the couch. There must have been someone still awake when he went to sleep.

Dolly handed him his worn wallet and winked. She said she took it to protect his bankroll. He was beginning to like this woman more and more. His $11.00 was still there.

For the car, Luke bought gas, a quart of oil and added air to that right rear tire that had a slow leak. For themselves, he got lunch materials and smokes. The store owner gave him a couple of sacks because he promised to sell his rice there.

As he drove to the lake, memories of past ricing seasons came to him. His earliest memories were of playing on the shore while his parents were out ricing. He knew the people enjoyed ricing and there were good feelings all around. The years seemed to melt from people. Grandparents moved about with a light step and without their canes. Laughing and loud talking broke out frequently. The cool crisp morning air, the smell of wood smoke, roasting meat and coffee were all part of these early childhood memories.

When he grew older, his responsibilities increased. He took care of his brothers and sisters. He cleaned the canoes and rice boats of every last kernel of rice. He learned how to make rice poles and knockers. He learned how important ricing was to the people.

His thoughts were jolted back to the present when his left rear tire blew out. He thought, "Gee that was my good tire too." As the car lurched to a stop, he knew he didn't have a spare cause he hocked it last week. He took the offending tire off because he knew he'd have to eventually. He looked down the road.

He saw one of his uncles coming down towards the rice landing. When his uncle saw what was wrong, he stopped and opened his trunk. He had a snow tire in there that still had some air. Luke shared a smoke and a beer with his uncle as he put the good tire on. As they sipped and gossiped, Luke found out that his uncle was not planning on ricing this year but was just going down to the landing to see if anyone needed a partner. His uncle was known as a good knocker so finding a partner was not going to be a problem.

The tire change made them late and they had to park way back on the road. The canoe and all their stuff had to be packed a long way to the lake. Everyone else was lined up and ready to go.

The ricers laughed as he was getting in the water because his face showed what he'd been doing the night before. In the face of all this teasing, he could hardly wait for the jokes and jibes to be aimed at someone else so he could join in the laughter. It was good to see his relatives anyway.

Dolly was standing in front of the canoe with her pole as he arranged his sacks, water jug, and "oops," must have left the lunch in the car. They drifted out to where the eager ones were waiting to blast off. Luke was knocking because this was his partner's first year ricing. He had looked at the rice while hunting and he knew where on the lake to go.

He repeated the string of instructions to Dolly as they began. "Don't break the rice, stay out of the open water, keep the canoe moving, watch for the color of the ripe rice, if you feel yourself falling, jump in and save the rice in the canoe."

Dolly looked comfortable in the front of the canoe and they didn't feel tippy as they started off. She poled to the rice and the sound of the other ricers swishing through the rice made a nice rhythm. Luke chuckled when he heard the unmistakable sound of a knocker hitting a canoe instead of the rice. While loosening up his arm and shoulder muscles, he saw the heavy heads were hanging at just the right angle for easy knocking. The sound of the rice falling in the canoe made Luke feel good.

Everywhere he looked, there was good rice. This good patch went all the way across the lake. He saw a bald eagle circling above them. He interpreted this as a good sign.

After a couple hours, Luke's stomach reminded him of the lunch in the car. The rice had bearded up pretty good and was clean and free of debris. Not too shabby, thought Luke.

They stopped to visit with his first cousin who stopped for lunch. The fried bread, deer meat, and green tea gave Luke and Dolly enough strength to finish the day. Luke thought he'd bring his cousin some of the next deer he shot.

After getting off the lake, they sacked up on the shore. Both Luke and Dolly joined in on the laughing and exaggerating as people told stories about what happened on the lake that day. The harvest was good and everyone was happy with the way the rice was falling.

This was true except for the greedy ones who wouldn't have been satisfied with seven canoeloads of rice. They would have wanted eight.

While sacking up, they laughed because one of the greedy ones tipped over right in front of the landing. The rice would grow good there next time.

At the auction, the bids were all pretty good and they ended up selling their rice to that buyer from McGregor. The buyer knew he was getting quality rice at a low price. The buyer didn't know, in addition to the good rice, he bought half a muskrat house, wet blue jeans and some rocks with zero nutritional value.

As the sacks were being weighed, the buyer was pulling up on the sack to decrease the weight. On the other side a skinny brown hand was pulling down just a little bit harder.

The people laughed as they watched this ancient tug of war. They were familiar with this yearly ritual.

Luke and Dolly looked forward to the next day of ricing. It should be a better one because now she knew what she was doing out on the lake. "She is pretty and pretty good at ricing," thought Luke.

Yup, ricing was here again.

Coffee Donuts

T HE SEMITRAILER trucks roared down the highway on this, a rainy October morning. The car waiting to enter the highway was rocked by the wind and washed by the spray as the loaded grain trucks went by.

Three "skins" from the Fond du Lac reservation didn't mind the wait. It was raining and they didn't have to go to work. This meant they had nowhere to go and a long time to get there.

The driver was bragging about his car and was giving the boys a demonstration ride through the ditchbanks. The driver had just bought the car and paid the insurance with his earnings from the job at the reservation housing project.

It was a pretty good car and it looked like it would last through two winters. The tires were good, the lights worked, the radio was loud and the heater blew hot; hell, even the cigarette lighter worked.

The job at the housing project added stability to the driver's life. The Friday paychecks seemed to mellow out his old lady and she didn't seem as snaky as before when they were on welfare. Since he wasn't drinking anymore, the driver spent more time with his kids instead of hanging out at the local tavern. Because of the size of his family, he was next on the list to get one of those new houses they were building. He was thinking these things as he slid sideways around the corner on the empty gravel road.

As he was bragging how well the car held the road, the passenger in the middle slid into the guy riding the shotgun. The passenger in the middle was just happy to be riding. He was happy to be out.

The past year had been spent in and out of jails and treatment centers. His troubles began last year over an open bottle charge. Instead of jail and a fine, he chose to pay his debt to society by going to a treatment center for chemical abusers. After a few hours in the facility, he left. This meant the law was looking for him. After a few months of freedom, he was caught and had to go back and do his time in the county jail.

Finally, it was all behind him on this, his second day of real freedom. He had been told to report for work the next day at the housing project.

The passenger in the middle knew of a pick-up truck he could get cheap. He could drop the engine in from his old car and fix that truck up pretty good now that he was going to be cashy. He was explaining how he was going to hook up the transmission as they slid around another corner. As he slid on the seat, his elbow dug into the shotgun's rib.

The elbow in the rib brought the shotgun back into the conversation. The shotgun had been looking at the edge of a field for a deer. True to his name, the guy riding shotgun had a shotgun. The rusty, trusty 12 gauge was deer hungry.

When riding with shotgun it was hard to talk to him cause all you could see was the back of his head as he looked for deer.

Shotgun was happy cause he was working. He was happy about the job at the housing project. The job paid for a new deer rifle and a canoe. He was happy he didn't have to work today so he could go hunting.

He remembered giving the driver a similar ride a couple weeks ago when he got his new truck. The shotgun's new truck was a four wheeler and it allowed him to go deeper into the brush before getting stuck.

The driver chuckled as he remembered how long it took to dig the truck out of that last swamp. The driver thought, "Enough of this crazy driving," as they approached the state highway and civilization again. As the three "skins" entered the state highway, they began to argue about where to go next. The driver wanted to go home and take his old lady and kids shopping. He also wanted to continue the riding and hunting.

The passenger didn't care, he was just happy to be out and riding. The shotgun wanted to go get his truck and continue the riding and hunting.

The driver was adjusting the rearview mirror, the passenger was digging under the seat for his stolen jailhouse copy of O. Henry stories. The shotgun was again looking for deer.

They didn't see the grain truck with the sleeping driver coming at them in their lane.

The Time King Ate Puppy

L UKE WARMWATER's sister Nita is blessed with dogs. She's got big dogs, little dogs, inside dogs, and outside dogs. She's about three dogs short of being considered weird.

Nita's son, Eddie, had his own dog. He was a round brown ball of fluff. He was named Puppy. Eddie and Puppy were outside enjoying life in Sawyer. Life was a lot simpler there than in the big city. The quiet was broken by the noise Eddie and Puppy made as they played. Hide and seek, exploring and wrestling kept Eddie and Puppy happy.

One of Nita's other dogs was King. He was a Doberman. He was definitely an outside dog. He lived at the end of a logging chain attached to his house. King used to drag the dog house around until Nita had one of her brothers stake the house down. Now the house was inside a circle of bare ground. King would bite and growl at the wind that dared blow on him. King was the kind of dog that mean dogs took lessons from. King watched as the kid and Puppy played.

Eddie had to go inside to pee and get a drink of water. He was also going to get some of his Ma's home-made cookies. While he was inside, he noticed his favorite cartoon was on TV. The TV caught and held his attention as he ate the cookies. He forgot about Puppy who was still outside as the TV mesmerized him.

When Eddie's cartoon was over he went back outside to play with his puppy. He couldn't find him anywhere. He looked around the yard; he looked all the way to the tar road. He couldn't find him. He went inside to tell his Ma. Nita came out and helped him look. They couldn't see or hear him anywhere.

Nita went over by King's house. She couldn't see the pup but she found some brown fluff and a puppy sized flea collar that was chewed in half.

That's it, she thought, King ate Puppy. The decision was made for her by

Eddie's crying. Nita had a hard time dragging him off King. The four-year-old, forty-pound fighter was attacking the Doberman who ate his puppy.

King was tried and convicted. He was scheduled for execution for the heinous crimes of murder and cannibalism. Nita put out a contract.

Nita's brother volunteered as the hit man. He was still carrying a grudge and some tooth-shaped scars from King. He hadn't believed Nita when she said that she and Eddie were the only humans that could feed or even approach King.

A single shotgun slug ended the career of King the puppy eater. The next week, Nita had replacements for King and Puppy. The King is dead, long live the King.

Son and Sunshine

A FOUR-YEAR-OLD boy named Joseph and his 42-year-old father went for a walk one day. It was a special day. The boy was happy because he had his father's undivided attention. The father was happy because when he was with his son, he could forget past wars, present worries and future problems.

Time was put on hold on this bright sunshiny day as the two began their trip through reality. They started with a pancake breakfast. Joseph's father didn't care if syrup was dribbled and spilled. There were more important things to do and see.

As they walked along the city streets, Joseph saw some empty store fronts. He asked about them. His father gave a marginal explanation about them and this explanation was accepted without question. The trust between the two could almost be seen. It was agreed that Joseph would walk a block and then be carried on his father's shoulder's for a block.

Their next stop was at a neighborhood park. The green grass invited Joseph to run. He ran and his father ran to catch up with him. The swings caught Joseph's eye so he ran there. Joseph wanted to be pushed high enough so his tummy would tickle. Joseph's father stood behind as many fathers through the ages have done and pushed until the squeals and giggles scared the robins away.

The two then continued their walk. They were careful not to step on cracks in the sidewalk. Neither one wanted to be responsible for anyone's broken back.

Joseph's observations and perceptions continually surprised his father as they walked and talked along the city streets. Joseph wanted to show his father that he could write his name. He found a stick and began drawing letters in the dirt. As he was struggling with the "s" in his name, an ant walked through. Joseph used the stick to squash the ant and then went back to his name. For some unknown four-year-old reason, Joseph scratched out his name when they left.

Their next stop brought a decision. Should they look at the creek splashing under the bridge or should they look at the bright red fire engine parked on the bridge? The splashing water won and they looked and talked about that. The fire truck was then examined. The truck held their attention for quite a while. This was Joseph's first close up look at a fire truck. They saw the hoses, ladders, helmets and axes. They could almost see the red lights flashing. They could almost hear the wail of the sirens as they studied the fire truck.

The splashing water called them back and they began their walk along the creek. Joseph found a stick and then found one for his Dad. The sticks were important and were used for many purposes. At times they were guns, mountain climbing staffs, and just plain sticks. At times they were carefully stashed because two hands were needed for climbing on the rocks.

Joseph was the leader of the expedition as they walked up the creek. He chose the trails and the things they stopped to examine. The creek gurgled along as they climbed. The sun made them take off their shirts. The wind caressed the sweat from their bodies as they climbed.

They stopped to climb rocks, skip rocks, look at leaves beginning to bud, and watch birds. The hours flowed by like the creek as they explored.

Joseph's father was in more of a hurry to get to their destination until Joseph reminded him that they were there to have fun.

Some overhead electric wires were blasted out of the sky by Joseph with his laser gun stick. They didn't look like they belonged there. They saw no other humans as they climbed.

They thought of crawling on a tree trunk to cross the creek but after a practice session, Joseph decided it was too scary. Joseph didn't want to ride on his father's shoulders because he couldn't go where he wanted or touch what he wanted.

Throwing rocks in the water was fun. Watching water bugs run on top of the water was fun until Joseph saw some minnows. They lay on their bellies to watch them. They lay on their backs to watch the clouds.

Because they were Anishinaabe, they talked about Mother Earth and all the beauty they saw. Joseph's father taught him about the different trees, bushes and plants as they walked along. The flowers nodded in agreement as they walked by.

They stuck the sword sticks in their belts as they climbed the final hill to the playground. Joseph was not afraid as they climbed the steep hill, his father was right behind him. The playground was thoroughly used. Smiles and laughter were natural as they played.

The walk back home was finished on Dad's shoulders because the four-year-old legs were getting tired. They completed their walk and this completed a circle in the hearts of the father and son. Good memories were made that day.

Stories and Stories

L UKE WARMWATER's kids were crabby. One of them was coloring on his younger brother with a magic marker, another was kicking the table to see if he could spill the milk using only his feet, and the youngest was just whining.

There was nothing good on TV. They had seen all the movies on the VCR. Luke stopped it all when he offered to tell them stories. He gathered his children around his chair.

He told his kids about the time everyone was crabby when he was a kid. There wasn't a dance or funeral close by. There were no rabbits to snare. Luke said, "Grandpa used to tell us stories. Grandpa told us about a guy from around here who used to like to walk. He was a pretty good walker. One time he walked in the direction the sun comes from. He walked until he came to the ocean and couldn't walk any more. He was a walker not a swimmer, so he stopped.

"We went along with the walker as he went through the woods to the ocean on the East coast. We learned about the people that were friendly and those who were mean.

"We saw the lakes and rivers, we saw the valleys and mountains, we saw everything the walker saw as Grandpa told the story. After Grandpa told us that story, he got up and went outside to the toilet. When he came back, he continued to tell us about the walker. Grandpa said the walker was gone for three ricing seasons before he came walking back.

"The walker told stories to all the people around here, he never had time for a wife or family. A couple years after he came back from the ocean, he took off again. This time he went in the direction the sun goes down. He didn't come back from that walk. We like to think he made it to the other ocean, anyway. Yup, he sure liked to walk, Grandpa said as he closed the story. He then got up to holler at the dogs who thought they smelled waboose or something.

"Grandpa sat back down and told us about the brave warriors who used to live around here. He said when they used to go to war with the Sioux, the people would gather here from Portage, Nett Lake and what is now called Wisconsin. They would travel night and day to go fight the Sioux. Grandpa told us about the guy who was captured after he was wounded. The shin nob was tortured and then they cut off his feet. The Sioux tied him to a stake and were going to roast him with a fire.

"While standing on his cut off feet, the warrior pulled the stake up out of the ground. He used that stake as a huge club and was chasing the Sioux around until a dozen arrows cut him down. 'That's the kind of warriors that used to live around here,' Grandpa said.

"We sat around his feet as Grandpa told us stories. He was dressed in dark green wool pants, thick wool socks, wide suspenders, a long john shirt and mischievous eyes.

"While he was telling the story, he kept time by tapping a drum only he saw. His hand was shaped around an invisible drum stick as he kept time on the arm of his chair.

"Grandpa got up to put wood in the stove. A puff of good smelling smoke came out and joined us in the room, listening.

"His calloused, thick fingered hands told more than half of his stories. His hands, arms, shoulders and eyes all added to the stories as he was telling them. He got up, got some green tea and came back and sat down.

"Grandpa said, 'One time I was walking in the woods, I was over by, you know where the plum bushes are by Perch Lake? Well, I was right there. I don't remember where I was going that day. It was just getting to be spring, the leaves were just starting to come out. It wasn't really thick yet, you could see pretty far in the woods. The loons were back, I could hear them.

" 'I just came to that last turn in the trail there when, HOLY JEEZ, a big deer jumped up right in front of me. The deer stood broadside and looked at me. We must have stared at each other for 20 minutes before I made my move.'

"Grandpa's hands and arms slowly raised a rifle. His hands and arms settled that rifle into a good firing position. His head dropped down to look over the sights at his supper. His trigger finger slowly pulled back on the trigger. BOOM, he said. We could see the recoil rock him back.

"Grandpa looked over the rifle with his eyebrows signifying surprise. The deer was still standing there, looking at him. He sighted in again, he slowly brought his trigger finger back. BOOM, the recoil drove him further back in his chair.

"Another look, another surprise, the deer was still standing there, looking at him. He tried a third time. He pulled that mighty deer slayer in tighter, he took his time sighting in, it was a long time before we saw his trigger finger creep back, every so slowly.

"Some of us watched him, some of us watched where the deer was going to fall, some of us watched both places, back and forth. BOOM, the recoil this time drove him all the way back in his chair. It knocked him speechless. We all began to ask questions, How could you miss? How far away was he? Whose gun did you have? My Grandpa don't miss. How could you miss? Was that a magic deer?

"He sat up, raised that mighty deer slayer up again, sighted in and slowly began to draw back on the trigger. Before it went off this time, he looked at us with smiling eyes and said, 'I didn't have a gun.'

"We knew this was the last story of the night, we went to our beds happy because we had a Grandpa who told us stories. Some of us were repeating, 'I didn't have a gun,' as we went to sleep."

Luke Warmwater looked around, his kids were sleepy and asleep. He got up and carried them to bed.

Your Standard Drunk

LUKE AND HIS cousin, Dunkin, were on a dirty drunk.

"Have a beer," said Luke, one fine summer morning.

"How long we been doing this now?"

"About three weeks, I think," said Luke.

They were drinking at Dunkin's house at Perch Lake. It was far enough in the woods that cops didn't visit. It wasn't too far for people who wanted to drink. It was a good drunk, no one went to jail or the hospital. It was a mecca for the drinkers in the community. It also was like a magnet for runaway wives, husbands and children.

Luke and Dunkin has many visitors during their drunk. Some came to drink, some came to talk and all came to eat. The visitors brought food and more to drink. Whatever was needed to continue the drunk was carried in by the next visitor.

During the day, they drank by the lake, at night, they drank by campfire.

Jack Sky came to drink and talk. He told his favorite story, his life story. "Damn right, I'm Ottawa and proud of it. I've lived around here longer than most of you," said Jack.

Jack came to the reservation when he was a little guy. He grew up and married a local woman. He now had children and grandchildren living all over the rez.

"Just when I think I belong here, someone makes a smartass remark about Ottawa Indians," Jack complained. "I've lived here for forty years but someone has to remind me I'm not really from here," said Jack, as he took a long pull from his bottle.

The story was good enough to get him drunk and fed many times. He was getting kind of old so he was only good for a week and four tellings of his life story.

Another one of the visitors was a young girl. She told her life story which didn't take too long. "My Ma is mean, she won't get me a phone or color TV for my bedroom, I showed her, I took off," said the young girl as she began her crying jag.

Dunkin handed Luke a beer and said, "Remember what it was like when we were kids?"

"Yah, sleeping four to a bed with the snow blowing through the cracks and piling up on the blankets."

"How about hauling water in a cream can, a sled in the winter and a wagon in the summer."

"Yah, I sure hated the days when my Ma washed clothes."

"All she's got to worry about is a phone and a TV."

The people sitting around began to laugh and tease her.

"I want a color TV," begged an old man with a falsetto voice.

"I want a phone in my bedroom," giggled an older woman.

As the teasing went on, the young girl was looking for a way out of the teasing. Her mother drove up and grabbed her. She threw the young girl in the car and threw threats around about allowing kids at parties like this one.

Luke handed Dunkin a beer as they watched them drive away.

"Some parents wouldn't come after their kids," said Luke.

"Uh huh, some kids wouldn't come after their parents either," agreed Dunkin.

Wild Man showed up one day. "I was down in the cities when I heard about this drunk," he said, "no one came into the Corral Bar and offered me a job so I came home."

"Look who I invited," Wild Man said as he went to the back of his truck. In the back of the truck was a deer.

The deer was a fat juicy one and he was skinned and cleaned immediately. Wild Man gave the younger ones a lesson in skinning and cleaning a deer. He also told them where he shot it and how he offered the deer spirit some tobacco.

When Wild Man kicked back and opened a beer someone else began the cutting and cooking. It wasn't too long after that everyone was eating. There was grease from ears to elbows. The drinking and eating continued on through the night.

The next morning they heard a big truck rumbling up. It was a beer truck. A couple of Luke's cousins got out when it stopped. They went around and helped the driver out. He was a white man.

"We were drinking with this white guy last night."

"He said he wanted to come out here and drink with the Indians."

The white guy looked like he was ready to pass out, he looked around and said, "I've got a lot of Indian friends, help yourself to some beer." He sat down and then fell over side ways and began snoring. Whenever he'd wake up, someone would hand him a beer or a shot of whiskey. He'd take a drink and then pass out again.

Luke thought this was too much good luck. This much good would also bring an equal amount of bad luck, not to mention the cops.

Luke and Dunkin passed out a couple of 12 packs and loaded the driver back into his truck. They wrote out an IOU and a thank you note. They pinned the notes on the driver and locked the truck.

On the way back home, they decided the drunk was about over.

"Let's send everyone home when we run out of beer."

"Yah, time to get ready for ricing, anyway."

Both of them were dreading the three week's worth of hangover they had coming.

Bloody Money

L UKE WARMWATER was broke, not short of money, but broke. The kind of broke that is all pervading. Everyone he knew was waiting for a check, not him though.

He knew there was nothing coming down the road for him. The ship he was waiting for must have sunk. He was so broke, he had to mix his metaphors so he'd have enough. He was so broke, he was telling stories about a guy he knew who had a dollar.

But, as the man said, he was broke, nor poor.

He had a solution to the problem in mind. Moneyless Luke went down to the bleeders at the Blood Donor Center. He had heard this place was called Dr. Dracula's Bank. He also heard the workers there were called vampires.

He thought about the whole thing before he went through the door. If blood plasma was worth $10, what was the value of his other body fluids? What was the going rate for ear wax? Does anyone buy spit or sweat? What about liver bile? Where do you donate sperm?

The cheerful mood of the vampires worried him. How can a person be so happy when you make others bleed? The bright lights of the place showed him some of the plasma producers.

They all looked like people who needed $10. That was the common thread running through them. There were hippies, winos, Indians, street people, college students, blacks and some who defied a label.

The vampires looked like they were all stamped from the same mold. The white uniforms and artificial smiles made them look alike. The vampires acted like the people selling plasma were some kind of livestock. They were efficient as they went about their duties. Luke had seen the same look on farmers' faces as they milked their cows.

Luke entered the process. First was a blood test. The prick on the finger didn't hurt as much as the humiliation of having to sell his blood. He thought about buying food with his blood money. This completed the cycle somehow. Next in the process was a procedure that can best be compared to a jail booking. Identification, mug shots, and a medical history interview. The only thing missing was the fingerprinting.

The next room was a waiting room. After leaving a little cup of piss, Luke had another interview and a cursory physical exam. He then passed to the next room.

This was the bleeding room itself. The room was large and barnlike. Instead of cow stanchions, there were rows of green vinyl beds.

He watched a vampire wiping down the vinyl bed that was temporarily between plasma producers. He saw a plasma producer walking slowly off to collect his $10. The whole place was a flurry of activity. The vampires were doing most of the moving around. The plasma producers were horizontal with the white clad vampires hovering like bats around them.

Luke went in and lay down. He was mentally prepared for the bloodletting. The vampire cheerfully explained what she was doing as she was doing it. Not once did their eyes meet.

The needle was about the size of a 60 penny nail. He felt two punctures as she pushed the needle in. One as the needle stretched and perforated the skin and the second as the needle perforated the vein. He noticed that the vinyl bed was still warm from the last occupant.

About this time, Luke's cousin came in. He lay down on the next bed to be bled. They told each other stories and gossiped the rest of the process away. The last Luke saw of his blood was when the vampire whisked the plastic bag away.

Luke left with $10 in his pocket. He had a bandage on his arm and when he got outside, he saw the parking ticket on his car. He must have been hooked up to corporate America too long. The $4.00 ticket reduced his profit to $6.00.

While driving home, Luke saw his brother-in-law, Dave, at the drive-up window at the bank. This was the same Dave that owed him money from last fall. Luke had sold Dave a canoe.

Dave looked cashy as he left the bank. Luke followed him. When Dave pulled into a cafe, Luke followed him. Luke had coffee and they entertained each other telling stories.

Luke's stories always centered around a canoe. Pretty soon Dave remembered that he still owed Luke for the canoe. He paid up.

When Luke got home, he checked the mail. As he was dividing the envelopes up, he noticed one from an attorney. That one would stay in the pile of envelopes that had picture windows on them.

After reading the mail from his relatives, he began opening the picture window envelopes. The one from the attorney had a letter, a release form and a check. The check was for an accident that happened a couple years ago. Luke could hardly remember the accident but knew it wasn't his fault.

The $1700 check plus the $200, plus the $6 for his blood gave him a net profit of $1906. Not bad for one day. He wondered how long this prosperity part of the cycle would last.

The first thing he bought was a box of band-aids for that hole in his arm.

Work Ethic

N OW THAT ricing was over, Luke Warmwater began to think about getting through the winter. What he needed was a job. A job to pay for food, child support and recreational drugs. He also thought he would need a winter jacket, boots and mitts. His old car had snow tires from last year, it had three of them still on.

After thinking about working in the woods, cutting firewood, Luke remembered wading through the ass deep snow, digging out frozen birch with frozen fingers. No, it seemed like an inside job was the answer to the problem.

Luke went to the state employment office because he heard they sometimes had a line on available jobs. After looking at the list of jobs open to any Sawyer Indian who was a chemical engineer or a technical sales representative, he narrowed his choices to the ones he though he could bullshit his way into.

The one that called for a management trainee looked promising. It was a hamburger franchise and if nothing else, he would be near food during the cold days coming. With his referral slip in hand, he made it to the interview with three minutes to spare. He interpreted this as a good sign.

The manager got things off to a bad start when he asked if Luke would cut his hair for the job. The only other choice was to wear a hairnet like his Grandma wore. He didn't want to smell like hamburgers and a daily diet of fast foods would get pretty tiring after a while so the career of retail food sales was out.

The next referral slip directed him to report to the personnel office of a large pizza making factory. He filled out the forms and the secretary told him to report for the second shift. He didn't know he automatically qualified for the job when he was able to fill out the forms without assistance.

His first night on the job went okay. He was given a push broom and told which areas to sweep. He thought, not too bad, the broom wasn't heavy and the building was warm. He also thought, I never really noticed the smell of pizza before.

After steering the broom around for a couple of hours, he began to think of ways to advance from this menial, manual labor. The next time the foreman came by, Luke asked about it. The foreman showed him a guy who was sweeping around the next conveyer belt. The foreman said the guy had been there for almost a year and at the next opening would be promoted to the production line.

Luke took a closer look at his fellow workers and came to the conclusion that some of them were from a sheltered workshop someplace.

At the lunch break of pizza, he tried to strike up a conversation with some of the other workers. The conversation didn't get very far unless he spoke in one syllable words, nodded his head and smiled a lot. He got tired of the vacant smiles and when he noticed he was beginning to smile like that, he thought of other jobs he could handle.

He knew that the Indian Center always had a job or two in one of their programs. With resume in hand, he showed up to meet the screening committee. The screening committee was all white and most of them looked like ex-radicals or ex-hippies. These former "flower" children had gone "to help the Indians" and were now in positions of authority at the Indian Center. The positions they held were probably the first rung on the ladder of success.

In spite of the brilliant answers he gave during the interview, he didn't have a prayer of getting the job. He didn't know it then, but one member of the screening committee had a friend that needed a job. While waiting for the phone call about the job, he remembered the story of the Indian who showed up for an interview wearing a blond wig. Neither one of them got the job.

Luke was getting desperate and thought he'd either have to get a job or pull a job. He knew if he didn't make a child support payment pretty soon, the court would repossess him and put him in jail for at least 90 days. This wouldn't get him all the way through winter so he continued his job-seeking efforts.

While walking through the shopping mall, he noticed a new waterbed store opening up. He went in and asked for a job. The sales manager had a great idea for a marketing gimmick. Luke got the job. His job was to sleep on a watered in the front window of the store. This was all too good to be true and he had trouble falling asleep the first couple of days on the job. He wondered if he was sleeping open-mouthed, if he was drooling or thrashing around while he slept. He got used to people staring at him because this new job was a dream. He could party all night and still get up and go to work. Luke's job ended when he was caught demonstrating another use of the water bed to the sales manager's wife.

By this time the long arm of the law reached out and snagged Luke. It was about his child support and unless he came up with the money for them, the judge would see that he had a warm place to sleep in the county jail. The judge sitting on the bench knew Luke from their previous encounters. He didn't want to send him off to be fed and sheltered at county expense. The judge proposed a solution. Luke began to work around the judge's house as a handyman. He figured the judge wouldn't get mad if he charged up a rifle and shells where the judge did business. He was wrong and after getting an ear beating about trust and credit, he found himself back on the street looking for a job. He did get to keep the rifle and shells though.

He finally found a job at a machine shop. This one paid better than all the others he had worked at all year. With this income he paid the judge for the rifle and shells. He got caught up on his child support. He ate good. He began to look at the finer things in life. One of the finger things in life was a different car.

His old car was loud, drank oil and the missing window made the wind chill unbearable. He hated to take it to the scrap yard but took a small pleasure in knowing he was the last person to ever drive the car.

The job at the machine shop was pretty easy. He drilled four holes in a piece of metal. After a little time on the job, he was able to get his entire day's quota done right after lunch. The money was good and it was warm in the building so he hung in there for the rest of the winter.

One fine spring day after lunch, Luke was looking out the window. He thought how good it would feel to have the sun shining on his face. He reached over and shut off the machine. He thought back to how close he and the machine had become. He was the part of the machine that went home at night. He went out the door, never to return.

Luke had a cousin who was a pusher on a big construction project. He thought his cousin could get him on at that job.

Yep, next week he'd look up his cousin.

The Jail Trail

THE COMMODITY cans were just melting through the snow when Luke Warmwater went to jail this time. It wasn't his first time in the barrel. He knew all the jailers by name and disposition. He was disgusted to be in jail and was also disgusted that the whole routine was so familiar to him.

The jailer who let him in was friendly as he booked him. He even greeted him by name. The poor bastard, Luke thought, he's been doing his time, eight hours at a time since the last time. Life in jail on the installment plan.

Empty pockets, a shower and clean, green jail jumpsuit completed the metamorphosis of the free Sawyer Indian to a number. He did remember to ask for a large jumpsuit. It wouldn't bind in the long hours coming. He also asked for an extra blanket because the pillows in this jail were always small.

He wondered who he would know in the cellblock he was assigned to. There were always Indians in jail. He also thought no more food worries. He had to catch himself. He almost thanked the jailer who opened, held and then locked the steel door behind him.

He looked for an empty bunk to claim as his space. He spotted one the same time he spotted his cousin, Dunkin Black Kettle.

His cousin quit the solitaire card game he was playing and began to deal a cribbage hand for Luke. All right, thought Luke. He adjusted to jail immediately. While Luke and his cousin played cards, they caught up on each other's life and crimes.

Getting used to jail did take some time, though. That was okay because Luke had nothing but time. Sleeping in the same large room with mostly strangers, mostly criminals was a shock at first. After listening to these strangers belch, moan, snore and talk in their sleep, they didn't stay strangers long. Some did remain criminals though.

Jail quickly settled into a routine. Eat, sleep, play cards, watch TV. It went on and on. Eat, sleep, play cards and watch TV. Incarceration was too nice sounding a word to describe their plight.

One of the guys in the cellblock would begin each day by sighing. There were heavy sighs, mournful sighs, laughing sighs and sighs of all sizes. Luke got to know everyone's habits in no time.

After conferring with his jailhouse lawyers, the other prisoners, Luke decided that treatment at a chemical abusers place was the way out of his current predicament. Abusing whiskey had gotten him in jail, he wanted to see if it would get him out. The jailhouse lawyers had all been through the mill and knew the drill.

Luke began the steps that would lead to the 12 steps at the treatment place. The last untreated Sawyer Indian was going down. He did get out of jail.

Just about everyone else of treatable age had been through one of the facilities. Some relatives from Sawyer had counted coup thirteen or more times.

There was one story going around that the State Hospital was going to rename one wing of their facility. They were going to rename it for one of Luke's uncles because he had been there so many times. Luke thought the story was slightly exaggerated because he had another uncle who had been there just as many times. They were not going to name anything for him. The story was good for a chuckle though.

He walked through the door of the treatment place. He was supposed to report in sometime in the morning. He walked in at one minute to noon. No sense rushing things, he thought.

Strangers, look at all the strangers. There must be a least fifty white people wandering around that he didn't know. Culture shock! Wait a second, on the other side of the room was a skin he recognized from the rez. It was a woman he was in jail with. She must have used the same trail to get out of jail. He threw her a Sawyer wave and she smiled a greeting back. Good, another skin. He adjusted to treatment immediately.

Food, Luke saw food he hadn't seen in quite a while. So much of it too. Luke wondered if a guy could go back for thirds or even fourths as he shoveled the food in. He didn't have to buy it, fry it, or clean up after it. Luke thought he was in food heaven.

Treatment. Generally what it consisted of was sitting around and talking about memorable drunks. During these soul-searching, guilt-provoking sessions, if one could work up a good cry the story was accepted as a true revelation. Whimpering alone was not enough, it had to be wailing, gnashing of teeth and heaving sobs. Certain rooms were designated as the crying rooms. Luke could tell which ones they were, they had Kleenex boxes strategically placed about.

Since he had quit crying for good in the fourth grade, Luke was at a slight disadvantage. He couldn't get extra points or credibility for tears. He did have some good drunk stories though.

Since he was a storyteller, he was ahead of the others in the "group grope" sessions. His stories were memorable and repeated throughout the facility. So much for confidentiality; you can't hold a good story down, he thought.

Anything that was said or unsaid, done or undone was a symptom of the problem that brought a person to the facility, Luke quickly learned. He thought if the only tool you have is a hammer, everything begins to look like a nail. That was the feeling of the place.

Guts, the whole place seemed to operate on guts. If you were not spilling your guts on the floor, you were not trying hard enough. He wondered if the people working there ever got tired of wading through human guts.

After getting the skinny from the other skin about how to get along, Luke began to live the role of the drying-out-drunk. The other skin, who shall remain nameless because of the confidentiality rule, helped him along in the treatment place.

One day, when it was her turn to raise the flag, Luke helped her. Since it was a treatment place, they solemnly placed their hands over their livers as they raised the flag.

After successfully going through the phases of the program, Luke found himself ready to graduate out into the real world. He wondered how many of these strangers he'd know in three months; he wondered if he'd ever drink again. He wondered if the place did him any good. He didn't have to wonder if he was free. He knew he was. He was an ex-jailbird, spun-dry Sawyer Indian.

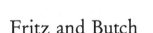

Fritz and Butch

"NO SHIT, it was the Vice President of the United States."

"Sure it was and I suppose he brought the Pope with him," said Dunkin Black Kettle.

"No, it was just him, he had all kinds of Secret Service guys with him," said Luke Warmwater. "See, I even got his autograph," he said as he handed his cousin a piece of paper with a signature scrawled on it.

"Yah, right, anyone can write like this. You can't even make out what it says."

"It says, Walter F. Mondale, see right there. It's his name, right there in front of you, in black and white."

"Give me another piece of paper like this and I'll make you another autograph, what name do you want me to scribble?" asked Dunkin.

"Watch the TV news tonight, see if they talk about the Vice President visiting Duluth today."

Luke and Dunkin were in the bar at the Radisson Hotel. A housing conference was being held there. Luke had just joined the Indians who were celebrating the end of the day's business.

Dunkin was making his moves on three women from the White Earth Reservation. He'd called his cousin to come and help snag up the three women. He'd also called another cousin, Butch Storyteller to come join them.

As usual, Butch was late, so Dunkin and Luke were doing their best to entertain the three out of town visitors. Just as Dunkin was getting started on one of his best stories, a Secret Service guy came in the bar, gave it a professional once over, and stood by the door.

The Indians were curious now. "See, I told you," said Luke as the Indians watched to see what was going to happen. Walter Mondale and his entourage walked by the entrance to the bar and proceeded to the elevator.

"I'll be damned, I caught you telling the truth," said Dunkin as he resumed his snagging. He wasn't getting very far because the conversation kept returning to the subject of the Vice President.

Since they were talking about the Vice President instead of vice like Dunkin wanted, he put his snagging moves on hold. He figured he could use the Vice President's visit to his advantage. The Indians drifted out to the hall to catch a glimpse of the Vice President when he came back down in the elevator.

"I wonder if Butch got lost, he was supposed to be here a half hour ago." muttered Dunkin as he watched the White Earth women wander off.

"How could he get lost, he's lived around Duluth all his life," answered Luke.

"He'd better get here pretty soon or there'll be no reason to come down here."

"Ding," said the elevator as it opened and disgorged four Secret Service guys. They fanned out and checked the hall for possible danger. The Indians were all lined up along one wall, sipping their drinks, waiting for Fritz to make his appearance. The Secret Service was lined up on the other side of the hall, watching the Indians and the rest of the crowd that was gathering. The Indians talked, joked and laughed as they waited.

About this time, the local TV crews arrived and set up their lights and cameras. They were going to tape the Vice President as he walked by.

"I'll get his autograph for you," Dunkin told one of the White Earth women, as he resumed his snagging moves.

"Ding," said the elevator. The TV lights came on, the crowd collectively leaned forward, the Secret Service tensed up. All eyes were on the door, waiting for it to open.

The door opened and Butch came strolling out. He was whistling a nameless tune. The lust in his eyes was replaced by a look of fright as he saw the lights and all the people standing there looking at him. He was dressed in a Levi jacket and was wearing a bone choker on his neck. The Indians recognized him right away. They were laughing and applauding.

"Speech, speech, can you comment on your policy on Indian housing, Mr. Vice President?" the Indians asked Butch. Butch walked out about four steps, froze, then spun around and tried to get back in the elevator. He was there to snag, not meet the media or be escorted by the Secret Service. The doors closed in his face. He tried to pry them open with his fingers but that didn't work. He faced the doors for a long three seconds and then finally turned around.

He recovered his composure and in his best Richard Nixon impression ever, threw his arms in the air, made two peace signs with his fingers, shook his jowls and said, "My fellow Americans." The TV lights were turned off.

"Ding," the elevator doors opened again and Fritz came out. He looked slightly confused as he saw the Indians gathered around Butch, laughing.

The TV lights came on again and Fritz walked through the crowd, shaking hands and smiling. He was also signing autographs. Dunkin went up to Fritz and got his signature on a piece of paper. It was the same piece of paper Luke had showed Dunkin earlier. Fritz smiled as he recognized his signature. He signed it again and gave it back to Dunkin.

"Anybody can get an autograph, I got you two of them," Dunkin told the White Earth woman. She put it in her purse and they all went back to the bar. The White Earth women and the Fond du Lac men sat down and began to get to know each other.

"Let me tell you about the time the three of us jumped on a plane and went to a party in Wisconsin," said Dunkin as he gazed deep into the eyes of the woman he was sitting with.

"This isn't the first time this has happened to me, I think Fritz kind of looks like me," Butch told the woman he was sitting with.

Luke smiled, life was back to normal.

Culture Clash

LUKE WARMWATER and his old lady Dolly were riding down a gravel road on the reservation. Luke and Dolly were just on a ride because they had the gas.

It was ricing but the lakes were closed so they could rest. The wind was combing the tangles out of the rice. They were glad because they knew they could make rice the next day.

Down the road they saw someone shambling along.

"A way day," said Luke, pointing with his lower lip.

"A yah," agreed Dolly. "That's your brother, the one they call Almost, isn't it?"

"Yah, I wonder what the hell he's doing around here," wondered Luke.

From the way he walked, Luke knew Almost had been on a drunk. There was nothing unusual about that. What was unusual was the bloody washrag he held against his head.

Almost got into the car and said, "Hey, brother, you got a smoke?"

As Luke handed him one, he began complaining and explaining. He was complaining about the cut on his head and explaining how it happened.

"This gash must need 37 stitches. How about a ride to the hospital?" Almost said.

"No problem," said Luke, "put your seatbelt on — we're not riding in an ambulance."

"That old girl broke her frying pan over my head, you know, one of those cast iron ones. I knew I shouldn't of gone home yet," Almost moaned. "Sure, I've been on a drunk, but she was laying for me when I got home. She used that frying for something besides fried bread."

"We went ricing yesterday," Luke said.

"That bonk on the noggin did nothing to improve my hangover. She was yelling about that skinny Red Laker I was passed out next to. I got out of there before she really got mad," Almost continued.

"We got 150 pounds of rice at Dead Fish Lake yesterday," Luke said.

He began the ritual of "Rushing Him to the Hospital." He felt good about driving so fast. He was on a genuine mission of mercy and he could bend and even break the traffic laws.

Luke's old car was holding up pretty good on the high speed run. "She'll need a quart of oil by the time we get there," he said.

The cops sitting at the edge of town eating donuts didn't know of Luke's mission of mercy. All they saw was a carload of Indians weaving through traffic.

Donuts and curses flew through the air as they began one of their own institutions called "High Speed Chase."

One cop was screaming on the radio about the chase. The other was trying to keep track of all the laws that were being bent and broken.

"Hey, all right, we got an official police escort," said Luke, when he saw the red lights in his mirrors.

By this time Luke's escort had grown to three city squads and deputies were coming to join the chase.

The car/ambulance came sliding into the hospital parking lot and stopped by the emergency room. Dolly got Almost out of the car and helped him into the building.

Luke drove over to where you're supposed to park and began congratulating himself on the successful run to the hospital. His troubles began when the cops got to the parking lot. They were excited about the chase.

"What's wrong with you, driving like that?" yelled a cop as he came running up to Luke.

"I wanna see your license!" screamed the second cop as he tried to wrestle Luke to the ground.

"Good, he's gonna resist arrest," said the first cop as he drew out his nightstick.

"My brother, Almost, is. . . . " Luke got out before a nightstick glanced off the side of his head and shut him up.

Luke gave up trying to explain and just began to fight back. He was holding his own and even took one of the nightsticks away. He threw that thing up on the roof so they'd quit hitting him with it.

The balance of power shifted towards law and order as more cops piled into the battle. Pretty soon Luke was sitting on the pavement, a subdued and hand-cuffed Indian. There never is an easy way to end these things, he thought.

The cops jerked Luke up on his tiptoes and marched him into the emergency room. Luke's head needed some doctor attention after all those nightsticks. They laid Luke down on the table next to Almost.

"Matching stitches," growled Luke to his brother.

"Ah neen da nah," said Almost and then shut up when he saw the cops and cuffs.

There was something ironic about the whole situation but Luke couldn't figure it out as the doctor stitched the brothers up.

The cops took Luke to jail. On the ride, Luke saw the ripped uniforms and lumps on the cops. That would explain why they put the cuffs on so damned tight.

Luke was pushed into his usual cellblock and he checked himself for damages. It was good to get those cuffs off.

A cop came in and handed Luke his copy of the charges. In addition to traffic charges, there was one for theft of city property. They couldn't find the nightstick he threw away.

The cellblock door clanged open and Almost was pushed in.

"We gotta quit meeting like this," sighed Luke. "What they got you for?"

"Disorderly conduct, and of course resisting arrest," said Almost.

"We'll go to court this afternoon," calculated Luke.

"When I got out of the hospital, the cops were still outside. They must have been mad yet because when I offered to drive your car home, they attacked," said Almost as he rubbed his cuff-damaged wrists.

So Almost went to jail, the car went with the tow truck and Dolly went visiting relatives to raise bail money.

She got back to the jail as the brothers were being taken to court.

"Got you covered," she said as she flashed the bail money.

Luke grinned hard at her.

In court, the brothers Warmwater pled not guilty and demanded a jury trial. A new court date was set and the matter of bail came up.

Luke got up and addressed the judge.

"Your honor, I hate seeing you under these conditions. I've been here before and as you may recall, I've always showed up on time for court.

"Ricing only comes once a year. The harvest is good this year and my old lady, Dolly, is finally learning how to make rice, I'm sure you know how important to the Indian people the rice crop is.

"The reason I'm telling you all this is because I'd like to request a release on my own recognizance."

"Request granted," the judge said as he gaveled the case down the court calendar.

As long as he had the judge's ear, Luke got brave and said, "Oh, yeah, your honor, all that stuff is true for my brother too."

The judge cut them both loose. They walked out of there free ricing Indians. They used the bail money Dolly raised to rescue the car and also that quart of oil they needed.

They dropped Almost off at home. His old lady was kind of sorry about hitting him. When he promised to buy her a new frying pan, she forgave him. They began making preparations for ricing the next day.

Luke and Dolly continued their ride down the gravel road on the reservation. Down the road, they saw someone walking.

"A way day," said Luke, pointing with his lower lip.

"Don't you dare stop, Luke Warmwater!" said Dolly.

M.A.Y.B.E.　　　　　　　by B. Wallace

I T WAS A DARK and stormy afternoon, of course, when I received a most unusual telephone call from a Dr. Moreland at the University of Minnesota. His assistant had been sifting through some old documents in their storage area in the Anthropology Department. He had stumbled upon a rather old and rusty file cabinet with the label on the front drawer identifying the contents as D.U.S.U.M. The second drawer had been labeled M.A.Y.B.E. The cabinet, government green in color, was pried open and inside the good doctor and his assistant had discovered a number of rather dusty and faded folders. Most were indistinguishable but some were readable and Dr. Moreland was quite careful with the fragile papers. While he spoke to me he seemed quite puzzled and curious.

He told me the dates on some of the papers and wanted to know if I had been around the "U" at that time – had I been a student in the early '70s? If so, he felt I may know something about the contents of the file cabinet. My curiosity was sparked as I was certainly a part of the University during the '70s and had been involved in a number of "movements," some of them serious some of them just for plain fun. I was hesitant to confirm my presence during those days as I was always nervous taking to Anthro's.

He began to read from one of the files titled, "Department of Undecided Studies, 1970." It was stamped "CONFIDENTIAL" in bold caps which only told me that everyone and his brother had read the material at some point. He said it appeared that some sort of Task Force had been formed and was attempting to create a bonafide Department of Undecided Studies. This Task Force had modeled their work after the Department of American Indian Studies, the Department of American Studies and the Department of Third World Studies. Every campus had one of these in the '60s and '70s and most of us involved in the "movement" radically supported these departments as crucial to the development of our young minds. He found fragments of minutes from one of their marathon meetings where an anonymous member was quoted: "I am going to save myself a lot of aggravation and tell everyone that I am a manic depressive, paranoid schizo fetish freak with klepto-frigid tendencies and be done with it!" Now that's radical!!! "But," he said, "a Department of Undecided Studies?" What would its purpose be? Who would it serve? Did the University actually accept such a premise? He began to describe proposed courses the Department hoped to offer but I stopped him in mid-sentence and asked him if he wouldn't mind if I paid him a visit in the near future. He invited me. Old Moreland was pretty conservative, and I had read some of his work, and I knew the man lacked a sense of humor. Before ending our phone conversation he indicated that he was feeling quite offended by this "latest finding" and it simply appeared to be another attempt at embarrassing the University in its divine wisdom.

My work at a small private college continued as usual with my latest research paper titled: "Do All Children of Single Heads of Households Resemble the Non-Participatory Parent?" My survey and subsequent lengthy paper had now become quite controversial in the tri-state region, and while I never intended to offend or embarrass anyone the calls and letters just kept coming. The negative responses were primarily from the so called "non-participatory parent" or to put it simply, the fathers of these many children. I found most of the comments quite humorous in content – most of these fathers were adamant in insisting their children did, in fact, resemble them. Most fathers had little contact with their children and most of them had never even seen the child yet they were defending a concept I had no argument with. It's true, these kids generally look like the father.

Now, I'm not picking on men but by gawd you can ask any single mother who her kid(s) look like and watch her roll her eyes back, squish up her mouth, flare her nostrils and groan, "just like the father!" Listen, girls, I have two children, I am single (by choice I might add) and you guessed it – both my children look just like good old dad. Now I don't believe in coincidence – everything happens for a reason. Even this! While we single parents truly end up loving, nurturing, guiding, disciplining and providing for the children there is that constant daily reminder – yes, you all know what I mean. The daily interaction with the little kid with the big cow eyes (same color and long lashes just like dad!) looking up to you for love and assurance yet the physical attributes and mannerisms of your former better half is ever present. Thank god most single parents have a good sense of humor and can laugh at themselves as they describe each other as "dying on the vine." That is not a term I feel is derogatory. It is simply a term that sometimes describes our sexual and social activities. We know what feast or famine is all about!

My interviews with friends, colleagues and numerous people chosen at random kept me quite busy and I had put my appointment with Dr. Moreland on the backburner. My interviews were pretty informal and I found most of the stories similar with all the tragedy and humor intact. Because our community is so small most of us knew these "non-participatory parents" and we were able to recall certain incidents that have stayed with us for many years. Stories poured from our mouths as we laughed, cried, and hugged one another.

One particular story stands out. A Red Lake woman told of the time she simply got fed up with her old man sleeping around, not coming home, and generally mistreating her. She tracked him down on Saturday night at a party and knew he would eventually pass out and not come home. He, of course, attempted to bed another woman but both had had far too much to drink and they were not successful. They did end up in the same bed and that's how our scorned friend found them. To say, "They fell asleep" would be too kind she told us. She came prepared — with a large tube of Super Glue. You can guess what she super-glued to his left leg. When he awoke in the morning and attempted to take his morning leak he found himself in a great deal of pain. He tried to wake the woman next to him but decided against it as he was totally humiliated. To walk only caused him more pain but he stumbled to the next room and woke up his buddy who finally drove him to the emergency room at the County Hospital. We all wondered how he explained all this to the attending physician when his "weenie" had to be pried off his leg. The Red Lake woman never let on to what she'd done and just let him think it was the other woman.

I never tire of the stories and actually found them to be quite therapeutic — not only for myself but for the parents being interviewed. I often think that if we ever formed a "support group" it would, no doubt, be the largest in the state.

Of course my mind kept drifting back to Moreland at the University. Did he really say, "Department of Undecided Studies"? What was M.A.Y.B.E.? Finally, it was time to go over. Moreland was just as I had expected. Tall, bony, very thin lips. I seem to have this aversion to thin-lipped people — most are rather cold in their approach, myopic in their thinking, and lack a sense of compassion not to mention humor. Now, I suppose I'll be hearing from the thin-lipped people reading this . . . please don't send any letters or make threatening phone calls.

He guided me to the bowels of Ford Hall, his assistant (more thin lips) continually rattling off in academic jargon. Finally, he opened the door to the storage area and the old green file cabinet stood out just like a sore thumb. Moreland gave me permission to go ahead and explore. They left to go into another storage room.

As I began to sift through the dusty, moldy files I began to chuckle to myself. I found bits and pieces describing an entire department. A job description fell out of the file and I was able to decipher what some of the qualifications were for the Chairperson. For instance: Must have Masters Degree from Third World Unaccredited College, Must have potential of being a follower, Must have transferred jobs at least 6 times in the last year, Must have extraordinary glandular control over palms and must be indecisive, unwilling, uncooperative, unknow-ing and unscrupulous. The rest of the job description was too damaged and fragile so I set it aside.

Another folder held a number of very professional looking resumes, apparently from people seeking the position of Chairperson. Some of the names were borderline obscene and some were just plain funny. An Indian woman from a federally unrecognized tribe boasted the name of Sarah Suckem Sillie and de-scribed herself as Chippewa/Polish/Red Laker who was 5'7" and stacked! She appeared to be the Task Force's number one candidate. Her background was quite diverse. For example: She studied "Flatus Differentiation" at The College of Last Ditch Efforts, she completed a degree in Multiethnic Cosmetology at the Yucatan School of Social Graces. She was an excellent maker of Fry Bread and had a special knack for mud wrestling.

The only other resume that was salvageable was one describing a Vito Run-ning Rabbit. His background was real sketchy but I managed to put a few sentences together. He studied Photography (when asked what he did for a living he always said, I shoot Indians), Anatomy and Flamenco dancing. His work experience in-cluded being a bed pan pusher, chief cook at Tight Spot Cafe in St. Paul and male stripper at the Corral Bar.

Another folder contained proposed courses. This folder was quite thick in content but I could see that the mice had chewed their way through most of it. Some of the courses I found only contained the titles such as:

Ind. Arts. 101 . . . . Nude Welding
Anat. 339 . . . . Anatomy in Braille
Sci. 244 . . . . Vegetating in Public
Psy. 260 . . . . Psychology of the Past; BIA
                                  Boarding School Freaks and
                                  other Misanthropes
Bio. 303 . . . . Seminar on Nutrition: Grab
                                  Your Mate Instead of Your Plate
AIS. 212 . . . . Faking 49er Songs
Anthro 440 . . . . Seminar: The Study of
                                  Neanderthal Mooning

I then found another folder titled: M.A.Y.B.E., the acronym for Minnesota Anishinabe Youth Believing in Education. Apparently this was a student group affiliated with the Task Force. Their motto: Undecided for One, Undecided for All.

There was a Search Committee that reviewed all resumes for the Chairperson and it seemed to consist of anywhere between 5-9 people, Chaired by Wanda Wigwas. The Curriculum Committee consisted of 3 people, Julio Left Moccasin and Roman Iron Hands, and Bonnella Big Canoe. I believe Bonnella was a Shinabe from our home state. I continued to roar with laughter and read on. This entire Department was based on rumor, humor and hearsay! Students who completed the "needs assessment" had all indicated "UNDECIDED" as their major area of study. There wasn't any specific registration time, only pre-registration. Classroom numbers were non-existent with only the names of the buildings. All classes started on Indian time.

After several hours of laughing and breathing in all that old University dust I came up for air. Moreland and his assistant were still busying themselves down the hall. I hesitated to tell them of my discovery! It became obvious to me that this self-appointed Task Force planning the new "Department" had been seeking grants from private and corporate foundations to match a University award. There were several copies of proposals (all enclosed in heavy plastic folders) that had been sent to various places that were sensitive to the indigenous cultures in the five state region. I mean these folks knew the corporate and foundation world and their approach was most professional. All the documents were immaculately typed and color coded.

In the last file in the very bottom drawer of the file cabinet I found several "tickle files" – reminder files that contained written notes of every contact made. This last folder seemed to be tucked away, almost invisible, but I struggled carefully to remove it. It was more than dusty, it was more than a little moldy and the mouse droppings inside told another story. The folder contained several damaged papers but one in particular caught my eye. It was not a full sheet of paper but maybe quarter size. It was light green in color and stapled on to a letter of some sort. Maybe it was some sort of "voucher." I inspected it more closely and almost fell over. I burst out laughing, not believing what I was seeing and touching. My heart pounded and I shook with some weird sense of delight!

The light green "voucher" was actually a check, a very large check. A very large check that had never been cashed. A check made out to M.A.Y.B.E. attached to a letter from the Chair of the Board at a rather prestigious corporation. The letter began with a hearty "Congratulations" – the rest was difficult to read but I did manage to decipher the intent – to be used as seed money for the creation and development of the Department of Undecided Studies, University of Minnesota.

I gently reattached the fragile check to its cover letter. I continued to chuckle to myself all the while thinking that if this Task Force ever *decided* anything then we certainly would have been in trouble! I gently closed the drawer of the cabinet, caught up with Moreland in the next room, thanked him and bid him a fond adieu.